Adulthood and Other Fictions

American Literature and the
Unmaking of Age

SARI EDELSTEIN

OXFORD
UNIVERSITY PRESS

Great Clarendon Street, Oxford, OX2 6DP,
United Kingdom

Oxford University Press is a department of the University of Oxford.
It furthers the University's objective of excellence in research, scholarship,
and education by publishing worldwide. Oxford is a registered trade mark of
Oxford University Press in the UK and in certain other countries

First Edition published in 2019

Impression: 1

Published in the United States of America by Oxford University Press
198 Madison Avenue, New York, NY 10016, United States of America

British Library Cataloguing in Publication Data
Data available

Library of Congress Control Number: 2018947646

ISBN 978–0–19–883188–4

Printed and bound by
CPI Group (UK) Ltd, Croydon, CR0 4YY

For Holly Jackson

Acknowledgments

It gives me great pleasure to recognize the many people that helped bring this book into being. I am grateful to Jacqueline Norton at Oxford University Press for her commitment to the book and for shepherding it into print and also to Brendan O'Neill for his initial interest in this project. The peer readers offered indispensable suggestions; this book is much improved for their incisive and generous feedback.

This book also benefitted from the insights and suggestions of a wide range of scholars, who gave me confidence that it had a potential readership even when others seemed stymied at the prospect of a book on age. Anna Mae Duane has been a champion of this project from the beginning; I am inspired by her collegial spirit and lucky to be the recipient of her intellectual generosity. Likewise, Pam Thurschwell, Melanie Dawson, Sarah Chinn, Nazera Wright, Aaron Lecklider, Duncan Faherty, Karen Kilcup, Aneeka Henderson, Anna Mae Duane, Lara Cohen, and Nadia Nurhussein read portions of the book and shared crucial feedback along the way.

I am also indebted to a growing network of scholars whose work takes up questions of age, from an array of vantage points, and enables and enhances my own thinking; thanks especially to Corinne Field, Nick Syrett, Nate Windon, Habiba Ibrahim, Allison Curseen, Marah Gubar, Margaret Gullette, Robin Bernstein, James Dobson, Lucia Hodgson, Nazera Wright, Samaine Lockwood, and Nat Hurley. For inspiring conversations and encouragement, I am also grateful to Nicole Tonkovich, Catherine Keyser, Jennifer Tuttle, Cindy Weinstein, Denise Knight, Sam Alexander, Patrick McKelvey, Julia Dauer, Peter Betjemann, Danielle Coriale, Lori Harrison-Kahan, John Patrick Leary, Emily Goard Jacobs (for teaching me about the telomere!), Laura Korobkin, and Jean Lutes. Jackie Penny at the American Antiquarian Society provided careful archival sleuthing and support and located some of my favorite images. I miss Michael T. Gilmore all the time; his example continues to guide my scholarly endeavors.

My friends, in academia and beyond, have sustained me in countless ways. Aaron Lecklider and Brian Halley, your enthusiasm for this project has been a source of reassurance and immense pleasure. Lara Cohen, John Patrick Leary, Nadia Nurhussein, Jennifer Delton, Mason Stokes, Cecily Parks, Ashley Shelden, Elizabeth Wilson, Bess Rouse, Jennifer Winn Aronson, Jill McDonough, Josey Packard, Emily Greenstein, Munirih Yeshwant, Dana McSherry, Kent Greenfield, Melissa Axelrod, Emily Wiemers, Dennis Rasmussen, Brooksie Robbins, Bobo Widing-Jonsson: I am lucky to count you as friends.

I feel fortunate every day to work at the University of Massachusetts, Boston. My colleagues, including Louise Penner, Betsy Klimasmith, Judith Goleman, Cheryl Nixon, Jill McDonough, Emilio Sauri, Matthew Davis, Eve Sorum, Alex Mueller, John Fulton, Susan Tomlinson, Len Von Morze, and many others, supported my work on this book by asking probing questions and suggesting useful sources. My students, especially those in English 379 and 463, helped me work through these ideas, shared their own, and sharpened my understanding of adulthood as an unstable and privileged category. Samantha Regan made sure I had a working computer, a quality office space, and hot coffee; she is a model of professionalism and kindness. I am grateful to the UMass Boston Office of Graduate Studies for publication subvention support.

And finally, this book reflects the influence of people who make my life as a scholar possible. Diane Duggan has given me the time, space, and peace of mind to think and write; this book would not exist without her. My family—Robin and John Hendricksen, Marcy and Leo Edelstein, Robert and Josie Edelstein, Karen and Percy Jackson—thank you for all the ways you have supported me as I wrote this book.

Jane and Adam, thank you for keeping me young and making me old at the same time; I love you both more than I can say.

Holly Jackson, you are my dearest interlocutor, my best friend, and the love of my life. Let's always be old little girls together.

A portion of chapter 1 appears in "'May I Never Be a Man': Melville's *Redburn* and the Failure to Come of Age in Young America." *ESQ: A Journal of the American Renaissance*, Vol. 59.4 (2013): 553–84, and an excerpt from chapter 4 appears in *Common-Place: A Journal of Early American Life* 17. no 25 (Winter 2017).

A part of chapter 3 was included in "Louisa May Alcott's Age," *American Literature*, Vol. 87:3, pp. 517–45. Copyright 2015, Duke University Press. All rights reserved. Republished by permission of the rightsholder. www.dukeupress.edu. I am grateful to those publications for allowing me to reprint and expand my arguments here.

Contents

List of Illustrations

Introduction

"For age is opportunity no less
Than youth itself, though in another dress,
And as the evening twilight fades away
The sky is filled with stars, invisible by day."

Henry Wadsworth Longfellow[1]

"Nature is full of freaks, and now puts an old head on young shoulders,
and then a young heart beating under fourscore winters."

Ralph Waldo Emerson[2]

Adulthood is a fiction. With no consistent biological boundaries, it is at once a disciplinary ideal, a prized status for those who comply with gender norms and the ethos of capitalism, and a political rank long reserved for a small subset of the population. A central claim of this book is that adulthood functions ideologically and that age itself is a political instrument, though seldom recognized as such, which is intrinsic to how other social hierarchies operate and to the distribution of power more broadly. The "other fictions" to which I refer in my title are not only the novels under analysis in the subsequent pages but also the presuppositions about age that construct our understandings of development, maturity, ability, and independence. Along with adulthood, I read all age categories—including old age, adolescence, and childhood—as narrative constructs, and this book seeks to interrogate the fictions about aging and maturity that circulate in US culture, to excavate their history, and to acknowledge their wide-ranging implications.

Adulthood and Other Fictions attends to age as an analytic category to shed new light on our most familiar narratives. It shows how a diverse array of nineteenth-century writers, thinkers, and artists responded to the emergence of age as a regulatory category linked to gender and sexuality and a demographic data point tied to the bureaucratization of the life course and the management of populations. These nineteenth-century discourses established an age culture that we continue to inhabit, and this book helps us to reencounter its formation as a political and narrative construct.

Our classic texts represent age as a significant cultural and political coordinate, impelling a range of interpretive questions. For instance, why does the narrator of *Bartleby, the Scrivener* open with a description of himself as "elderly"? Why might Walt Whitman, in the 1881 edition of *Leaves of Grass,* describe himself as "thirty-seven years old, in perfect health," despite the fact that he was actually sixty-two years old when he added this line?[3] What does the literature of slavery reveal about the politicized and gendered function of age under this regime, from Frederick Douglass who reported that he "never met with a slave who could tell how me old he was," to Harriet Jacobs' description of the specific age of fifteen as "a sad epoch in the life of a slave girl"?

Although literary studies for decades have rigorously addressed the identity categories of race, class, gender, and sexuality, age—with the exception of childhood—remains conspicuously absent from scholarly discussions of nineteenth-century American literature and culture.[4] I argue that these other measures of social location are articulated through the seemingly more natural and essential identity defined by age to a surprising extent.[5] That is, age operates in conjunction with discourses of power to naturalize other hierarchies. Indeed, the quantitative nature of numerical age lends itself well to the project of buttressing other statuses, as it provides an ostensibly objective basis for claims about development and ability.

Childhood studies scholars have importantly uncovered the ideological work of real and symbolic children in the projects of nation-building and racial formation, but this book argues that we must move beyond the figure of the child to consider age as a continuum.[6] The institutionalization of childhood studies unwittingly elevates youth over all other ages and reifies the stages of life themselves as essential categories rather than as cultural constructs, even as childhood studies is premised on the notion of childhood as such a construct. As age studies scholar Margaret Gullette writes, "No age class exists in a capsule."[7] In many cases, the compartmentalization of childhood from "adolescence," "adulthood," and "old age" as distinct categories obscures the underlying scholarly premise that these life stages are culturally produced and profoundly disciplinary. By focusing on childhood in isolation, as though it were a discrete or stable designation, divorced from other ages, scholarly studies of childhood risk reinforcing the false binary between children and adults that the field means to destabilize.[8]

Adulthood and Other Fictions instead draws attention to how taxonomies of age serve political ends. To be clear then, this is not a book about adulthood as a coherent category; rather, it aims to reveal life stages themselves as cultural constructs, devoting particular attention to the ideological work of adulthood as the most privileged age status. Bringing critical age studies to bear on nineteenth-century American literature, I consider literary treatments of childhood, youth, midlife, and old age in an effort to reveal age as a preoccupation of the US literary tradition and to reveal that the criteria for adulthood are shifting and unstable. That is, whether one qualifies as an adult depends less on chronological age than on the other criteria used to define the category.

Throughout this book, I employ a range of terms that may seem self-explanatory but which are freighted with ideological significance and political import. I use "age" to refer to numerical or chronological age, that is, the number of years an individual has been alive.[9] While age seems to be a private or individual signifier or a purely biological marker, the meanings of this number are produced by ideological and cultural contexts. Numerical age is imbued with cultural meanings and expectations, as individuals are plotted on developmental trajectories and expected to comply with a range of scripted age norms.

I use "adulthood" to refer to the period of life associated with autonomy, legal and political rights, financial independence, and the initiation of a heteronormative life trajectory. Adulthood functions less as a biological status than a social achievement; it is best understood as an ideal rather than an inevitability. Indeed, we might think of the notion of the adult as comparable to the category of woman or man, which are also cultural fantasies anchored in bodily scripts and behavioral norms but which can never be wholly attained or perfectly executed. I use "maturity" to refer to the social performance of adulthood, a sign of "successful" aging, rather than the inevitable outcome of aging itself. Maturity signifies compliance with expectations for adulthood; it makes legible the markers of conventional development, and it accrues the privileges linked to adulthood, which can be political or social.

Adulthood and Other Fictions denaturalizes the relationship between age and maturity, revealing that the developmental logic that undergirds commonplace understandings of maturity is an imposition rather than an expression of self. Likewise, it demonstrates that maturity is a core element of class, gender, and racial privilege in the United States. As I show here, nineteenth-century American literature acknowledges how age is deployed as a regulatory device, and it aims to make space for conceptualizing and recognizing alternative forms of maturity.

* * *

The nineteenth century witnessed a seismic shift in the political and cultural significance of age. Over the course of the century, the demographics of the nation transformed to include an unprecedented number of people over sixty, a significant precursor to the "graying" of the American population so often discussed in our own moment. Along with this demographic change, the nineteenth century saw the rise of age-graded schooling, age-specific medical treatments, and the emergence of a commodity and periodical culture that enshrined age as socially meaningful. Age segregation, and the move away from multigenerational contexts, was a core component of modernization.

The US census reveals this profound change in thinking about the human life course: the 1790 census simply recorded whether free white males were older or younger than sixteen (and significantly did not even ask women and people of color to report their ages), while the 1850 asked individuals to report a specific numerical age. With this addition as a primary identifier on the census, age was enfolded into a governmental project of tabulating citizens' biopolitical information. As Judith Treas writes, chronological age became the "linchpin of a host of standards for stratifying individuals in a uniform fashion—a practice that gives rise to the standardization of the life course."[10] What seemed like a new data point for establishing individuality actually served to plot individuals along normative developmental trajectories; indeed, the ostensibly democratic project of the census enlisted the populace in age awareness, making individuals complicit in the project of monitoring and acting their ages. That the first commercial birthday cards were printed in the United States just a few decades later suggests the extent to which observing numerical age became a core aspect of social identity as well as of the consumer economy.

This is not to say that age was meaningless before the nineteenth century. Eighteenth-century Americans unevenly relied on age qualifications for militia duty and jury service, and many Americans recorded their births, deaths, and developmental benchmarks like marriage in family Bibles.[11] But even when Americans acknowledged the stages of life or numerical age prior to the mid-nineteenth century, age seldom served as a primary marker of identity or as a principal means of classifying individuals.[12] Beginning in the first decade of the nineteenth century, however, age, rather than property ownership, became the relevant qualification for voting (for white men) and age-segregated institutions, such as convalescent homes and children's hospitals became mainstays of the American cultural landscape.[13] In this sense, age usurped class as the major social distinction that served as the basis for full citizenship and political entitlement.

The nineteenth century also gave rise to what we now call the "cult of youth" and to an anxiety about old age that historian David Hackett Fischer refers to as "gerontophobia," displacing a longstanding tradition of reverence for elderly people.[14] Old age was increasingly regarded as a medical condition; indeed, one late-nineteenth-century medical researcher described old age as "an infectious, chronic disease."[15] In his 1858 bestselling treatise, *Medical Common Sense*, Dr. Edward Bliss Foote went so far as to caution readers about the dangers of exposing children to prolonged physical contact with elderly people: "When, by contact for long nights with elder and negative persons, the vitalizing electricity of their tender organizations is given off, they soon pine, grow pale, languid and dull, while their bed companions feel a corresponding invigoration."[16] Thus, older people could sap the strength and vitality from children by sheer proximity. In the face of a rapidly industrializing economy, old age became a liability rather than a benefit in a workplace that came to value expertise and professional credentials over experience and seniority, though it is worth noting that the condition and status of older people has always varied more by class and race than by historical period.[17]

In the final decades of the nineteenth century, age became a field of study. Social theorists, including Herbert Spencer, George Beard, and G. Stanley Hall, set the terms for modern conceptions of age with the science of human development. They developed new medical fields and new terminology and also published in popular periodicals so that their ideas about age and the life course came to seem like scientific truths about human nature.[18] By the dawn of the twentieth century, elderly people, for example, were understood to occupy a discrete stage of life, and obituaries referred to "old age" as a cause of death, cementing an association between old age and death even as babies and children were far more likely to die than the elderly.[19] In truth, as historian Howard Chudacoff puts it, "Death was not age-related."[20]

Just as the science of sexuality produced a discourse of non-normative identities and behaviors, so too did the science of human development result in a host of ways in which one could conceivably age wrongly. Indeed, discourses of age and the life course drew upon and ushered in normative conceptions of sexuality, paving the way for the Freudian understanding of adulthood as defined by progressive development through psychosexual stages. For nineteenth-century doctors and social theorists, precocity was a particularly troubling concern, as it exposed a possible disjunction between chronological age and maturity. In his enormously popular book, *Plain Facts for Old and Young* (1879), John Harvey Kellogg, cereal maven and medical doctor, worried that women were beginning their families too young: "With so many girl-mothers in the land, is it any wonder that there are so many thousands of unfortunate individuals who never seem to get beyond childhood in their development?"[21] Women's untimely conception could lead to a range of diseased ages:

"spoilt childhood, feeble and precocious youth, extravagant manhood, early and premature death."[22] As Kellogg's formulation indicates, inappropriate development as well as acting *other* than one's age became sites of cultural concern and anxiety. Chronological age thus served a supervisory function, scripting individuals into age-appropriate behaviors, affects, and relationships, and these nineteenth-century discourses produced the intense age consciousness that is still with us today.

*   *   *

Adulthood and Other Fictions foregrounds imaginative literature as one of the most significant discourses of age. Nineteenth-century fiction was attuned to the increasing relevance of age and life stage discourse and actively participated in establishing—and deconstructing—the meanings attached to age. Consider, for example, Nathaniel Hawthorne's short story "Dr. Heidegger's Experiment," first published in 1837, which centers on a group of "melancholy old creatures" who join the eponymous doctor for dinner.[23] According to the narrator, "They looked as if they had never known what youth or pleasure was, but had been the offspring of Nature's dotage, and always the gray, decrepit, sapless, miserable creatures, who now sat stooping round the doctor's table, without life enough in their souls or bodies to be animated even by the prospect of growing young again."[24] The narrator proceeds to describe these friends as "wasted," "melancholy," and "ruined"; over the years, they have lost money, good reputations, health, and predictably, the one woman in the group has lost her beauty. These descriptions of the elderly resonate in *The Scarlet Letter's* Custom House sketch, in which Hawthorne refers to his older co-workers as "a set of wearisome old souls, who had gathered nothing worth preservation from their varied experience of life."[25] They sit around all day listening to the "several thousandth repetition of old sea-stories and mouldy jokes, that had grown to be passwords and countersigns among them."[26] For Hawthorne, it seems old age is inherently unattractive, tied inexorably to dead economies and declining bodies.

Dr. Heidegger offers his "ruined" friends drinks supposedly from the "Fountain of Youth," and warns them to "draw up a few general rules for your guidance, in passing a second time through the perils of youth."[27] But they disregard his words of caution and proceed to drink with abandon and return to the "happy prime of youth." Their recklessness suggests that they have gained nothing with the passage of time, least of all the ability to control their impulses. As the elixir takes effect, the doctor watches his friends return to their youthful selves: "The most singular effect of their gayety was an impulse to mock the infirmity and decrepitude of which they had so lately been the victims."[28] In other words, the story imagines a disdain for elderly people as the signal characteristic of youth, thereby naturalizing generational antagonism.

But while the story might seem to offer an essentialist view of old age, it actually suggests that age is more powerful as a cultural construct than as a biological reality. As the narrator observes, "By a strange deception, owing to the duskiness of the chamber, and the antique dresses which they still wore, the tall mirror is said to have reflected the figures of the three old, gray, withered grandsires, ridiculously contending for the skinny ugliness of a shrivelled granddam."[29] In other words, they are not *truly* young again, or even young-looking; rather, the elixir merely enables them to *experience* themselves as young, which frees them from the cultural constraints that come with old age. And as in many narratives of age, the mirror tells the "truth," reliably reflecting chronological age even and especially when it conflicts with the psychic experience of age. In this sense, the magic of the "Fountain of Youth" seems to be a kind of placebo; it relieves individuals from awareness of their age and consequently from the work of disciplining themselves according to age expectations.

Dr. Heidegger's experiment thus reveals age to be a prescribed subject position rather than a fixed aspect of identity. One does not outgrow the selves that predominate in our youth; rather, we subordinate them as we grow older and learn to regulate ourselves according to age norms. However, even as the story acknowledges them as culturally constructed, Hawthorne does not endorse the subversion of these norms. On the contrary, the story portrays "young" behavior in the old as revolting and inappropriate and conflates old-ness with the grotesque.

This story allegorizes the paradoxical relationship to age that developed in American culture over the course of the nineteenth century. It simultaneously mocks the doctor's friends for their immaturity—and for their desire to regain youth—even as it denigrates their elderly bodies. Significantly, the doctor's decision to refrain from drinking from the fountain suggests that he has acquired a kind of perspective that his friends lack. His friends' ludicrous, juvenile behavior enables him to come to terms with his own condition as "old and rheumatic."[30] Indeed, the story might well serve as a cautionary tale for a nation beginning to fetishize perpetual youth, one that would eventually turn to elective surgery and other modern fountains of youth or elixirs in order to stave off the effects of biological aging.

The novel form, as it emerged in the American tradition in this period, helped to circulate and shape the new logic of age as well as offering savvy deconstructions. Indeed, as the novel form conventionally relies on the logic of maturation, a character changing over time, aging is its defining subject.[31] Literary studies thus offers indispensable insight into the ways that coming of age has been narrated and how the stages of life have been naturalized; by the same token, an interdisciplinary analysis of age discourses more broadly in the nineteenth century reveals that the novel's construction of age as the core of identity is not merely a preoccupation of this form but rather part of culture-wide phenomenon.

Scholars of European and British literature have contributed important theorizations of the *Bildungsroman,* or coming-of-age novel, particularly in relation to nineteenth-century political contexts. For example, Franco Moretti reads the *Bildungsroman* as the "symbolic form of modernity," arguing that the genre's definitive focus on youth is a way of reckoning with the revolutions and upheavals that ushered in modernity.[32] More recently, Jed Esty has considered the figure of the "frozen youth" in modernist fiction, persuasively observing that "uneven development" in this period is often tied to colonial migration and displacement. For Esty, the stunted, thwarted, untimely plots of modernism take on new significance when read in relation to globalization.

But the nineteenth-century American coming-of-age novel has not received such elaborate consideration nor have studies considered age itself as a subject, except insofar as it serves as a metaphor for national development. In large part, this may be because it is hard to know how to define the genre. Leslie Fiedler's classic study *Love and Death in the American Novel* famously describes the American literary tradition itself as "innocent, unfallen in a disturbing way, almost juvenile."[33] For Fiedler, the absence of heterosexual romance, particularly marriage plots, in American literature is a sign of the tradition's immaturity, its refusal to engage with real adult concerns.

Adulthood and Other Fictions responds to Fiedler's characterization of the tradition as inherently juvenile. While it recognizes that many of our canonical texts do reject heteronormative romance and conventional forms of maturity, it seeks to politicize this refusal to acquiesce to the normative social order and the ideological imperatives of adulthood. By revisiting Fiedler's classic account of the tradition through the lens of age studies, *Adulthood and Other Fictions* illuminates nineteenth-century American literature's attention to age, and more specifically to adulthood, as an ideological instrument and provides a more thorough consideration of how literature participated in constructing age and development in our cultural imagination. While some authors reinforced age norms, many others used fiction to articulate alternative understandings of age and maturation. They imaginatively critiqued their culture's demands that people grow up by a certain age, questioned and disrupted mainstream assumptions about age and identity, and tended to see "growing up" as equivalent to the assumption of appropriate positions in economic, racial, and gender hierarchies. Moreover, if as Esty puts it, "the *Bildungsroman* stabilizes the protagonist's aging process within and against the backdrop of the modern nation," then we might also read the distorted American configurations of this classic European form in relation to anxieties about the methods by which the United States itself was maturing.[34]

But *Adulthood and Other Fictions* also moves beyond the *Bildungsroman* to expose treatments of age at the center of texts that are not manifestly about youth or growing up in a traditional sense. In this vein, I consider texts that feature elderly and middle-aged protagonists; I focus on the significance of cross-generational relationships, and I examine texts in which conventionally defined adulthood is off-limits or undesirable. *Adulthood and Other Fictions* demonstrates that American literature is a tradition rife with what might be called "novel forms of aging," or texts that resist commonplace ideas about development and reveal conventional understandings of adulthood as oppressive and exclusive. As Patricia Meyers Spacks observes, novels "imply theories of development and powerfully reinforce them, but—unlike didactic manuals—they do not necessarily describe idealized development sequence."[35] The novel, in other words, creates, enforces, and circulates normative ideas about development and age, but it also provides a space for imagining alternatives to the teleology of modern aging. *Adulthood and Other Fictions* sounds the nineteenth-century tradition to ask how we might conceptualize aging apart from a model of decline or progress. That is, if we abandon the linear model of aging, what other shapes can a life take? To what extent are discourses of aging produced in conjunction with those of gender, race, class, and sexuality? For whom are aging and maturation synonymous, and is maturity always desirable? And what definitions of maturity might proliferate if we destabilize market success and marriage as the only viable criteria?

In nineteenth-century fiction, we repeatedly encounter characters who refuse to inhabit age appropriately; they undermine the supposedly natural linkage between numerical age and maturity as well as the notion of aging as a linear, irreversible process. Rebecca Harding Davis' story, "Anne," which appeared in an 1889 issue of *Harper's*, offers a theory of age that departs from contemporary scientific efforts to pathologize old age as a discrete and knowable life stage. The story opens with the protagonist, Mrs. Nancy Phillips, awakening from a daydream in which she has imagined herself as a young girl, beautiful and full of potential. As she tells her daughter, "'I fell asleep out on the porch awhile ago, Susy, ... and I dreamed that I was sixteen again. It was very vivid. I cannot even now shake off the impression that I am young and beautiful and in love.'"[36] Over the course of the story, we learn that "Anne" was the name Mrs. Phillips went by as a young girl, before her marriage, and the daydream resuscitates this younger self. "She ought to think of that old long-ago self as dead. But it was not dead."[37] Indeed, it becomes clear that Anne remains unsettlingly alive. Upon looking in the mirror, she thinks, "They were Anne's eyes, and Anne had never been Job Palmer's wife."[38] Through the eyes of her sixteen-year-old self, Mrs. Phillips sees her life as boring, narrow, even tragic.

Her two children, James and Susan, treat their mother as a helpless infant, referring to her passionate responses to art as "childish outbreaks."[39] Upon discovering that her mother has gone for a walk, Susan chastises her: "'Oh no, but you are not young, darling mamma. You are just at the age when rheumatisms and lumbagoes and such things set in if one is not careful. Where have you been?...Walking in the woods! Really now that is something I cannot understand'—smiling at her mother as though she were a very small child indeed."[40] Such infantilizing rhetoric chafes Mrs. Phillips and stokes her desire for independence and autonomy. Moreover, Susan expresses the conventional notion of chronological age as a stable truth: to be an old woman, she implies, is to be debilitated and immobile. She finds incomprehensible her mother's desire to be outdoors and free from the domestic setting.

Davis rejects the patronizing assumption that old age is a "second childhood" and instead represents it as an unpredictable period in which multiple selves collide and coalesce. "She remembered that when she had been ill with nervous prostration two years ago she had in an hour suddenly grown eighty years old. Now the blood of sixteen was in her veins. Why should this soul within her thus dash her poor brain from verge to verge of its narrow range of life?"[41] According to this story, aging does not occur in a linear progression nor is aging necessarily permanent; rather, aging is figured as an unruly, disordered phenomenon that happens to the body and the mind at different times and manifests in unknowable ways. Davis turns to the gothic to represent the uncanny aspects of aging, the persistence of prior selves into the present.

Davis' story thus aligns with the claims of age studies scholars, who have urged us to abandon limited, monolithic concepts of aging and to acknowledge that our assigned age is often an inaccurate indicator of the age with which we most identify.[42] Leni Marshall, for example, writes, "you do not lose the other ages that you have been, but practically, they are inaccessible to people who meet you after those years are behind you."[43] For Marshall, literature can portray this accretive model of aging; it can remind us that aging need not entail alienation from one's prior selves. As Amelia DeFalco succinctly puts it: "Identity need not be mono-narratological";[44] in other words, we don't have to live by a single, continuous narrative that reveals a more coherent self over time. Such theories run counter to psychoanalytic models of "healthy" development, which entail the subordination of childish pleasures and the lockstep procession through discrete stages.[45]

In its attention to the interpellative work of age, critical age studies intersects with and supplements a range of cultural studies methodologies that similarly aim to destabilize identitarian categories and allow for more malleable ways of imagining subjectivity. Queer theory, in particular, shares with age studies an incentive to consider how disciplinary labels establish the illusion of coherent identity, police behavior, and regulate sexuality. The work of scholars such as J. Jack Halberstam and Sara Ahmed reveals how linear models of development administer age norms as well as those of gender and sexuality and to recognize how disruptions and delays thwart the momentum of heterotemporality.[46] Halberstam defines as queer those subjects whose lives are "unscripted by the conventions of family, inheritance, and child rearing."[47]

But while Halberstam oddly defines this alternative mode of temporality in terms of an "epistemology of youth," we might fruitfully consider how old age also offers possibilities for inhabiting time that do not merely ensure generational continuity or correlate to respectability.[48] That is, we need not tether old bodies to conservatism when in fact the circumscribed expectations for aging contain radical potential to disrupt heterotemporality and normative gender expectations. As Jane Gallop recently asked, "What if, following [Lee] Edelman's resistant logic, old people took up our place as augurs of mortality, refusing to subordinate our present lives to the worship of the future?"[49] The repudiation of longevity for the sake of it, the failure to plan and save for retirement, the refusal to subordinate oneself to younger generations: these practices disturb ostensibly natural ideas about aging and offer a sharp rebuke to normative expectations for being elderly. Even just inhabiting an elderly body seems to fly in the face of our repression of all that is not vigorous and autonomous.

Ultimately, we might read as queer any failure to abide by age expectations or to identify with appropriate age norms. Such failures diverge from and destabilize gender and sexual norms of development, and they help us to see the supervisory work of milestones that delineate normative life stages and reward conventional success. That is, disruptions to what Dana Luciano has called "chronobiopolitics" unmoor age from socially sanctioned versions of maturity and cast into relief the project of maturity itself a somewhat suspect enterprise.[50] These refusals of normative life itineraries and age identities might involve what Kathryn Bond-Stockton calls "growing sideways"; they may entail stasis and non-development; or they may carve out new routes that move at an irregular pace or encompass episodes of recursivity.[51]

Nineteenth-century American writers anticipated such conceptions of aging, and they highlight numerical age as prescriptive more than expressive. Women writers, in particular, are attuned to how age norms circumscribe their life narratives. Sarah Orne Jewett, for example, spent her life outside of heteronormative teleology, choosing instead to devote herself to same-sex intimacies and to authorship. On her forty-eighth birthday, she wrote, "This is my birthday and I am always nine-years old."[52] For Jewett, childhood could be a permanent state, a lifelong identification, rather than a biological stage, a way of circumventing the oppressive demands of womanhood. The thirteen-year-old Louisa May Alcott similarly felt estranged from her assigned age, noting in her diary: "I am old for my age, and don't care much for girl's things. People think I'm wild and queer."[53] Both of these queer age identifications suggest the imbrications of age with ideologies of sex and gender, suggesting the appeal of non-reproductive ages for women who chose against the gendered meanings of adulthood and opted out of normative age schedules.

Adulthood and Other Fictions demonstrates that age and gender ideologies are mutually constitutive, one becoming legible when refracted through the other.[54] Where white men could come into majority and gain political privileges with age, the passage of time entailed the diminishment of social influence rather than the acquisition of rights for women.[55] Significantly, white women could legally consent to sex at ten years old in many states without ever achieving political maturity.[56] In other words, adulthood was meted out to women in accordance with the logic of patriarchy. Indeed, long before Susan Sontag observed the "unequal distribution of adult roles between the two sexes" in a 1971 essay in the *Saturday Review,* many nineteenth-century writers were attuned to what she called the "double standard of aging."[57]

Once we begin to read with age in mind, it becomes clear that feminist critique often involves protest against disciplinary age norms. For example, Charlotte Perkins Gilman's classic story "The Yellow Wall-Paper," centers on a nameless female narrator who is put on bed rest in a nursery by her doctor-husband, who refers to her as a "blessed little goose" and a "little girl." The narrator's ultimate act of creeping around the room on all four offers a nightmarish vision of devolution for a grown woman deprived of the opportunity to accrue the privileges of maturity and to develop with age. Indeed, the story reveals acquiescence to normative expectations for age and gender as debilitating rather than empowering.[58] Lilian Bell's *The Love Affairs of an Old Maid* (1893) makes this point even more vigorously, taking aim at how age propriety, like gender compliance, redirects women's energies toward the body and the self rather than toward the public sphere. As she succinctly puts it, "We have so much to think about more important than our stupid ages."

Where queer and feminist theories illuminate the ideology of hetero-linear development, the field of disability studies offers a critical precedent for reading bodies that defy normative expectations.[59] Even though old age is often linked to disability in the cultural imaginary, literary studies scholars have directed surprisingly little attention to the intersections of age and disability.[60] While we cannot equate old age with disability, these embodied, stigmatized statuses overlap as similarly subject to regulation, rehabilitation, and pathologization. Like age and race, the modern concept of disability was the product of the nineteenth century's regime of bodily classification, and it is largely through age that mainstream science measures whether individuals are bodily appropriate and developmentally on schedule. Moreover, if we live in what Robert McRuer calls a world of "compulsory able-bodiedness," we also live in one of compulsory youth, in which the body itself becomes deviant as it ages past a certain point, no longer serving capitalism or its reproductive imperatives.[61]

Age studies must follow disability studies in its incitement to think about the representational work of socially devalued bodies, and in particular to attend to the axes of dependence and autonomy. If adulthood is equated with autonomy and self-sufficiency, then those individuals who need assistance or who lack bodily or intellectual autonomy are conceived of as immature or child-like. Indeed, the interpellation of subjects into specific age groups and the annual function of the birthday work to ensure cooperation with existing systems and to maintain the status quo. Maturity thus serves as a regulatory ideal, a way of enshrining those forms of living that comply with the ableist expectations and demands of capitalism.

* * *

While it is tempting to organize a book on age according to the chronology of the normative life course, *Adulthood and Other Fictions* resists the appeal to reaffirm this teleology. Instead, the book addresses the cultural and literary engagements with age norms as they were formalized over the course of the century, highlighting the social production of ostensibly biological life stages. To this end, I largely refrain from considering life stages separately and therefore reifying them. Nor does this book offer a comprehensive treatment of all age categories; indeed, scant attention is paid to infancy or childhood, already richly discussed in literary and cultural studies, and certainly an entire book still remains to be written on old age alone. Each chapter is anchored in a close examination of one or more major authors, including Herman Melville, Louisa May Alcott, Frederick Douglass,

Harriet Jacobs, Sarah Orne Jewett, Mary Wilkins Freeman, and Henry James, whose work meditates on the burgeoning significance of age as well as the limitations and possibilities inherent in the notion of adulthood. My hope is that an attention to these canonical figures will indicate that age has been hiding in plain sight, an unacknowledged but integral site of meaning in even the most familiar works. I begin in the 1840s, with Melville, and conclude at the close of the century with James, using these figures as bookends for a period that gave rise to the modern culture of age. Indeed, by the turn of the century, Americans had developed what historian Howard Chudacoff calls "age consciousness," and the life stages as we roughly conceive of them today were firmly institutionalized.[62]

The first chapter reads Herman Melville's semi-autobiographical novel *Redburn: His First Voyage* (1849) as an anti-coming-of-age novel that exposes maturity as profoundly ideological, tied to capitalist and nationalist agendas. Published during a moment in which calls proliferated for individual Americans and the nation at large to grow up, *Redburn* rejects the trajectory toward adult masculinity defined exhaustively in this moment as the basis of American development. The chapter positions Melville's work amidst the cultural preoccupation with linear life-course trajectories, represented in popular broadsides and lithographs enshrining the stages of life. Melville's career, which took a well-known plunge after *Moby-Dick*, might be recast as a refusal to embrace the terms by which market society defined adulthood and success.

The second chapter examines slavery's distorting effects on age. It reveals how racism and slavery operate *through* age, buttressing a system that distributed maturity, and humanity, according to an invented logic that age discourse helped to naturalize. The chapter explores the vexed status of age under slavery in Frederick Douglass' *My Bondage and my Freedom* (1855) and Harriet Jacobs' *Incidents in the Life of a Slave Girl* (1861) as well as Federal Writers Project interviews with formerly enslaved people who seem to defy the boundaries of human longevity. These narratives acknowledge not merely the corruption of childhood but the exclusion from adulthood as among the most troubling aspects of slavery. Ultimately, they lament enslavers' use of age as a metric of economic value and a tool for dehumanization, and their narratives stage willful refusals to accommodate this logic.

The third chapter exposes the exclusionary status of adulthood and the disciplinary work of age from a gendered perspective. Women were, in the words of one historian, "perpetual minors," and this uneven distribution of rights perverted female development and preoccupied one of the most celebrated novelists of the century. Louisa May Alcott's *Little Women* (1868) reveals the rhetoric of age as a core disciplinary idiom in the lives of girls and women, who must constantly calibrate their behavior and appearance to their chronological age. In *Work: A Story of Experience* (1873), she ventures that numerical age might serve as a viable measure of maturity for women, but she denaturalizes the seeming inevitability of gendered norms and the developmental teleology that underwrites them. For Alcott, it was essential to envision alternative versions of female maturity, departing from linear models of aging as decline.

Adulthood was not merely withheld from white women and all people of color; it was also a status that one could outgrow if one lived long enough. That is, if adulthood is linked to autonomy, independence, and the privilege of visibility, then by the end of the century, elderly people were disqualified from adulthood. The fourth chapter reads New England regionalism as a response to this pathologization of old age. The old maids, spinsters, and widows that populate the short fiction of Mary Wilkins Freeman and Sarah Orne Jewett stage a subversive dialogue with the scientific and cultural denigration of the elderly, particularly elderly women, and resist the homogenizing effects of this discourse. While much scholarship acknowledges the prevalence of elderly people in regionalism, linking old age to the passing of old modes of living, this chapter urges us to see the elderly characters in this genre not as metaphors for dying ways of life but as representations of elderly bodies and subjectivities in their own right. These authors force us to question the celebration of independence and autonomy imbricated in fantasies of adulthood and in American identity itself.

The final chapter turns to Henry James, often hailed as the "Master" and the only mature American novelist, and yet, James' fiction actually unsettles the notion of adulthood, complicating rather than consolidating this category. In *What Maisie Knew* (1897), James exposes the various inflections that compromise the autonomy of the adult subject, suggesting that age alone does not produce independence, rationality, or maturity. Indeed, the notion of adulthood as an epoch of independence and self-determination may be a fiction not unlike that of childhood innocence. His work highlights how adulthood derives much of its cultural authority through an enduring association with independence, particularly financial independence, and suggests that interdependence and caregiving may entail forms of maturity that are not rewarded, sanctioned, or made legible in a culture that confuses coming of age with class assent and individualism.

* * *

The cultural meanings of age continue to change even as I write this book (I hesitate to use the words "evolve" or "develop," which might imply that we are approaching a final, culminating, "true" kind of knowledge about age). Economic downturns and medical breakthroughs have simultaneously altered the normative life course and increased life expectancy, leaving social scientists scrambling to coin new terms for ostensibly new stages of life. For instance, noting that many young people are choosing marriage and parenthood later in life, sociologist Jeffrey Arnett has dubbed the late teens and early twenties "emerging adulthood,"[63] and the media remains fixated on the notion of the "boomerang generation." Young people in the twenty-first century often refer to the act of "adulting," acknowledging that maturity is a culturally scripted performance that requires conscious effort rather than an inevitable and intrinsic stage of life.[64]

However, the surfeit of social science data and research on the aging experience masks a failure to imagine age beyond the models we have inherited from nineteenth-century precursors. Indeed, books are still being published by chief historians of age and the family that naturalize the normative telos of heterosexuality as the sole pathway to adulthood.[65] *Adulthood and Other Fictions* argues that nineteenth-century writers questioned this trajectory even in its nascence, railing against the insistence on marriage, the requirement to participate in the capitalist economy, and the imperative to reproduce. American writers have long sought alternative ways to conceptualize age and have questioned the limited terms by which maturity is defined.

Though this book seeks to denaturalize age and to historicize the stages of life, it does not disregard the biological aspects of age. Instead, as Anna Mae Duane writes, "we must rigorously engage science's biological parameters in relation to, rather than treat them as the ontological opponent of, other forms of knowledge."[66] Indeed, the false dichotomy of biology and culture prevents us from seeing how cultural shifts incite biological changes and vice versa.[67] For example, research in neuroscience suggests that chronological age and biological age may not be synonymous. The 2009 Nobel Prize in Medicine was awarded to Elizabeth Blackburn for her discovery of the telomere, a bit of DNA attached to chromosomes. Studying the telomere has enabled scientists to see how the psychological stress of caring for sick children affected the biological age of mothers. Their research demonstrates that "age" is not merely produced by chronological years but by a host of other factors, such as stress, which is often linked to socioeconomic class and gender-specific labor. Indeed, such studies explode the phantasmatic unity of age, as they reveal that "age" can refer to a range of different statuses. Chronological age thus fails as universal or wholly reliable measure of age such that we might revise the chafing popular adage that "age is just a number" to "age is a few different numbers" or even move away from quantitative measures altogether as they are clearly indeterminate.

Likewise, scholars have drawn attention to how the economic consequences of neoliberalism have rendered the traditional pathways to adulthood "obsolete, unattainable, or undesirable."[68] Sociologist Jennifer Silva's
research reveals that the precarity of working-class existence makes conventional adulthood—as defined by stability and dignity—unattainable
and elusive. In a related vein, Julie Passanante Elman notes that the category
of the teenager has increasingly been used as a counterpoint to the "adult
citizen, a rational and stable subject position," making teens "development
opportunities" who must learn that "endless self-surveillance and enhance-
ment are not only innately healthy but also central to good citizenship."[69]
Such studies remind us that age categories and expectations for human
development are themselves the products of socioeconomic circumstances
rather than inherent aspects of the human condition.

Indeed, we must acknowledge how social inequalities unevenly age
disadvantaged populations. As Toni Calasanti, Kathleen Slevin, and Neal
King put it, "The point at which one becomes 'old' varies with these other
inequalities."[70] Just as slavery used age as a metric of economic value and
a tool for dehumanization so too does contemporary racism pervert the
life course. As Ruth Wilson Gilmore writes, racism "intensif[ies] the
anxieties that lead to premature deaths due to alcoholism and drug addic-
tions (including cigarettes), heart disease, suicide, crimes of passion, and
other killers that relentlessly stalk the urban working poor."[71] Surely, we
can add police murders and hate crimes to this list. In other words, the
stresses of racism result in premature aging and shorter life spans, revealing
that age is a measure wholly inflected by other subject positions and must
therefore be considered from an intersectional perspective.[72]

Ultimately, age is neither entirely biological nor completely cultural.
As British historian Pat Thane maintains, age "cannot simply be a social
construct, an artifice of perception, or fashioned through discourse—
unquestionably bodies age, change, decay—but the images, expectations,
and experience of older men and women have been constructed in different ways at different times and for differing people at any one time."[73] In
other words, while we cannot overlook the material realities of aging and
death, the embodied aspects of growing older, this book urges us to see
many aspects of age as naturalized more than natural.

As social scientists and Hollywood blockbusters cast the early twenty-first
century as a watershed moment in terms of American aging, we might well
remember that the nineteenth-century United States witnessed the incep-
tion of this paradigm: an unprecedented number of people entering old
age, the rise of "new" life stages, scientific discoveries about the aging process. By tracing the rise of age culture in the nineteenth century, this book

seeks to show how deeply cultural discourses, especially narratives and images, shape conceptions of growing older as well as convert cultural beliefs into common sense. As Pierre Bourdieu reminds us, classificatory systems, like age, "are not so much a means of knowledge as of power, harnessed to social functions overtly or covertly aimed at satisfying the interests of a group."[74] If we begin to read with an eye for age ideology, then we can become attuned as well to how it operates in tandem with other subject positions and forms of social organization to police individuals and to bolster existing power relations.

1

"May I Never Be a Man"

Immaturity in Melville's America

"There is no steady unretracing progress in this life; we do not advance through fixed gradations, and at the last one pause: —through infancy's unconscious spell, boyhood's thoughtless faith, adolescence' doubt (the common doom), then scepticism, then disbelief, resting at last in manhood's pondering repose of If. But once gone through, we trace the round again; and are infants, boys, and men, and Ifs eternally."

Herman Melville, *Moby-Dick*

After Melville's death in 1891, a quotation was found affixed to the inside of his desk: "Keep true to the dreams of thy youth." Scholars have interpreted Melville's affinity for this adage, by the German poet Friedrich Schiller, in a number of ways: as an attempt to "persuade himself of the transcendent, if not, transcendental, value of his life," as a reference to his father, and as a reminder of early religious aspirations.[1] But we might also consider Melville's attachment to this motto as a point of departure for thinking about his representation of youth as an endangered realm of dreams and ideals that one must protect. The quotation suggests that one should remain faithful to the "dreams of thy youth" rather than replace them with more mature or appropriate ambitions.

Melville's work offers a point of entry into the intensifying discussions about age and development that arose in the mid-nineteenth century. When we revisit his work through the lens of age, it is apparent that his fiction champions the "dreams of youth," rejecting the trajectory toward adult masculinity defined exhaustively in this moment as the basis of American development. In his oeuvre, he exposes adulthood as an ideological construction rather than a biological inevitability and questions the value of maturity and development for individuals and for the nation itself.

Historians have dubbed the nineteenth-century America's "adolescence," a period of growing pains and turmoil that ultimately resulted in the economic prosperity of the twentieth century.[2] Carroll Smith-Rosenberg, for example, writes that in the nineteenth-century "America itself was the adolescent," and Joseph Kett similarly describes Jacksonian society as adolescent.[3] Beyond these retrospective descriptors, however, many contemporary Americans thought of themselves and their period this way. In the antebellum United States, immaturity and youth were buzzwords.[4] Henry David Thoreau revered youth, rejecting the notion that the old have anything worthwhile to impart to younger generations. As he writes in *Walden*, "Practically, the old have no very important advice to give the young, their own experience has been so partial, and their lives have been such miserable failures."[5] He went on to claim: "I have lived some thirty years on this planet, and I have yet to hear the first syllable of valuable or even earnest advice from my seniors." This contempt for the old bespeaks the transcendental commitment to personal revelation over received wisdom, linking Thoreau to the project of generational self-definition, which hinged on dismissing the lionized founders. Moreover, Thoreau's rejection of "earnest advice" gestures to the popularity of advice manuals and guidebooks, which sought to ensure that young men would come of age appropriately.

This exultation of youth penetrated even Harvard University, the oldest American institution of higher learning. Echoing Thoreau's contempt for preceding generations, Charles Russell Lowell's 1854 address to Harvard's graduating class was provocatively entitled "The Reverence Due from Old Men to Young." Lowell told the audience: "The old men, the men of the last generation, cannot teach us of the present what *should* be, for that we know as well as they, or better." Lowell's inversion of the idea that young people can learn from their elders was part of a broader cultural turn toward age as a consequential site of difference and meaning. In his *Harper's* column, Samuel Osgood gestured to the intensity of this generational rhetoric, asking, "Why should there be this harsh antagonism between youth and age?"[6]

The identificatory appeal of youth was perhaps most explicitly displayed by the Young America literary movement, a loose collective of New York City intellectuals, which included John O'Sullivan, Cornelius Matthews, Evert Duyckinck, and Walt Whitman.[7] Beginning in 1837, these writers and thinkers gathered in barrooms and basements in the city and published their ideas in the *United States and Democratic Review*. They admired Andrew Jackson's fervent populism and rejected the cultural elitism of the Whigs, aspiring instead to be the "roughs" of Whitman's famous formulation. They lamented being born too late to participate in the Revolution and therefore decreed that the Revolution was unfinished; Americans were too dependent on their forebears and European counterparts and needed to finally break away and begin anew. As Emerson bemoaned his generation's dependence on the "dry bones of the past," these writers actively sought to embody the present and to produce works of literature that represented the nation in all its vitality.[8] By 1845, they had begun to refer to themselves as "Young Americans," celebrating youth and newness as core values and emphasizing the need for a new vision of national futurity distinct from the plans of previous generations.[9]

Over the course of his career, Melville's relation to the Young America movement shifted from ardent support to ambivalence and ultimately to disaffection. While he was often vocal about his commitment to literary nationalism, most famously in "Hawthorne and his Mosses" in 1850, he satirized the group in his 1852 novel *Pierre; or the Ambiguities*. In a chapter titled "Young America in Literature," Melville describes a literary market-place in which authors are "haunted by publishers, engravers, editors, critics, autograph-collectors, portrait-fanciers, biographers, and petitioning and remonstrating literary friends of all sorts."[10] This description seethes with Melville's hostility toward a marketplace that makes crass, commercial demands on authors and thrives on networking and publicity; these were precisely the expectations that the Young America literary circle placed upon him.[11] Coupled with his frustration with such demands and with the group's unenthusiastic response to *Moby-Dick*, Melville also found himself less aligned with the movement's ideological underpinnings, particularly its commitment to westward expansion and slavery. Melville's complicated relation to the Young America movement—and the political commitments it came to embrace—is a defining feature of his fiction.

Published in 1849, Melville's semi-autobiographical fourth novel, *Redburn* centers in the problem of maturity. While some have read it as a classic story of initiation, *Redburn* fits more comfortably in a tradition of nineteenth-century American novels that thwart the conventional coming-of-age plot and instead offer delayed, inverted, rerouted, interrupted, or otherwise unconventional life narratives.[12] As failed *Bildungsromans*, such fictions disrupt the traditional linkage of narrative development and character maturation.[13] Certainly other scholars have read classic American litera-ture as childish or hostile to the demands of adult masculinity. Leslie Fiedler famously diagnosed the American literary tradition as "almost juvenile," noting the compulsive "return to a limited world of experience, usually associated with his childhood."[14] But rather than read the retreat from adult heterosexuality as a rejection of politics and as anti-feminist escapism, we might see such narratives instead as politicized refusals to acquiesce to the normative social order and its ideological imperatives.[15]

In recent years, the field of childhood studies has generated a robust body of scholarship focused on illuminating the multivalent significance of the child in nineteenth-century American literature and culture. Karen Sanchez-Eppler's pioneering work has directed attention to children as historical and cultural actors, as both "forces" and "objects of socialization."[16] Anna Mae Duane has examined the "child's role in mediating cultural and colonial violence" while Robin Bernstein's work uncovers the inextricability of childhood innocence from the production of racial ideology.[17] This chapter seeks to build upon this work, but it is focused less on childhood than on immaturity itself, unmoored from a corresponding biological age.[18] Instead, it addresses the ideological demand to "come of age" in the mid-nineteenth century, drawing attention to the cultural preoccupation with the transition to adulthood and the anxieties that attended this ostensibly natural development.[19] Nineteenth-century writers, such as Melville, acknowledged the disciplinary function of age scripts, and far from representing childhood as a stage from which one inevitably advances, they explored dilated adolescence in ways that prefigure twenty-first century anxieties about the "boomerang generation" and the "failure to launch."[20]

ENVISIONING THE STAGES OF LIFE

With the emergence of what Charles Sellers calls the "market revolution," the Jacksonian period gave rise to altered expectations for coming of age.[21] Young people, specifically young white men, were expected to embrace the ethos of capitalism and to assume trajectories that often departed from those of prior generations, thus destabilizing models of development that presumed the generational continuity of rites of passages and occupations.[22] By 1850, Hawthorne looks backward at a culture in which occupations were reproduced in a generational cycle. As he writes in the Custom House section of *The Scarlet Letter*:

> From father to son, for above a hundred years, they followed the sea; a gray-headed shipmaster, in each generation, retiring from the quarter-deck to the homestead, while a boy of fourteen took the hereditary place before the mast, confronting the salt spray and the gale, which had blustered against his sire and grandsire.[23]

Hawthorne's reflection describes a not-so-distant past in which occupations were transmitted lineally; sons experienced the same rites of passage ("confronting the salt spray and the gale" and moving from forecastle to the cabin) as their fathers and grandfathers. To mature and achieve manhood meant encountering the very same obstacles as one's predecessors.

However, as innovations in transportation and communication transformed the US economy, men moved from agricultural and family-run operations to factory jobs and urban businesses in large numbers. Consequently, white boys grew up without their fathers present in the same ways as in the past.[24] As economic and cultural changes gave rise to new experiences of white boyhood, so too were mainstream ideas about coming of age thrown into crisis. As Steven Mintz observes, "At no time was the passage from adolescence to adulthood less predictable, orderly, or uniform than in the early nineteenth century."[25]

The emergence of a working-class youth subculture in New York, as well as in Philadelphia and Boston, exemplified the feisty democratic spirit of the era and the newly meaningful generational gap that separated sons from their fathers in this tumultuous period. The Bowery "b'hoys" and "ghals," for example, spoke in their own slang parlance, adopted a unique flashy style, and flouted middle-class expectations for domesticity and refinement [see Figure 1.1].[26] Like Melville and his literary Young Americans, the working-class b'hoys transformed youth into a style and a political statement that challenged reigning age and gender expectations.

Because the appropriate development of young men was considered integral to the course of the young nation, popular art and literature fixated on the proper development of young people, particularly boys.[27] Cultural authorities sought to channel juvenile energy in productive ways and cautioned that disproportionate amounts of recreation were dangerous.[28] In his "Lectures to Young Men," delivered over the course of 1843 and 1844, Henry Ward Beecher urged adolescents to temper their passions and to avoid those "amusements which violently inflame and gratify [men's] appetites."[29] He cautions against "strange women," certain "popular amusements," and "gambling." An abundance of publications centered on what one writer called the "elements of a manly course," likening coming of age to a voyage or journey and urging young men to weather this passage on the straight and narrow. In his manual, John C. Todd, for example, referred to "discipline [a]s the life and salvation of such a ship in a such a storm."[30]

In the same vein, periodicals such as the *Youth's Penny Gazette*, a weekly paper published by the American Sunday-School Union, advised young men to avoid excess and idleness and to commit to religious study. The 1846 masthead of the *Youth's Penny Gazette* depicts manhood as four distinct stages, reminding readers of the proper course of life [see Figure 1.2].

Such popular iconography stressed the linear path of development, as if to remind Americans that life cycles remained constant in spite of uncertainties in social and political life. These images constructed the pathway from youth to adulthood as a turbulent journey that would conclude with discovery, arrival, and completion of the self. Among the most famous paintings of the mid-nineteenth century were Thomas Cole's *Voyage of Life* paintings (1842), a series of four images that represent an allegory of the four stages of human life: childhood, youth, manhood, and old age. As art historian Alan Wallach notes, "Cole's *Voyage of Life* enjoyed a popularity

Figure 1.1. Nicolino Calyo, "Soap-locks, or Bowery Boys", *c.*1847, watercolor on paper. Collection of the New-York Historical Society.

Figure 1.2. Masthead, *Youth's Penny Gazette c.* 1846. Courtesy of the American Antiquarian Society.

equaled by few works in the history of American art."[31] These paintings are sweeping panoramas in which a maturing individual is set against a massive landscape. For example, Cole represents childhood as sailing smoothly on a glassy river, while manhood is set on a turbulent river beneath ominous clouds [see Figure 1.3].

Figure 1.3. Thomas Cole, *The Voyage of Life: Manhood*, 1842.

The series depicts a set of assumptions about the stages of life, including that one should naturally progress according to a timeless, linear model of development and that manhood should be a period of physical and spiritual testing.[32] In Cole's painting, the rudder is lost, and the voyager prays to God. Significantly, adulthood is defined by masculinity; the very term "manhood" reminds us that maturity is a gender-specific construction. The stark solitude of the figures in the panoramas suggests the individualist spirit of the era, affirming the notion that the journey through life is fundamentally about the development of the self.[33]

In the wake of the astounding popularity of Thomas Cole's *Voyage of Life* series, Nathaniel Currier, George Cram, and James Baillie were just a few of the artists to gravitate toward the stages of life as subject matter for paintings.[34] Their images of the life course were posted on bedroom walls and printed as broadsides, and in the words of one historian, the popularity of this theme reveals "just how obsessed Americans really were with the life cycle during the middle decades of the 19th century."[35] Both Currier's woodcut engraving, *Life and Age of Man* (*c*.1848) and Baillie's "The Life and Age of Man" (1848) depict man at eleven stages of life, emphasizing a linear development that peaks after youthful military service [see Figure 1.4].[36] In both images, two full stages of life are defined

Figure 1.4. James Baillie, *The Life and Age of Man: Stages of Man's Life from the Cradle to the Grave*, *c.*1848. Library of Congress.

by military service, perhaps unsurprisingly given that 1848 was a landmark year in the history of American conquest.[37]

According to the illustrations, the height of male development and success culminates in planting an American flag at the top of the arc, a gesture that resonates with the expansionist aims of the era. As Thomas Cole puts it, "This iconography of the life course reveals the middle-class quest for a normal life course, increasingly defined in terms of health and material self-reliance."[38] In addition, it affirms the expectation that men should devote their adolescence and early adulthood to the service of the nation, eventually transitioning to the business world. Thus, this image naturalizes a life course centered in militarized national service and capitalist wealth acquisition.

Significantly, the same artists depicted the "Life and Age of Woman," and women's development appears markedly different from her male counterparts, revealing that the meanings of age and the expectations for development were deeply gendered. Based on the Baillie and Currier illustrations, women appear to be in their prime at stage three, just before marriage; by stage six (the height of the male arc) the women already appear haggard and hunched [see Figure 1.5]. Of the differences between

Figure 1.5. Nathaniel Currier, *The Life and Age of Woman: Stages of Woman's Life from the Cradle to the Grave*, c.1848. Library of Congress.

the "Age of Man" and "Age of Woman" illustrations, art historian Claire Perry notes, "The man gesticulates energetically throughout the tableau, communicating to viewers about where he had been and where he will go. In contrast, the young girl is moored in place, assuming a fixed and neutral stance that she will maintain until her back is stooped by old age."[39] While women's lives are rooted in caregiving and domestic duties, men should experience development as tied to movement, action, and experience. When juxtaposed, the male and female "stages of life" clearly reinforce a middle-class ethos of "separate spheres." Moreover, with their emphasis on militaristic nationalism, business, and reproduction, the images demonstrate how the social and cultural meanings given to specific ages correspond with the economic and ideological investments of the state.

These renderings of the life course rely on a view of development as stadial, with images of discrete stages, separated by stairs and distinctive backgrounds and contexts. This genre's reliance on the trope of stairs to denote the "stages of life" implies the extent to which development was expected to follow a clear, undeviating course; reaching the top stair is depicted as an accomplishment, the achievement of gender compliance and the expression of conventional maturity. However, as Jay Prosser reminds us, "gender is not a teleological narrative of ontology at all."[40] Rather, it is circular, discursive, and performative; repeated acts congeal over time to produce the appearance of substance. In other words, one does not inevitably pass *through* a set of stages ultimately arriving at the destination of man or woman. By disseminating this linear view of development, nineteenth-century visual culture participated in naturalizing gender performance and established the mutually constitutive norms for both gender and age. Moreover, the stark whiteness of these renderings of the life course implies the racial logic that informs cultural ideas about development and maturity.

REDBURN AS FAILED *BILDUNGSROMAN*

The proliferation of gender and age-prescriptive images and texts that circulated in this period find clear counterparts in American literature, a tradition rife with narratives that celebrate self-making and individual ascent. However, beyond vaunting individualism and the consolidation of the self, nineteenth-century fiction also functions as an imaginative space that enabled critiques of the rigid expectations for development and maturity. In spite—or perhaps because—of the national zeal for stories of progress and linear assent, a countertradition of fiction narrativizes the unmaking of the self and dwells in stasis, juvenilia, and circularity.

Published during a moment in which calls proliferated for individual Americans and the nation at large to come of age, Melville's *Redburn,* exposes maturation as profoundly ideological, tied to capitalist and nationalist agendas. In *Redburn,* Melville debunks maturity—for the individual and for the nation—as desirable, espousing a politics of refusal and unmasking mature manhood as corrupt, limiting, and unnatural. Departing from the Young Americans' belief in the necessity of national progress, *Redburn* endorses circularity over linearity, homosocial play over heterosexual closure, and the irreverence of youth over the inflexible requirements of adulthood.[41] It asks: How does the imperative to mature ultimately mask a demand for normativity? At whose expense does such maturity occur, and what values does the ideal of maturity naturalize? In an era defined by the rapid rise of market capitalism and national growth, *Redburn* interrogates the costs of the frenzy to profit, expand, and develop.

Initially, *Redburn* seems to be a conventional coming-of-age novel, centered in a classic story of male "voyage."[42] The novel tells the story of the naïve Wellingborough Redburn's journey aboard the *Highlander,* a merchant ship bound for Liverpool. Its opening chapters and subtitle, "His First Voyage, Being the Sailor Boy Confessions and Reminiscences of the Son-Of-A-Gentleman in the Merchant Navy," signal an interest in rites of passage and initiation. Like his literary descendant Ishmael, young Redburn is avid for life experience, having gleaned a romantic view of the sailor's life from novels and family stories, but from the moment he boards the *Highlander*, Redburn's preconceptions about the sailor's life—and about life in general—are repeatedly shattered. "Was this the beginning of my sea-career? Set to cleaning out a pigpen, the very first thing?" Redburn wonders.[43] He does not anticipate the cold and authoritarian Captain Riga, the brutal hazing rituals, or the squalid conditions of life aboard the ship.

Narrated retrospectively, "after the lapse of so many years," Redburn notes that when he first joined the merchant marines, he "was then but a boy" with a "young inland imagination."[44] He hints at the novel's backward orientation when he notes that he had already "learned to think much and bitterly before my time; all my mounting dreams of glory had left me; and that early age, I was unambitious as a man of sixty."[45] Of his premature encounter with life's hardships, Redburn laments, "It is a hard and cruel thing thus in early youth to taste beforehand the pangs which should be reserved for the stout time of manhood."[46] Thus, his oceanic voyage is linked with a desire to regain what Melville called the "dream of youth."

For much of the novel, the narrator reinhabits the consciousness of his younger self, calling attention to his naïve and idealistic perspective.[47] For example, of his ignorance of the workings of the marketplace, Redburn recalls: "I never thought of working for my living, and never knew that there were hard hearts in the world...How different my idea of money now!"[48] Later, he observes a scene of wrenching poverty: "I stood looking down on them, while my whole soul swelled within me; and I asked myself, What right had any body in the wide world to smile and be glad, when sights like this were to be seen?"[49] Redburn's immaturity works as a mechanism for defamiliarizing the adult world and revealing its inadequacies; "may I never be a man," he thinks to himself while observing the cruelty of his fellow sailors. The ostensibly childish questions and observations of young Redburn call into question the qualifications for and desirability of adulthood, as they suggest that to grow up is to become accustomed to "hard hearts" and disturbing injustices.[50] In other words, immaturity serves as a critical stance, a position that casts the social constructions of contemporary society into stark relief.

Redburn's disillusionment with the sailor's life and the knowledge he gleans about society would seem to be necessary elements of his maturation. Indeed, coming-of-age novels are all in some sense about coming to understand the harsh realities of the adult world. But what differentiates *Redburn* from the conventional novel of development is its revelation that one need not accommodate these imperatives. Moreover, the novel exposes maturity as a construction that corresponds with capitalism, nationalism, and other ideological systems; it is thus attentive to the biopolitical function of coming of age as a trope and to the naturalization of developmental discourse as a political tactic. In *Redburn,* coming of age is synonymous with coming to accept the demands of capitalism, the brutality of masculinity, and the corruption of authority figures; rites of passage do not usher one into a deeper sense of individualism but rather impose a monolithic set of normative values.

Melville represents scripts of development as inseparable from gender scripts, and thus the novel's contempt for development takes the specific shape of a critique and dismantling of manhood. Early in the novel, Redburn's older brother offers him his shooting jacket and fowling-piece to bring on his overseas voyage, but these items prove to be cumbersome and outdated. The fowling-piece, at once the ultimate phallic symbol and a mockery of that symbol, is mocked by the ship's captain, and the shooting jacket becomes the butt of numerous jokes. Redburn is re-christened "Buttons," a dig at the jacket's prissy buttons and a sign of the journey's infantilizing rather than ennobling effects. Thus, from the moment he leaves home, the novel stages a disjunction between inherited ideas about sailors' lives and new, less romantic realities. The old emblems of male autonomy are irrelevant, even laughable, in a market-based world in which Redburn lacks even the funds to pay his passage to New York. Indeed, Melville emphasizes the impotence of these older tokens of male prowess when Redburn is unable to sell them, except very cheaply to a pawnbroker; they carry little value in a capitalist market.

Similarly, Redburn receives a copy of *Wealth of Nations* from Mr. Jones, a friend of his brother. Redburn finds the book as "dry as crackers and cheese" and wonders whether Mrs. Jones or his father or "anybody had ever read it, even the author himself."[51] At length I fell asleep, with the volume in my hand; and never slept so sound before; after that I used to wrap my jacket round it, and use it for a pillow."[52] Thus, from his brother's shooting jacket and fowling-piece to the copy of *Wealth of Nations* he receives from an older friend, Redburn is encumbered with the paraphernalia of normative masculinity but he cannot make proper use of it—these items are unwieldy rather than instrumental, soporific rather than edifying.[53]

Bequeathed to him by male role models, Redburn's alienation from and subsequent rejection of the inherited fowling-piece and the copy of *Wealth of Nations* suggest his disillusionment with both residual and emergent, market-oriented versions of conventional masculinity. As Sara Ahmed writes: "Objects are not only material: they may be values, capital, aspirations, projects, and styles... Through objects," she explains, "we also inherit orientations, that is, we inherit ways of inhabiting and extending into space."[54] The objects that are meant to orient Redburn, to locate him within the values of normative, middle-class white masculinity, are rendered meaningless—and their function is denaturalized by Redburn's incapacity to utilize them properly.[55]

Most significant among the array of objects that Redburn takes with him on the voyage are his father's guidebooks from his own days as a sailor. Annotated with "half-effaced miscellaneous memoranda in pencil," the guidebooks are supposed to enable Redburn to experience Liverpool as his father did."[56] As it turns out, the books are out of date and thus cannot orient him in time and space. Upon asking about a hotel highlighted by his father, Redburn is told that the establishment was torn down many years ago, leading him to realize the futility of the guidebook:

> The book on which I had so much relied; the book in the morocco cover; the book with the cock-hat corners; the book full of fine old family associations; the book with seventeen plates, executed in the highest style of art; this previous book was next to useless. Yes, the thing that had guided the father, could not guide the son.[57]

This obsolete inherited text indicates that the old rules of conduct no longer apply. Whereas Hawthorne recalled an era in which life at sea was inherited lineally from father to son, Melville narrates a generational rupture, suggesting that prior models need to be jettisoned.[58] The elaborate description of the book's ornate and artful design points to its status as iconic, enduring, and vaunted, which makes its inutility all the more striking. The disconnect between the father and the son's experience of Liverpool, and of boyhood more generally, fits into a culture-wide awareness of the generational rift occasioned by the expansion of market society. According to Smith-Rosenberg, "Sons found themselves within a world neither they nor their fathers understood... The men of Jacksonian America experienced themselves both as loosed from the fathers' ways and fathers increasingly troubled as to how to provide for, control, or even to understand the experiences of their sons."[59]

While Redburn bemoans the inutility of the guidebooks, Melville thematizes this generational distancing and reveals the pitfalls of inherited patriarchal logic. Redburn's attempts to use the guidebooks make him a kind of Rip Van Winkle, thrown out of time by rapid social changes, unable to retrace the routes of previous generations. But rather than pathologize this failure to progress according to the path of maturation proffered by preachers, popular artists, and paternal figures, Melville dismantles and interrogates received ideas about progress and maturation. Only through accepting discontinuity with the past and abandoning what

Michel Foucault calls the "consoling play of recognitions" can we achieve knowledge; old guidebooks offer a comforting connection to a family history and seem to provide a reassuring roadmap for how to live, but they are utterly worthless in Redburn's own moment.[60] Thus, the novel indicates that the failure of his father's map opens up the liberatory possibilities that inhere in doing away with the old conventions. Moreover, the novel's attention to guidebooks echoes the contemporary obsession with advice manuals and guidebooks for young men, which Melville seems to be parodying as irrelevant and non-functional.

It is surely no coincidence that Redburn's realization of the guidebook's obsolescence is followed closely by his encounter with Harry Bolton, a British youth described as "one of those small but perfectly formed beings, with curling hair and silken muscles...with a complexion as feminine as a girl's" and "large, black, and womanly" eyes.[61] Redburn first notices Harry "standing in doorways" near the docks and is struck by the "beauty, dress, and manner" of this "delicate exotic." From his association with liminal spaces to his dandyish manner, Bolton is characterized as deviant in multiple ways, most visibly in his gender behavior. His entrance in the novel is directly linked to textual and narrative perversion; he takes Redburn to places that make no appearance on the maps of Redburn senior. Among them is Aladdin's Palace, a London gambling den and male brothel, described by Melville as a "semi-public place of opulent entertainment."[62] Upon entering this Wildean world of decadence, Redburn thinks, "My head was almost dizzy with the strangeness of the sight."[63] Whereas Redburn experiences his first encounter with England as a disappointment, thinking, "If *that's* the way a foreign country looks, I might as well have staid at home," Bolton introduces him to a truly foreign world; it is the only time that Redburn is truly transported in a novel ostensibly about a voyage. Redburn begins to "fancy I had not friends and relatives living in a little village three thousand five hundred miles off, in America."[64] Thus, Redburn's experience in Aladdin's Palace dislocates him from family as well as nation. Moreover, a devout member of the Juvenile Temperance Society as well as the Anti-Smoking Society, Redburn is aware of breaking the rules of his middle-class culture and of his family: "What would my brother have said?" he wonders as he strays from the conventional path.[65] While he is disconcerted by the aesthetics of this queer space, Redburn's mysterious night in London cements his break from his family and from the normative capitalist logic of the *Highlander*.

Literary criticism has long acknowledged that the novel form is defined by its reliance on character development and on the logic of progress. In his landmark work *The Rise of the Novel*, Ian Watt distinguishes the novel from other forms of fiction by observing that "a causal connection operating through time replaces the reliance of earlier narratives on disguises and coincidences, and this tends to give the novel a much more cohesive structure."[66] In other words, the novel is premised on a linear temporal sequence. Of all novel forms, the *Bildungsroman*, or coming-of-age novel, best exemplifies this sequential plot. Marianne Hirsch, for instance, defines the *Bildungsroman* as the genre in which "the events of the hero's life are chronologically and causally connected, portraying an individual process of becoming... The novel of formation is founded on the belief in progress and the coherence of selfhood."[67] Like the "Stages of Life" paintings, the *Bildungsroman* celebrates the overcoming of obstacles and inevitable unfolding of adulthood.

With the rise of queer theory, many scholars have observed the ways in which such a structure relies on and reinforces heteronormativity. For example, novels rely on heterosexual coupling and/or childbirth for closure, and those characters that cannot or will not mature are made peripheral, even antagonistic, to the development of a normative protagonist. Judith Roof claims that narrative itself relies on and reinforces linear heterosexual development, which she dubs "narrative's heteroideology."[68] She writes, "narrative's apparent rendition of life experience, then, is already an ideological version of (re)production produced by the figurative cooperation of a naturalized capitalism and heterosexuality."[69] Thus, for Roof, narrative is inseparable from a heterosexual telos; narrative undergirds and naturalizes normative sexual and gender development.

In *Redburn*, Melville disentangles narrative from normative sexuality and the developmental logic it instantiates. *Redburn* thwarts the teleology of the novel, and of the *Bildungsroman* more specifically, not only by denaturalizing the processes of development, but also by figuratively halting the progress of both the individual and the nation.[70] While contemporary popular culture idealized and naturalized development as a journey, Redburn's voyage is defined instead by circularity and repetition instead of a linear arc.[71] His queer experience at Aladdin's Palace incites a regression in the development of Redburn as a character and heralds an abrupt turn in the novel's geographic trajectory. The morning after Redburn's experiences in Aladdin's Palace, the *Highlander* begins its return voyage to the United States, with Harry as a new member of the crew. The foray into Harry's mysterious underworld thus incites the perversion of narrative development, aligning with Roof's observation that queer characters "contribute to the perversion of narrative's reproductive aegis."[72] Where *Redburn* may have seemed like a conventional *Bildungsroman*, preparing us for progress and becoming, we are instead rerouted; in the parlance of sailors, the novel "comes about."

Redburn's "coming about" is a recoil from adult masculinity and compulsory heterosexuality and is also a response to the force of what might be called a national *Bildungsroman*, a narrative of progress that endorsed territorial expansion and economic growth. Since the Revolutionary era, the American nation has been imagined as a child, and this rich metaphor has been invoked repeatedly to understand the country's genealogy, its revolution against a "corrupt parent" (in Thomas Paine's words), and its national character.[73] By the late 1840s, the use of age discourse to naturalize the nation and its progressive linear history became even more pronounced. The Young America movement had entered a new phase, often called "Young America II."[74] In this second wave, Young Americans supported the Mexican–American War, slavery, and the other projects that would ostensibly "advance" the nation. Edward Widmer describes "the metamorphosis of an innocent youth movement into a call for more territory, unleashing tensions over slavery and exposing democracy to ridicule."[75]

Melville, however, was increasingly skeptical about such modes of advancement and measures of achievement. According to Widmer, "More than any writer, Herman Melville registered an acute disappointment with the failure of Young America, a psychic wound that coincided with his thrust at greatness."[76] He was suspicious of an uninterrogated celebration of national progress through conquest. A fellow sailor seems to be speaking for Melville himself when he asks Redburn: "What's the use of bein' snivelized?... Are *you* now Buttons, any better off for bein' snivelized?... no, you a'rn' abit—but you're a good deal *worse* for it, Buttons... Snivelization has been the ruin on ye, and it's spiled me complete. Blast Ameriky, I say."[77] Though the dialect renders the sailor's speech comic, the sailor voices skepticism about civilization and progress, noting that in places like "Madagasky," one doesn't "see any darned beggars."[78] In other words, we should neither consider development a natural or inevitable aspect of any society nor should we presume that capitalist modernization is synonymous with improvement. As Redburn reflects on the return journey, "We may have civilized bodies and yet barbarous souls. We are blind to the real sights of this world; deaf to its voice; and dead to its death."[79] These concerns about the supposed superiority of Western civilization were already manifest in Melville's first novel *Typee* (1846), an "arrested romance," in the words of one critic.[80]

In *Moby-Dick,* he offers a similarly suspicious view of teleological development for individuals or nations, envisioning the course of life as cyclical, rather than linear. In a chapter called "The Gilder," he writes, "There is no steady unretracing progress in this life; we do not advance through fixed gradations, and at the last one pause:—through infancy's unconscious spell, boyhood's thoughtless faith, adolescence' doubt (the common doom), then scepticism, then disbelief, resting at last in manhood's pondering repose of If. But once gone through, we trace the round again; and are infants, boys, and men, and Ifs eternally."[81] This is a kind of rejoinder to the "stages of life" images that rely on sharp distinctions between youth, adulthood, and old age. Instead, Melville suggests an alternative understanding of aging, one that permits recursion and accretion rather than lockstep linear advancement.

In *Redburn,* Melville imagines the sea as a space apart from normative development. He describes the "certain wonderful rising and falling of the sea…a sort of wide heaving and swelling and sinking all over the ocean," an anti-linear movement associated with pleasure rather than progress.[82] Such movement reminds us that, as Hester Blum writes, sailors' "freedom from national belonging can make possible other ways of understanding affiliation, citizenship, mobility, and sovereignty."[83] I would add that Melville's sailors also experience freedom from the expectations for gender, sexuality, and age that are mandated by such institutions and structures.

Redburn explains that sailors abide by their own alternative age norms and vocabularies: "In merchant-ships, a *boy* means a green-hand, a landsman on his first voyage. And never mind if he is old enough to be a grandfather, he is still called a *boy*."[84] Thus, the status of a boy is divorced from age; in fact, anyone can be a boy. Moreover, the description of another member of the crew suggests that anyone can be an old man: Jack Blunt, was a "curious looking fellow, about twenty-five years old…but to look at his back, you would have taken him for a little old man"; his "large head of hair…was rapidly turning gray," and he regularly rubs potions and oils on his locks to restore their color. These details highlight the contingency of age, its reliance on geographic and cultural conditions. The sea thus serves as a space outside of conventional clock-based temporality, and consequently, as a realm in which age norms can be evaded and remade.

But the sea is not a wholly beneficent or innocent space. On the contrary, Melville acknowledges its inseparability from the horrors of the middle passage and its traffic in human bodies as well as violence against the natural world. He describes how the aptly named sailor Jackson, a member of Redburn's crew, claims he can deduce another sailor's age by examining his teeth. "His teeth were the evenest and most worn down; which, he said, arose from eating so much hard sea-biscuit; and this was the reason he could tell a sailor's age like a horse's."[85] The use of teeth as a metric for age gestures to the resonances between oceanic labor and slavery, a system that relied on bodily wear to determine numerical age.

The association between the ocean and the slave trade is made even more explicit when Melville writes that Jackson, "with a diabolical relish, used to tell of the *middle-passage,* where the slaves were stowed, heel and point, like logs, and the suffocated and dead were unmanacled, and weeded out from the living every morning, before washing down the decks." It appears that participating in the conversion of human bodies into property has warped Jackson's own development, as he seems strangely un-aged: "It was impossible to tell how old this Jackson was; for he had no beard, and no wrinkles, except small crowsfeet about the eyes. He might have seen thirty, or perhaps fifty years." As we come to learn, the consequences for this brutality have manifested *within* Jackson, leaving his exterior oddly unscathed but severely aging his interior. He is described, much like Ahab, "as being consumed by an incurable malady, that was eating up his vitals."[86] Jackson's youthful appearance, perhaps like the United States itself, conceals a corrupt, prematurely aged core. Indeed, many cultural commentators described the United States as inappropriately aged; at the end of the century, for example, G. Stanley Hall noted that the nation "lack[s] a normal development history … no country is so precociously old for its years."[87]

Redburn thus denaturalizes national and individual development, revealing both projects as oppressive impositions. Thus, while antebellum Americans were zealously pursuing John O'Sullivan's call to fulfill manifest destiny, exploring the so-called "untrodden space" of the future, *Redburn* offers a reversal of national narrative, beginning with a voyage to Britain and then a return to the United States.[88] The novel figures the routes of transatlantic trade as anti-linear, as the *Highlander* does not represent a progressive path toward a future but rather shuttles sailors back and forth between old and new, past and present, in a cycle of endless returns. On the return journey, Redburn witnesses the spontaneous combustion of a corpse, the death of many emigrants in a typhoid epidemic, and the suicide of the malevolent Jackson, who plunges himself overboard. These losses coincide with the return to the American shore, suggesting the human costs of commercial enterprise.

Wai-chee Dimock reads the novel's circularity and Redburn's failure to *go anywhere* as a marker of Melville's own sense of authorial futility. *Redburn* is "the exact opposite of a *Bildungsroman*," she claims, because Redburn's "infantilization is a metaphor for Melville's sense of authorial powerlessness."[89] For her, the novel functions as an allegory for Melville's hostility to an unappreciative literary market. But *Redburn* is less a lament for what is lost than an embrace of losing and a commitment to "infantilization" as a political position. Embedded in the narrative is a condemnation of those who "win" and who align themselves with the nexus of normative values linked to capitalism and maturity. It is in keeping with this sense of the market as unrewarding and unremunerative that the novel's darkly humorous conclusion reveals that Redburn does not earn any money from his journey but in fact *owes* money to Captain Riga, who declares: "By running away from the ship in Liverpool, you forfeited your wages, which amount to twelve dollars...You are therefore indebted to me in precisely that sum."[90] Thus, far from profiting or gaining in a conventional sense at the end of the journey, Redburn is in the red, as it were, leaving with less than he began; significantly, it was his queer sortie with Harry Bolton that economically queered him and steered him off the productive, wage-earning course.

Misreading his fellow crewmembers and accidentally becoming intimates with an alcoholic drifter, Redburn is an expert in what Judith Halberstam has termed the "queer art of failure."[91] He systematically flouts every one of Henry Ward Beecher's instructions and discovers instead the "unexpected pleasures" of "gender failure," and ends up renegotiating value itself.[92] Profit is refigured apart from capitalism and normative masculinity. That is, Redburn neither gains financially nor does he profit much in the way of experience or life lessons. Instead, the profit, if the word remains appropriate, is in his friendship with Harry and the pleasures of misbehavior. The novel's celebration of backwardness and queer immaturity over futurity-oriented adult masculinity is put boldly on display when the crew of underpaid sailors, safely back in New York, irreverently display their backsides to the aloof Captain.

At the conclusion of the novel, which takes places several years later, Redburn learns that Harry has died in a whaling accident. He is told that Harry first joined the "multitudes of young men, well qualified, seeking employment in counting-houses" and after failing to find a position, joined a whaling voyage and died when "jammed between the ship, and a whale, while we were cutting the fish in."[93] Critics have read Harry's death as a sign of his unfitness for the market-oriented world of the United States, but we might also consider his death as representative of what Elizabeth Freeman calls the "material damage done in the name of development."[94] In other words, it is not Harry's particular unfitness for the market that leads to his death but the normal functioning American marketplace itself, in which young men are smashed, "jammed," and destroyed. Like many of Melville's young male protagonists, including Pierre and Bartleby, Harry's fate bespeaks the unnatural violence of development.

Melville repeatedly deprecated *Redburn* as "a little nursery tale," a characterization that echoes Fiedler's eventual categorization of American literature in general. He told his father-in-law Lemuel Shaw that the texts of both *Redburn* and *White-Jacket* were "two jobs, which I have done for money—being forced to it, as other men are to sawing wood."[95] Ironically, he associated even this book with economic necessity, joyless labor, and adult male responsibility. He ended the letter by admitting that, "it is my earnest desire to write those sort of books which are said to 'fail.'"[96] In other words, Melville recognized how the dictates of commerce define failure, and he never internalized failure itself as undesirable.

Five years later, Melville's own career was taking its now well-known nosedive. *Pierre* had effectively alienated most of the loyal readers he gained with his earlier travel novels. Thus, we might read *Redburn* as a prescient embrace of failure in the name of freedom, experimentation, play, and adventure. According to *Redburn,* it is better to fail at adulthood (or never live to see it) than to align oneself with a civilization that forecloses rather than multiplies the possibilities for pleasure, artistic creativity, and friendship. Indeed, Melville articulated this notion in his 1854 story, "The Happy Failure," in which a young boy observes his uncle's repeated failures to achieve fame and fortune through a series of half-baked inventions. After failing to develop a contraption for draining swamps and marshes, the uncle remarks, "Boy, take my advice, and never try to invent anything but—happiness."[97] At the end of the story, on his deathbed, the uncle announces, "I'm glad I've failed. I say, boy, failure has made a good old man of me. It was horrible at first, but I'm glad I've failed. Praise be to God for the failure!" Failure is thus a preferable alternative to market profitability, an unexpected alternative route to happiness and to becoming a "good old man." This might very well describe Melville's own perspective on a marketplace that never recognized his genius. Thus, if we reread his failures as *refusals,* as strident commitments to the "dreams of youth," then *Redburn* is not so much a lamentation of "authorial subjection," as Dimock puts it, but a narrative homage to market disinterestedness, juvenile play, and adventure.[98]

BARTLEBY'S MOTIONLESSNESS

By 1853, Melville articulated this viewpoint even more forcefully in *Bartleby, the Scrivener; A Story of Wall Street,* a novella about what happens when individuals refuse to participate in or adapt to normative economic and social structures. But where *Redburn* entertains the possibility of happy failure, *Bartleby* envisions fatal consequences for those who refuse to adhere to the age norms that undergird capitalist culture. Moreover, *Bartleby* exposes life stages as arbitrary in a world that makes class the only viable hierarchy.

The very first line of *Bartleby* gestures to age as a meaningful site of difference and as a significant aspect of identity. "I am a rather elderly man," the narrator declares.[99] This mention of his status as "elderly" serves to telegraph the narrator's conservatism and complacency. Indeed, he is a Wall Street lawyer whose office operates as a metonym for his myopia. As he explains, his chambers offer an "unobstructed view of a lofty brick wall, black by age and everlasting shade."[100] In other words, the narrator is quite literally unable to see beyond the confines of his own position. The fact that the brick wall is "black by age" further shores up the implication that time truncates and taints one's perspective.

His three employees, Turkey, Nippers, and Ginger Nut, have nicknames that convey the dehumanizing effects of their work as copyists, but what has gone unacknowledged is that each employee occupies a specific stage of life: old age, adulthood, and youth. As the narrator explains of the eldest employee: "Turkey was a short, pursy Englishman of about my own age, that is, somewhere not far from sixty."[101] After noon, he becomes frenetic and incompetent, "boxing his papers about in a most indecorous manner, very sad to behold in an elderly man like him."[102] Turkey's demeaning labor reduces him to "indecorous" and undignified behavior, making his performance of age inappropriate.

Moreover, Turkey's inability to efficiently carry out his labor puts his employment at risk, and he attempts to evoke solidarity with his boss based on their shared age. As he puts it: "Old age—even if it blot the page—is honorable. With submission, sir, behold these hairs! I am getting old... With submission, sir, we both are getting old."[103] Turkey asks the narrator to read the blots as signs of age, as marks of their shared status, as old men, not unlike his graying hair. But the novella makes it clear that class position nullifies chronological age as a significant social position. While the narrator allows him to keep his job in spite of the blots, he disallows him from working on the more important documents.

The next oldest employee is Nippers, "a whiskered, sallow, and, upon the whole, rather piratical-looking young man of about five and twenty."[104] That Nippers is already "sallow" suggests that he is prematurely aged. Moreover, Nippers is plagued by "ambition and indigestion." The narrator tellingly reads this ambition as a kind of disease, given that Nippers will never ascend the corporate hierarchy, and in fact, the narrator sees this desire to exceed "the duties of a mere copyist" as "an unwarrantable usurpation of strictly professional affairs."[105] That is, the desire for advancement is linked with indigestion; both are pathological ailments rather than natural responses to menial labor in confined conditions. While the narrator notes that the work is "very dull, wearisome, and lethargic...and [for] sanguine temperaments it would be altogether intolerable," he nonetheless deems his employees' health problems and lack of job satisfaction as personal failings.[106]

The final employee is the office boy, Ginger Nut, "a lad some twelve years old."[107] As the narrator explains, "His father was a carman, ambitious of seeing his son on the bench instead of a cart, before he died. So he sent him to my office as student at law, errand boy, and cleaner and sweeper, at the rate of one dollar a week."[108] Again, it seems that ambition is fruitless, even pathetic, as Ginger Nut's primary pastime is "cake and apple purveyor for Turkey and Nippers."[109] In other words, far from learning about the law, Ginger Nut engages in lowly chores and errands for his fellow employees.

The novella suggests that Ginger Nut will eventually grow into Nippers, who will eventually become Turkey. None of them will outgrow infantilizing nicknames; none of them will ascend the class hierarchy. That these employees each occupy a distinct place along the human life course while retaining somewhat comparable positions within the workplace reveals the homogenizing and debilitating effects of corporate employment. *Bartleby* thus reveals how administrative labor co-opts the life course, confining individuals to stagnant roles, disregarding the possibility of real advancement or mobility. According to *Bartleby*, aging is grim and predetermined; indeed, Melville seems to be suggesting that market society, and its class hierarchy, flatten the course of life. The narrator's status as "elderly" is significant because his status as a lawyer and a member of the upper class enables him to enjoy the privileges of his old age, which include authority and a "remunerative" career that affords him the "easiest way of life."[110] Like Captain Riga in *Redburn,* the narrator is a figure for normative manhood, made possible by class privilege. It is as though Melville pinpoints the ages of the other employees only to reveal that numerical age is basically moot in a world in which one's position in the socioeconomic hierarchy is the only meaningful status.

Given the age-based characterizations of the other copyists, it is thus striking that Bartleby's age, like his provenance, remains pointedly unknown. Bartleby is a cipher, a "motionless young man," who, when asked to reveal "*anything* about yourself," famously replies, "I would prefer not to."[111] His refusal to give any kind of account of himself or to participate in the normative practice of self-identification is particularly significant in light of the novella's publication just three years after the US Census began asking individuals to report their specific ages. Bartleby's failure to provide personal details can thus be read as a form of resistance to the quantifying and standardizing measures that characterize market society, his silence signaling his status outside of classificatory regimes and potentially disruptive of capitalism's hierarchizing operations.

More specifically, Bartleby's failure to account for his numerical age might be read as a rejection of the bureaucratization of human time and the mandates of normative masculinity. In his popular 1846 book, *How to Be a Man,* clergyman Harvey Newcomb sought to teach "boys, or, if you please, *young gentlemen,* in early youth, from eight or ten to fifteen or sixteen years of age" how to properly enter the next stage of life, manhood.[112] His stringent instructions centered heavily on work: "He will never make a man, till he gets courage enough to face his work with resolution, and to finish it with a *manly perseverance. 'I can't.'* never made a man."[113] For Newcomb, "We may safely conclude, then, that, whoever despises labor is a fool; for he despises the only thing that can make him A MAN." Newcomb's guidelines align impeccably with the needs of an economy shifting away from home-centered agrarian labor to the administrative labor of market society. The emphasis on completion and resolution implies that finishing tasks is integral to the culmination of one's gender trajectory.

Read in light of Newcomb's directives, Bartleby's famous utterance— "I would prefer not to"—is then not merely a refusal to work but a refusal to identify with normative manhood itself. Bartleby's youth—one of the only knowable aspects of his identity—is a core aspect of his subject position, and his failure to meet the demands of the workplace can be read as a strident rejection of adulthood, a deliberate preference for an unfinished or unestablished identity. In a culture that deemed the efficient use of time essential to appropriate manhood, Bartleby's flagrant disregard for time management, his "motionlessness," is a repudiation of productivity and busyness and a rebuff to the enterprise of maturation. Where Redburn's trajectory is circular, Bartleby is simply static; neither protagonist moves along the linear pathway that connects youth to adulthood.

Moreover, Bartleby does not merely disregard the rules of masculinity; he serves as a threat to other people's masculinity and the hierarchy on which masculinity is based. His disruption of corporate culture "unmans" the narrator, who observes, "His wonderful mildness... not only disarmed me, but unmanned me, as it were. For I consider that one, for the time, is a sort of unmanned when he tranquilly permits his hired clerk to dictate to him, and order him away from his own premises."[114] Bartleby's unconventional gender performance destabilizes the narrator's own sense of his manhood, which derives from his authority in the class hierarchy. Indeed, so unsettling is their relationship that the narrator worries that Bartleby will "outlive" him and "keep occupying my chambers, and denying my authority." The fact that the narrator fears Bartleby's longevity reveals that age is supposed to function as a tool and a privilege of the upper classes. Bartleby, as a subordinate, is not supposed to have access to a long life, but his refusal to be anchored by a numerical age makes him ominous and threatening, a specter dislodged from the human life course.

By the end of the novella though, Bartleby—like Harry Bolton—is a casualty of a system that disposes of those bodies that cannot or will not insert themselves into the profit-making machinery. Where *Redburn* rejects a naturalized teleology of development, moving backwards and away from completion and progress, *Bartleby* opts for stasis and motionlessness. Both narratives eschew linear progress as they expose manhood as an unnatural subject position. To become a man, according to these texts, is to acquiesce to a world without feeling, friendship, or conscience. Beyond this, they show that adulthood is fundamentally reliant on and complicit with subjugation and inequality. Across both works, Melville reveals that coming of age as a white male in the United States is contingent not only upon oppressing oneself but upon exploiting others. Of that most famous of American coming-of-age novels, *The Adventures of Huckleberry Finn*, Toni Morrison observes, "What is not stressed is that there is no way, given the confines of the novel, for Huck to mature into a moral human being in America without Jim."[115] In *Redburn*, adult masculinity is a kind of pathology—it is to be evil like the "diabolical" sailor Jackson, aloof and unresponsive like Captain Riga, or obsolete like Redburn's father. It is to benefit from the poverty at the Liverpool docks that so transfixes and traumatizes Redburn, forcing him to recognize that "we Americans leave to other countries the carrying out of the principle that stands at the head of our Declaration of Independence."[116] In *Bartleby*, normative manhood means comfortably retreating to the privacy of one's "safe" circumstances rather than truly wrestling with the problems of inequality, disability, or exploitation.

Perhaps Melville's valorization of white male youth seems somewhat narrow and myopic when considered in his antebellum context, when the dehumanizing regime of slavery systematically revoked the markers of maturity from the individuals under its purview. Indeed, we should be wary of joining Melville in an unequivocal embrace of perpetual boyhood as a satisfactory mode of dissent or site of pleasure. The following chapter considers how enslavers distorted age norms and withheld adulthood from the enslaved. Frederick Douglass, for example, reflects upon this aspect of slavery in *My Bondage and My Freedom* when he considers his own prospects in relation to those of his white boy-master: "He could grow, and become a MAN; I could grow, though I could *not* become a man, but must remain, all my life, a minor—a mere boy."[117] The advice manuals and conduct guides that insisted on work as the key to manhood clearly do not apply to those enslaved and excised from the telos of development.

Douglass reveals that numerical age and development are brutally severed by slavery. No matter how hard he works, Douglass realizes he has no future, only the past and present: "The thought of only being a creature of the present and the past troubled me, and I longed to have a future—a future with hope in it." Douglass writes, "To be shut up entirely to the past and present is abhorrent to the human mind; it is to the soul—whose life and happiness is unceasing progress—what the prison is to the body."[118] Douglass' realization that slavery makes him a "mere boy" without a future underscores the relationship between adulthood, race, gender, and implicitly, the growth of US economy.[119] Douglass is deprived of self-determination and the developmental life narrative. Growing up is thus not simply the mark of one's American-ness or masculinity; it is also a white privilege.

2

Peculiar Forms of Aging in the Literature of US Slavery

"'Laws, Missis, those low negroes,—they can't tell; they don't know anything about time,' said Jane; 'they don't know what a year is; they don't know their own ages.'"

Harriet Beecher Stowe, *Uncle Tom's Cabin*

"I am 110 years old; my birth is recorded in the slave book. I have good health, fairly good eyesight, and a good memory."

Rosaline Rogers, formerly enslaved[1]

Herman Melville invoked the ship as a familiar metaphor for the "voyage of life," and in *Redburn,* he offers a critique of this linear developmental trajectory, unsettling the notion of maturity as inevitable and interrogating national progress. Frederick Douglass also recognized the literal and figurative possibilities of ships; a Baltimore shipyard is where he becomes a skilled laborer and plots his escape from slavery. In a famous apostrophe Douglass addresses ships directly as "freedom's swift-winged angels," and yet while they conjure mobility and possibility, ships are ultimately cruel reminders of his inability to advance and to gain access to the rights of manhood.[2] Indeed, when working as an apprentice shipbuilder while still enslaved, Douglass is subjected to violence from the white men working alongside him. He writes, "Fellow-apprentices very soon began to feel it degrading to them to work with me ... They, however, at length combined, and came upon me, armed with sticks, stones, and heavy handspikes ... I fell, and with this they all ran upon me, and fell to beating me with their fists." This brawl, which results in a severe injury to Douglass' eye, occurs in the shipyard and captures the extent to which the category of manhood itself, defined by physical prowess and labor, was viciously defended as a white realm.

Douglass is brutalized for daring to partake in the possibilities of the ship; the injury to his eye is thus a kind of punishment for deigning to visualize himself as a man. He notes, "As I look back to this period, I am almost amazed that I was not murdered outright, in that ship yard, so murderous was the spirit which prevailed there. On two occasions, while there, I came near losing my life."[3] For Douglass, the ship comes to serve as a reminder of permanent stasis, a site of potential annihilation, and a space in which he is repeatedly and forcibly reinscribed within an oppressive, racist hierarchy. He acknowledges that ships function as vehicles for coming-of-age in the cultural imagination but comes to see that opportunity as reserved for white boyhood.[4] It seems ships can only ever return him to the anti-developmental purgatory of slavery.[5]

While much scholarship focuses on what Hortense Spillers calls the "dehumanizing, ungendering, and defacing project" of slavery, little attention has been paid to slavery's deformation of age.[6] Like gender, age was withheld from enslaved people as a strategy to emphasize their non-humanness, excising them from the human life course and withholding the cultural markers associated with maturation and development.[7] While all life courses are culturally produced (not just those under slavery), slavery altered the conventional meanings attributed to age, uncoupling life stages from numerical age. The literature of slavery recognizes the appropriation of age as one of the most fundamental strategies that slaveholders used to delimit the category of the human as a white category, making the deformation of age and the denial of maturity a central subject.

Enslaved people were denied both the opportunity to age normatively and to identify with a numerical age or a stage of life. That is, slavery impeded the biological aging process *and* withheld the cultural meanings of age. The literature of slavery acknowledges that enslaved people were forced to relinquish the individualizing aspects of age, to give up their right to use age as a measure of life; they were victims of what might be called age theft. As Douglass famously writes in his first autobiography, "I have no accurate knowledge of my age, never having seen any authentic record containing it." He elaborates this point in *My Bondage and my Freedom,* noting: "I have never met with a slave who could tell me how old he was." As he goes on to explain, "Like other slaves, I cannot tell how old I am. This destitution was among my earliest troubles."[8] For Douglass, not knowing his age is a central deprivation, one that he recognizes as a core dehumanizing strategy of slavery.

This chapter reveals how racism and slavery exploit the metric of age to buttress a system that distributed maturity, and humanity, according to an invented logic. Rather than an in-depth treatment of a single text, this chapter engages with a range of sources in the hope of offering a sense of the breadth of engagement with the vexed status of age under slavery and to gesture to the multiple avenues for further study. To that end, I examine works by Douglass and Harriet Jacobs as well as Federal Writers Project interviews with formerly enslaved people who seem to defy the boundaries of human longevity. These narratives suggest alternative pathways to adulthood, as they acknowledge not merely the corruption of childhood but the exclusion from maturity as among the most troubling aspects of slavery. Ultimately, this chapter demonstrates how enslaved people resisted the classificatory regime that opportunistically manipulated numerical age and instead formulated alternative, or "peculiar," forms of aging.

"NOTHING BUT GROWN-UP CHILDREN"

Though enslaved people were kept from the knowledge of their numerical ages, age was a primary factor in the valuation of human chattel.[9] Younger men and women could typically do more manual labor, and they were also more likely to bear children, increasing a slaveholders' net worth. In his influential work *American Slavery as It Is* (1839), Theodore Weld establishes the economic import of age in the Southern slave economy.[10] He quotes several advertisements for slaves, which reveal the importance of age as a measure of a slave's worth: In the *Alexandria Gazette*: "I will give the highest cash price for likely negroes, from 10 to 25 years of age." Similarly, in the *Petersburgh Constellation*: "50 Negroes wanted immediately.— The subscriber will give a good market price for fifty likely negroes, from 10 to 30 years of age."[11] The advertisements reveal the premium placed upon youth.

Significantly, they suggest that age ten served as the crucial transition time; that is, rather than the midpoint of childhood, ten-year-olds were full-fledged members of the workforce, deemed adult in terms of their capacity for labor. Highlighting the strangeness of this age economy for her white northern female audience, Harriet Jacobs reflects on the high value placed upon her uncle, Benjamin, noting that, "though only ten years old, seven hundred and twenty dollars were paid for him."[12] Jacobs emphasizes the striking incongruity of his age and monetary value, drawing attention to how the potential of his young body for years of hard labor makes it more valuable than those lives that have accrued knowledge or expertise.

Conveniently, slavery itself tended to truncate the lives of those in its clutches, making old age not only less valuable but also less common. As Weld writes, "Another proof that the slaves in the south-western states are over-worked, is the fact, that so few of them live to old age. A large majority of them are *old* at middle age, and few live beyond fifty-five."[13] Weld's observations suggest both the high value placed on youthful vigor as well as reveal how fundamentally slavery warped the meanings of age, detaching numerical age from its normative significance. Frederick Law Olmsted, the famed landscape architect who toured the South, echoes this point when he observes, "'Old Man,' is a common title of address to any middle-aged negro in Virginia, whose name is not known. 'Boy' and 'Old Man' may be applied to the same person." These observations point to how age ignorance reinforced the de-individualizing premise of slavery; the lack of an age is linked to the lack of a name. Olmsted notes of another enslaved man: "He thought he was about twenty years old then, and that now he was forty. He had every appearance of being seventy."[14] The man's appearance thus belies his claims to being younger, hinting at the indecipherability of the body and the possibility for one's age to measure something other than biological years. Olmsted's observations suggest the intriguing possibility that enslaved people could occupy multiple points on the life span, inhabiting a world in which numerical age held no definite or stable meaning. While this resignification of age is the result of the oppressive age theft that I have been describing, I will be turning later in this chapter to a consideration of the subversive potential that such resignification sometimes offered.

Slaveholders and traders used age to divide black lives into economically discrete units. The price of enslaved men declined when they reached forty, and the price of enslaved women tended to depreciate when they reached their early thirties.[15] At age fifty, women were worth virtually nothing. In light of their decreasing use value, enslaved elderly people were often dubbed "half hands."[16] Olmsted notes "planters' practice of rating children, the aged, and disabled persons as one eighth, one quarter, or some other fraction of a prime-aged, healthy hand," thus linking age to disability and to an inevitable decline in value.

The plantation records of Isaac Franklin display the use of age as a principle tool for assessing the value of enslaved people [see Figure 2.1].[17] The paucity of individuals older than forty suggests that many did not survive into old age or were not considered worth keeping on the plantation. For example, "Charity," listed as age sixty-four, is worth "nothing," while men in their thirties are almost all valued at $900. "Sam Morrison," however, is already fifty-four, and consequently, his value has declined to only $400. The infant, "Eleanora," is valued only at $100, likely because her survival beyond childhood was not yet guaranteed, but her mother, "Sarah Henry," age sixteen, is valued at $700, already having proven herself a valuable asset. While the use of the term "griff," which refers to mixed race individuals, suggests that skin color was also a factor in valuation, the chart firmly demonstrates age as the primary measure of slave value.

Given the fact that age was a heavily manipulated figure, the ages recorded in plantation books cannot be read as reliable or wholly accurate. Corinne T. Field observes that such accounting tended "to reflect the

Isaac Franklin				Conveyances and Inventories, 1835–1850		
Sam Morrison,	54		400	Mason Thomas,	23 black	900
Daphney, his wife	49		500	Margaret, his wife	24 griff	700
Horatio, her child,	15		600	John, her child	2	200
Ned, do	11		400	Arthur Hill,	28 black	900
Sam, do	8		300	Sarah Henry, his wife,	16	700
Dick, do	6		250	Eleanora, her child	infant	100
Martha Morrison, do	26		700	Charity,	64	nothing
Henry, her child,	6		350	Henry Miller,	34	900
Ursilla, do	2		200	Elias Washington,	18	900
Adaline Blair,	29		700	Hannibal,	34	500
Francina, her child,	9		400	Alfred Murry,	31 griff	900
Rebecca, do	6		300	Pricilla Blount, his wife	20 black	700
Louisa, do	an infant		100	Ned Hawkins,	34	900
Adelle,	29		700	Tom Foster,	44	900
Louisa, her child	14	mulattress	500	Joe Cato,	33	900
Josephine, do	9	black	400	Cage Scott,	34	900
John Edward, do	5	griff	300	Samuel James Potter,	28	900
Susan Hunley,	34	black	700	Perry,	32	900
Alexander, her child	11		400	Isaac Wilson,	30	900
Victoria, do	infant	griff	100	Mary Foster, his wife	23	700
Emily Winchester,	29	black	600	William Harris,	29 griff	900
Turner,	29		900	Tom Sewel,	25 black	900
David Hawkins,	30		900	Washington Ford,	30	900
Martha Resaw, his wife,	29		700	Randall Williams,	23 griff	900
John Henson,	41		900	John Sims,	29 black	900
Mary, his wife	30		700	William Jenkins,	32	900
James Henry,	29		900	Watty Harris,	29	900
Ellen Roan, his wife	34		700	John Hall,	42	600
Jim, her child	11		500	Spencer,	44	900
Adalicia, do	9		400	Phill Johnson,	54	500
Louisa, do	7		350	Dick Kibbe,	25 mulatto	900
Anthony, do	4		300	Thornton,	34 black	900
Parthena, do	1		100	Windsor Cain,	25	900
Moses Pierce,	39		900	Nathan,	31	900
Rowden Jones,	30		900			
Bill Johnson,	31		900			$60,550
Treasy Butler, his wife,	30	griff	700	Movables, to wit:		
Matilda, her child	1	black	100	32 Mules and Horses, at $60 each		1920
Lewis Munco,	24	griff	900	60 Head of Cattle, 10 each		600

Figure 2.1. Excerpt from the plantation records of Isaac Franklin of Louisiana. Reproduced from Wendell Holmes Stephenson's *Isaac Franklin, Slave Trader and Planter of the Old South; with Plantation Record* (Baton Rouge, LA: Louisiana State University Press, 1938).

self-interest of those who sold and owned slaves, not the self-understanding of enslaved people themselves."[18] Moreover, because age served as a primary mode of establishing the value of individuals, traders were inclined to falsify the age of slaves in auctions. Slave narratives describe the various techniques employed to conceal old age, and slave auctions, in particular, regularly served as sites of age forgery. William Wells Brown refers to slave traders who "often bought some who were far advanced in years, and would always try to sell them for five or ten years younger than they actually were."[19] He goes on to describe preparing old slaves for market: "he was ordered to shave off the old men's whiskers, and to pluck out the grey hairs where they were not too numerous; where they were, he coloured them with a preparation of blacking with a blacking brush. After having gone through the blacking process, they looked ten or fifteen years younger."[20] This camouflaging of age reminds us of how enslaved bodies were utterly subject to the terms of the slaveholders, making age a compulsory performance rather than the measure of an individual's lifespan. In a lesser known narrative, fugitive slave John Brown develops this point: "Though he may be quite certain of the year, and might swear to it blindfold, he must say he is just as old as his master chooses to bid him do, or he will have to take the consequences."[21] Brown suggests that while an enslaved person *may* actually have knowledge of his age, he is prohibited from asserting it.

But it was not only numerical age that was wrested from enslaved individuals. The institution of slavery was premised on a racist construction of maturity; that is, the very meanings of age were racialized. Racial scientists, including George Fitzhugh and Louis Agassiz, claimed that African Americans were incapable of obtaining the same levels of intellectual or psychological advancement, and such theories were foundational to the rationalization of slavery and the paternalist arguments that propped it up.[22] William Wells Brown captures this racist logic in a poem called "My Little Nig," which he includes in *Clotel*: "I have a little nigger, the blackest thing alive, He'll be just four years old if he lives till forty-five." Inhabiting the perspective of a white slaveholder, Brown voices the prevalent antebellum assumptions about African American intellectual ability and maturity. If the "little nig" does live to be forty-five, he will nonetheless never become an adult; he will always be four years old.

According to the logic of the poem, he will never acquire the character and mental power of an adult nor will he attain maturity in a legal or political sense. The poem thus reveals the irrelevance of age; four and forty-five are synonymous because slavery—and its racist logic—saw African American intellectual growth as fundamentally limited. And it is not just adulthood that the poem withholds from the subject; the title's use of the phrase "little nig," an abbreviated racial slur, also clearly denies the subject access to gender and humanity. The jocular, playful tone and its light rhyme cement the poem's insidious racist message of African American non-personhood, demonstrating how perversions of age—along with gender—ensure that modern blackness, as Habiba Ibrahim puts it, is "constituted outside of the realm of the human."[23]

Slave narratives frequently draw attention to maturity and development as white privileges. In *Incidents in the Life of a Slave Girl*, Jacobs describes "an old black man, whose piety and childlike trust in God were beautiful to witness." However, this old man (later revealed to be fifty-three years old) "had a most earnest desire to learn to read" and comes to Jacobs for instruction. She notes, "I taught him his A, B, C. Considering his age, his progress was astonishing. As soon as he could spell in two syllables he wanted to spell out words in the Bible."[24] Jacobs uses this episode to reveal the intellectual deprivations of slavery, how it thwarts human potential, and in particular, how it makes an "old" man "childlike." By noting that his progress was "astonishing" considering his age, she suggests that "old" is not synonymous with being impaired or defunct. Jacobs thus redeems an old man who has been dismissed as worthless by the system, re-investing him with potential and disproving racist assumptions about black development. Conversely, when she reunites with her daughter who is living with a white family, Jacobs is shocked to learn that Ellen cannot read. "She felt ashamed of being unable to read or spell at her age, so instead of sending her to school with Benny, I instructed her myself till she was fitted to enter an intermediate school."[25] Ellen's shame at being illiterate "at her age" highlights how slavery uncouples age and maturity, and Jacobs' concern for her daughter's development suggests her own investment in normative age standards and her aspirational attachment to conventional benchmarks, like being able to read by a certain age.

A *Harper's Weekly* cartoon published in 1870 captures the age-perverting effects of slavery, highlighting the particular ways that slavery results in the denigration of old age [see Figure 2.2]. Titled "The Old Scholar," the cartoon features an elderly black woman holding a reading primer. In the background, children play at recess, and as the caption explains, the woman, "an old cook, 71 years of age" entered school and "got along very well until, perhaps, at the end of the second week, she missed her lesson, and *was kept in in play time.* The idea! an old negro seventy-odd years of age kept in in play time [orig. emphasis]." Like Jacobs' narrative, the caption registers outrage at the notion of an elderly woman, unable to read or write correctly, reduced to juvenile punishment. Her numerical age is rendered meaningless by a culture that has made her equivalent with elementary schoolchildren.

In fact, the cartoon indicates that she occupies a position inferior to schoolchildren. A young boy pokes his finger at the woman in a derisive way, suggesting that she is an object of ridicule and humor. Though the cartoon portrays the stunted condition—and infantilizing treatment—of African American adults, it also renders the woman in an unflattering light; her features are exaggerated, and her expression is one of bewilderment.

This concern with slavery's distorting effects on age permeates Harriet Beecher Stowe's best-selling novel, *Uncle Tom's Cabin*. Just as the elderly

AN OLD SCHOLAR.

"There is a negro school at Meherrin Station, on the Richmond and Danville Railroad, where the teachers receive scholars of all ages and both sexes. Mr. ARVINE, of Lunenburg, had an old cook, 71 years of age, who took it into her head to learn to speak and write the English language correctly; so she entered the school, and bringing her ten cents per day and regularly paying it over to the teachers, she got along very well until, perhaps, at the end of the second week, she missed her lesson, and *was kept in in play time.* The idea! an old negro seventy-odd years of age kept in in play time."—*Danville (Va.) Times.*

Figure 2.2. "An Old Scholar," *Harper's Weekly,* May 21, 1870.

woman in the *Harper's* image is illiterate and infantilized by slavery, so too does Stowe begin her narrative by describing how Uncle Tom, "a large, broad-chested, powerfully-made man," is dependent upon a white child to teach him to read.[26] Stowe introduces her readers to Tom as he is "carefully and slowly endeavoring to accomplish a copy of some letters, in which operation he was overlooked by young Mas'r George, a smart, bright boy of thirteen, who appeared fully to realize the dignity of his position as instructor."[27] The scene dramatizes slavery's perversion of age norms, as a "powerfully-made man" is forced to copy the work of a white child who possesses knowledge of his numerical age, the ability to read, and the dignity that derive from both.

When Tom is subsequently sold to a new master, he advises George on how to become a gentleman and a "good Mas'r, like yer father," a speech rife with the pathos of Tom's own exclusion from manhood and from the right to serve as a father to his own children.[28] It is significant that Tom must teach George how to be a "man of humanity" since Mr. Shelby,

George's father, has been exposed as unprincipled; indeed it seems that young George is only able to feel empathy for Tom and to feel repulsion from the practices of slavery precisely because he is *not* yet a man. In other words, white manhood seems to be the very status that dulls empathy and replaces morality with economic opportunism. Thus, like Melville, Stowe is suspicious of white manhood, which she repeatedly associates with cruelty, hypocrisy, and the decline of morality.[29] She underscores this point later in the novel when Ophelia tells the complacent St. Clare, "I wish you were as good as when you were a boy."[30] Douglass echoes this point when he observes, "I do not remember ever to have met with a *boy*, while I was in slavery, who defended the slave system."

While white children like young George Shelby and Eva St. Clare are able to perceive the evils of slavery, Stowe suggests that they also become "uncommonly mature" as a result of their unwitting complicity in and exposure to slavery; in other words, such children do not remain in childhood for very long. Eva's father is struck by the "daily increasing maturity of the child's mind and feelings," and as she becomes increasingly ill, he observes "a womanly thoughtfulness" in her face; we are told that "though but a child herself, [Eva had] by reason of long illness, grown old beyond her years."[31] As Lora Romero writes, "In her illness Eva, who is about eight years old, seems suddenly to undergo puberty."[32] For Romero, Eva's early-onset puberty is a sign of "Stowe's feminist critique of a patriarchal power that discourages proportional development in women and deprives them of self-government." We might also read Eva's accelerated aging as part of a more comprehensive meditation on how slavery inhibits the normative stages of life for every individual who directly encounters its brutality.

Eva's premature bodily aging and preternatural maturity serve as a counterweight to the enslaved characters detained in culturally enforced dependence and immaturity.[33] That is, where Eva's childhood is curtailed by her capacity to respond to the injustice of slavery, it is a correlative of the racist constructions of adulthood, which rendered African Americans inherently child-like, docile, and requiring of paternal supervision.[34] Eva's mother, Mrs. St. Clare, a villainous Southern matron, gives voice to this logic, referring to her "servants" as "nothing but grown-up children" and later telling Ophelia "you don't know what a provoking, stupid, careless, unreasonable, childish, ungrateful set of wretches they are."[35] Her benign but passive husband rightly notes how "the slave is kept in that dependent, semi-childish state."[36] In her untimely maturity and death, Eva seems to take on the thwarted development of the enslaved individuals, as her body registers a kind of hyper-maturity that points to how slavery has disrupted the age equilibrium and rendered normative development impossible for everyone in its purview.

While Stowe acknowledges the enlistment of age discourse to buttress the racial hierarchy, the obstructed development of African Americans is an afterthought to the novel's climactic scene of Eva's early death. And while the novel's black characters do exemplify the age theft committed by enslavers—Uncle Tom is often described as child-like while Topsy as "de-childed," to borrow Robin Bernstein's term—these representations also substantiate the claims made by racial scientists, who sought to biologize racial difference in terms of maturity and development.[37] Tom can only ever serve as the foil for the assertive, enterprising, light-skinned George Harris, and Topsy can never embody childhood innocence. In this sense, Stowe reinforces the racist logic that reserved the life stages for white people, enacting the representational analogue of the tactics of enslavers themselves.

Scholars, including Jo-Ann Morgan and Nathaniel Windon, have observed that subsequent editions and adaptations of *Uncle Tom's Cabin* further manipulated black age by depicting Uncle Tom as an elderly man [see Figure 2.3 and 2.4]. The transformation of Uncle Tom into a figure of old age likely allayed white readerly anxieties about his intimacy with

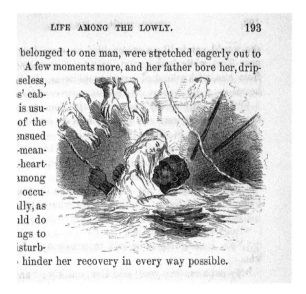

Figure 2.3. An illustration from an 1853 edition of *Uncle Tom's Cabin* depicts Uncle Tom as a strong, physically capable man as he rescues Eva from the river. Courtesy of the Harriet Beecher Stowe Center, Hartford, CT.

EVA AND UNCLE TOM.

Figure 2.4. This illustration from a 1900 edition of *Uncle Tom's Cabin* depicts Uncle Tom as elderly, with graying hair and glasses. Courtesy of the Harriet Beecher Stowe Center, Hartford, CT.

Eva as well as served mainstream nationalist desire to reimagine formerly enslaved people as figures of nostalgia and passivity.[38] To age Uncle Tom was to render him malleable, sentimental, and non-threatening. The very fact that Tom's age became a site for revision suggests the extent to which age serves a vector of power and for the entrenchment of racial hierarchy. Ultimately, *Uncle Tom's Cabin* highlights the freighted status of age under slavery even as it reserves normative age constructions for white characters.

SLAVERY'S PERVERSE *BILDUNG*

Because enslavers venerated young adulthood for its various economic potentials (productivity and reproductivity), coming of age became a site of anxiety and horror for the enslaved. Slave narratives are accounts of compromised and tortured coming of age, as they reveal what happens to "growing up" when it is linked to the constriction, rather than the expansion, of one's potential and the erosion of independence and autonomy.[39] The prohibition on literacy, relentless disempowerment, and the nullification of numerical age made childhood a sort of prison, rendering adulthood—as a cultural status defined by independence and self-determination—unattainable.

Douglass frequently juxtaposes his own adolescence with those of the white boys in his orbit, emphasizing his unnatural exclusion from their developmental trajectory. Reflecting on how divergent his path is from Tommy, his master's son, Douglass writes:

> He was no longer dependent on me for protection, but felt himself a man, with other and more suitable associates. In childhood, he scarcely considered me inferior to himself certainly, as good as any other boy with whom he played; but the time had come when his friend must become his slave. So we were cold, and we parted. It was a sad thing to me, that, loving each other as we had done, we must now take different roads. To him, a thousand avenues were open. Education had made him acquainted with all the treasures of the world, and liberty had flung open the gates thereunto . . . He could grow, and become a MAN; I could grow, though I could not become a man, but must remain, all my life, a minor—a mere boy.[40]

While boyhood creates a temporary illusion of similitude between Douglass and his young master, coming of age entails the revelation of their antithetical statuses. Tommy has "a thousand avenues" ahead of him, a multitude of ways to develop himself and to direct his life, while Douglass "must be confined to a single condition." This "single condition" is one of permanent boyhood; Douglass himself notes that he "must remain, all my life, a minor—a mere boy." In other words, slavery denies him the opportunity to mature and to develop as he ages, rendering manhood a white privilege.

Central to Douglass' prohibition from development is the co-optation of numerical age by slaveholders. When Douglass broaches the subject of his indefinite status as a slave with his white peers, he says, "'You will be free, you know, as soon as you are twenty-one, and can go where you like, but I am a slave for life. Have I not as good a right to be free as you have?'"[41] Douglass acknowledges that the age of twenty-one holds special significance *only* for white boys; his own numerical age is an empty signifier.[42] Ultimately, adulthood is denied to enslaved people who are systemically prohibited from accruing the benefits of age, and often from growing older at all.

While Douglass laments an enforced ignorance of his numerical age, Harriet Jacobs is by contrast attentive to specific numerical ages. And while we must be careful not to assume that Jacobs' narrative is representative of all female experience under slavery, her account nonetheless calls attention to the gendered realities of enslavement, to the fact that puberty starkly differentiated male and female trajectories. The title's use of the generic "slave girl"—in place of Jacobs' own name—suggests her investment in representing the universal trajectory of female coming of age under slavery as well as the de-individualization that occurs under that regime. The narrative's various chapter titles also signal its interest in the genre of the *Bildungsroman*: "Childhood," "Trials of Girlhood," "A Perilous Passage in the Slave Girl's Life," and "A Home Found." These titles, which gesture to the normative pathway of growing up, point to Jacobs' investment in revealing the distorted coming-of-age narrative produced by the system of slavery. The use of the term "incidents" in the title undermines the notion that the narrative is necessarily one of growth or development, positing instead that various events occur but do not inevitably produce a coherent developmental narrative.

Like Douglass, Jacobs frequently contrasts her experience of maturation with those of her white counterparts in order to expose the racialization of age norms and life stages. In one scene, she observes two young half-sisters at play: "The fair child grew up to be a still fairer woman. From childhood to womanhood her pathway was blooming with flowers, and overarched by a sunny sky. Scarcely one day of her life had been clouded when the sun rose on her happy bridal morning. How had those years dealt with her slave sister, the little playmate of her childhood? She, also, was very beautiful; but the flowers and sunshine and love were not for her. She drank the cup of sin, and shame, and misery, whereof her persecuted race are compelled to drink."[43] For one girl, the "pathway" of adolescence is bedecked in flowers and sunshine, a seamless set of transitions leading to normative adulthood and marriage. For her enslaved sister, there is no "pathway"; rather, growing up consists of degradation and shame; marriage is not an option, and motherhood will not necessarily happen on her terms.

We might read Jacobs' invocation of the *Bildungsroman* form as a particularly strategic choice in light of her desire to enlist the sympathies of white Northern women, already primed by Stowe's representation of families wrenched apart, in light of the fact that the proper development of young people is traditionally a maternal concern.[44] For Jacobs, girlhood is a period of "trials," culminating in the stark realization of one's status in a rigid racial and sexual hierarchy. Rites of courtship, religious ceremonies, and romanticized "firsts" are replaced by what Jacobs calls "A Perilous Passage in the Slave Girl's Life." Jacobs represents girlhood as a set of "perilous passages," exposing how slavery transforms rites of passage into rituals of violence. In particular, she singles out the age of fifteen as "a sad epoch in the life of a slave girl." In place of a quinceañera or a bat mitzvah, the primary rite of passage for the slave girl is the inauguration of harassment and the unceasing threat of rape. She observes, "When she is fourteen or fifteen, her owner, or his sons, or the overseer, or perhaps all of them, begin to bribe her with presents. If these fail to accomplish their purpose, she is whipped or starved into submission to their will."[45] Thus, instead of ushering her into autonomy and self-possession, Jacobs' describes her girlhood as a period of disillusionment and forced submission.

Jacobs vividly illustrates the anxiety linked to coming of age in a context that equates development with sexual exploitation. As she writes, "My master began to whisper foul words in my ear. Young as I was, I could not remain ignorant of their import."[46] Indeed, slavery created a world in which successful growth was desirable *only* in the eyes of masters. The fact that Jacobs' children are "growing finely" triggers anxiety, for it is linked to their increasing profitability in the market. Similarly, when Dr. Flint tells Jacobs, "I would make a lady of you," he links womanhood with sexual degradation and asserts his control over her developmental narrative.[47]

Where Douglass is kept a permanent "boy," Jacobs on the other hand must become "prematurely knowing," a phrase that suggests the perversity of her coming-of-age experience and implies that her entrance into womanhood—as defined by sexual knowledge and experience—occurs too early. Jacobs turns repeatedly to the word "prematurely" to underscore the unnatural *Bildung* of slavery and to highlight slavery's disordering effects on conventional age norms and stages of life. She opts to become pregnant with Mr. Sands' baby as a strategy of deflecting Dr. Flint and preserving her sexual agency. "When my babe was born, they said it was premature. It weighed only four pounds; but God let it live." Again, she uses the word "premature," suggesting the ill timing of her own entrance into this new stage.[48] In some sense, we might think of all babies born into slavery as "premature," as all they all enter a world unready to grant them equality and humanity, and as her son gets older, Jacobs observes that he is "prematurely cautious and cunning," implying that his childhood, too, has been warped by the need to develop survival tactics.[49] Near the end of her narrative, Jacobs makes more explicit her point that the nation is itself is immature and underdeveloped when she includes her "bill of sale," noting "it may hereafter prove a useful document to antiquaries, who are seeking to measure the progress of civilization in the United States."[50] A civilization that renders people into objects of sale, she implies, is not civilized at all.

Just as slavery turns puberty into a gateway into sexual violence, so too does motherhood—the ostensible apotheosis of womanhood—signify differently for enslaved women. For Jacobs, motherhood is far from a romantic passage into a new identity; indeed, a period that should ideally be an affirmation of life is closely associated with death.[51] In a context in which development itself has been co-opted, death presents itself as one method of opting out and seizing the terms of aging. Contemplating the inevitable separation from her children, Jacobs reflects on how the slave mother often "wish[es] that she and they might die before the day dawns."[52] Death thus functions as a potential escape from relentless abuse and a way to claim ownership of the life course, even as black bodies were often denied the right to rest in peace.[53]

"THE LAW OF RESPECT TO ELDERS"

Although the status of childhood under slavery has received much scholarly attention, the frequent attention to elderly people in this tradition has gone largely overlooked.[54] Along with very young children, elderly people were the least valued members of the economy; Daina Ramey Berry notes that "the monetary value of the elderly paralleled that of children ten and under."[55] Both ends of the age spectrum were associated with minimal productivity and death and therefore of little financial worth. Where enslavers often deemed old bodies disposable and worthless, slave narratives regularly draw attention to figures of old age, contrasting their crucial importance to the black community with their degrading treatment. While enslavers sought to turn age into a mere commodity, divorced from meanings apart from labor, the reverence for elderly people that surfaces in slave narratives suggests a willful refusal to accommodate this economic logic of age and a desire to destabilize age as an empirical metric.

Contrary to the systematic devaluation of old age, slave narratives represent elderly people as beacons of autonomy and figures of transgressive power. As Douglass notes, "Strange, and even ridiculous as it may seem, among a people so uncultivated, and with so many stern trials to look in the face, there is not to be found, among many people, a more rigid enforcement of the law of respect to elders, than they maintain."[56] Douglass' sarcastic emphasis on the strangeness of revering elderly people serves to suggest how much more civilized, more cultivated, the slaves were than their masters, who so utterly disregarded traditional respect and care for the elderly; indeed, the care for the oldest and weakest members of a society is often seen as a sign of how advanced a civilization is.[57] We might read the "rigid enforcement" of this respect for the elderly as a mode of resistance to the economy of age established by the slave system. The very fact that Douglass describes this respect for elders as a "law" suggests in itself the extent to which enslaved people saw the reclamation of age norms as politically significant and socially imperative.

Slave narratives draw frequent attention to the physical abuse and/or disregard of elderly people, and these instances of violence and neglect often function as catalyzing moments that put on display the barbarism of the slave system.[58] Where the totalizing economic worldview of slavery deems old people sub-human, slave narratives tend to invert this logic in their discussion of elderly people, describing slaveholders in bestial language. For example, Frederick Douglass writes:

> If any one thing in my experience, more than another, served to deepen my conviction of the infernal character of slavery, and to fill me with unutterable loathing of slaveholders, it was their base ingratitude to my poor old grandmother. She had served my old master faithfully, from youth to old age; she had been the source of all his wealth; she had peopled his plantation with slaves; she had become a great grandmother in his service...saw her children, her grandchildren, divided like so many sheep...and to cap the climax of their base ingratitude and fiendish barbarity, my grandmother, who was now very old...took her off to the woods, built her a little hut, put up a little mud chimney, and then made her welcome to the privilege of supporting herself there in perfect loneliness; thus virtually turning her out to die.[59]

Douglass describes the co-optation of his grandmother's life narrative: the way she served from "youth to old age," transforming her body into a vehicle for "people[ing] his plantation," and watching those children "divided like so many sheep." The shift in his language, from human to animal rhetoric, suggests the dehumanizing goals of slavery, which for Douglass is most apparent and egregious at the end of life. His grandmother's last years are reminder of the extent to which she is considered unworthy of the basic necessities of human life and dignity, and it is this treatment of his grandmother—and the sham "privilege" of a lonely impoverished death—that illuminates for him the absolute "barbarity" of the slaveholders.

That Douglass' grandmother is sent out to die in a little hut was not unusual. After lifetimes spent in service to their masters, elderly people were regularly sent out of the community and expected to care for themselves in their remaining years. Historian Dea Boster notes, "When the usefulness of slaves ran out, particularly due to old age or blindness, they were sent to rooms or cabins in the woods to live along and fend for themselves, separated from slaveholding families and the slave community."[60] While some cities and states pass laws requiring slaveholders to provide health care for manumitted older slaves, these laws were generally not enforced.[61]

Indeed, the older one became, the less s/he qualified for humane treatment. Jacobs notes, "Slaveholders have a method, peculiar to their institution, of getting rid of *old* slaves, whose lives have been worn out in their service."[62] Thus in contradistinction to the notion that one might earn some sort of recompense for years of servitude, older people were seen as extraneous drains on resources and often deserted or sent away. Jacobs later recalls that "a very old slave, who had faithfully served the Flint family through three generations...hobbled up to get his bit of meat... The mistress said he was too old to have any allowance; that when niggers were too old to work, they ought be fed on grass. Poor old man!"[63] The suggestion that an elderly person should be fed grass testifies to the view of old age as a sub-human status. Thus, in a world in which African Americans were only three-fifths human, elderly African Americans were even less than that.

Douglass describes the brutal treatment of an enslaved elderly man known as Old Barney whose years of service to Colonel Lloyd only result in harsher treatment. Just as Jacobs recounts her dismay at an older man's inability to read, Douglass is profoundly affected by the debasement of this elderly man:

> Old Barney was a fine looking old man, of a brownish complexion, who was quite portly, and wore a dignified aspect for a slave. He was, evidently, much devoted to his profession, and held his office an honorable one. He was a farrier as well as an ostler; he could bleed, remove lampers from the mouths of the horses, and was well instructed in horse medicines. No one on the farm knew, so well as Old Barney, what to do with a sick horse. But his gifts and acquirements were of little advantage to him.[64]

Douglass acknowledges that Barney possesses an immense skill set, the kind of knowledge one acquires over many years. But far from adding to his worth, Barney's years of experience and devotion to his "profession" stymie slaveholders by disrupting the prevailing logic of human valuation. Douglass recalls, "One of the most heart-saddening and humiliating scenes I ever witnessed, was the whipping of Old Barney, by Col. Lloyd himself. Here were two men, both advanced in years; there were the silvery locks of Col. L., and there was the bald and toil-worn brow of Old Barney; master and slave; superior and inferior here, but *equals* at the bar of God." Douglass' juxtaposition of these two old men casts into relief slavery's disregard for the elderly. In contrast with Colonel Lloyd's "silvery locks," Barney's "toil-worn brow" shores up the stark disparity in their experiences of old age; for one man, growing older enhances his status, while for the other, it simply makes visible the years of hard labor and indicates his devalued status. Indeed, it may the very fact that Barney "wore a dignified aspect for a slave" that galls Colonel Lloyd and prompts the assault, a reminder that Barney has no right to a dignified old age.

While the abuses of slavery are all horrific, Douglass is especially disturbed by the degradation of this old man: "down knelt the old man, his shoulders bare, his bald head glistening in the sun, and his aged knees on the cold, damp ground." He recalls, "The spectacle of an aged man— a husband and a father—humbly kneeling before a worm of the dust, surprised and shocked me at the time; and since I have grown old enough to think on the wickedness of slavery, few facts have been of more value to me than this, to which I was a witness. It reveals slavery in its true color, and in its maturity of repulsive hatefulness."[65] Douglass describes the scene as representative of slavery's "maturity," suggesting that it is the inevitable culmination—the full realization—of a system that turns people into things. Significantly, Douglass contrasts slavery's "maturity" with his own perspective, noting that he has "grown old enough to think on the wickedness of slavery." By juxtaposing his own maturity with that of the institution of slavery, Douglass draws attention to his moral development, upending the ideological basis for slavery. That is, in contradistinction to the institution, he has matured and gained the perspective that makes it possible for him to see how primitive the institution of slavery is.

While Douglass and Jacobs expose the inhumane treatment of elderly people, they also offer a competing age ideology whereby old age connotes achievement and industry. Indeed, this veneration of old age exemplifies how enslaved people formulated alternative ways to gauge the passage of time and to give meaning to the phases of life.[66] Thus, in response to efforts to wholly transform age into economic currency, enslaved people constructed an alternative paradigm for development that did not rely on numerical age. Jacobs describes her grandmother, "Aunt Marthy," as an icon of independence, self-sufficiency, and grit. Through this account of her grandmother, Jacobs rejects prevailing assumptions about elderly individuals. Instead of declining in value, her grandmother becomes ever more intelligent and self-sustaining over the years. It is, in this sense, a progress narrative, a narrative of growth and ascendance with age and time, rather than one of loss and affliction.

Moreover, this characterization of Aunt Martha challenges preconceptions about women in general. Not only does she defy the expectations associated with aging in slavery but she proves to be a superlative businesswoman: "The business proved profitable; and each year she laid by a little, which was saved for a fund to purchase her children." And as Jacobs insists, "It was *her* labor that supplied my scanty wardrobe." Despite a lifetime of deprivation and emotional hardship, she becomes evermore resourceful and industrious. Jacobs writes, "By perseverance and unwearied industry, she was now mistress of a snug little home, surrounded with the necessaries of life." Her home is an icon of independence and self-sufficiency. Thus, through this characterization of Aunt Martha, Jacobs upends the notion of older people, especially women, as inefficient dependents. Moreover, her grandmother manages to incite fear in the narrative's villain, wielding power with very few words. "Although my grandmother was all in all to me, I feared her as well as loved her... Though she had been a slave, Dr. Flint was afraid of her." Aunt Martha's economic savvy, her awe-inspiring independence, and her strict code of morality make her a formidable figure in Jacobs' narrative, and she emerges as a rejoinder to prevailing notions of the elderly as inefficient or tragic.[67]

The portrayals of elderly people—the very visibility of elderly people in these narratives—are reminders of how zealously the white ruling class guarded the privileges of old age, and they draw attention to the denial of maturity and dignity as profound injustices. Moreover, Old Barney and Aunt Martha are themselves embodied forms of resistance to the ideology of age that grounded slavery. As Leslie Pollard notes, "The maintenance of old and superannuated slaves could drain vital funds from the coffers of age-conscious masters."[68] Enslaved elderly people, simply by existing, were often obstructive to the workings of the economy. Leslie Owens reiterates this point, noting, "Elderly slaves could get in the way on a plantation, moderately disrupting operations by their slow labors and need for additional rest time."[69] Thus, longevity itself might be read as a mode of defiance, as a bodily refusal to accommodate the economic priorities of plantation culture.

EXTRAORDINARY AGING

Beyond the valuation of elderly people in slave narratives, we can find in postbellum African American culture an even more explicit repossession of age. In the 1930s, the Federal Writers Project commissioned writers to interview formerly enslaved people about their experiences under slavery, and the interviews typically began by inquiring about the age of their subjects. The Federal Writers Project resulted in an archive of more than three thousand interviews, recorded between 1936 and 1938, the largest trove of slave narratives in existence. Ben Brown voiced a representative response: "I don't know how old I am, dey never told me down dere, but the folks here say I'm a hunderd yeah old an' I spect dats about right."[70] While Brown does not know his numerical age, he gives the rather high estimate of one hundred years. Another interviewer notes of a man named Edward Taylor: "exact age not known, but he is positive he is over 115 years old."[71] The exceedingly high numbers of these ages coupled with the subjects' uncertainty of their exact numerical age is a pattern across the interviews that offers a lens into a strategy that survivors of slavery used to resignify the peculiar forms of aging enforced upon them.[72]

Without knowledge of their birthdays, many of the individuals interviewed calculated their ages based on their memories of major events, with the Civil War serving as a crucial temporal benchmark for numerous interviewees.[73] For example, George Greene notes, "I don't know when I was born. I don't know exactly, but I was born in slavery time before the War began. I was enough to wait on the table when they was fighting. I remember when they was setting the Negroes free...I figure out my age by the white woman that raised me. She sent me my age."[74] In another interview, Chaney Hews responded: "My age, best of my recollection, is about eighty years. I wus 'bout eight years ole when de Yankees come through."[75] Similarly, Ella Wilson explained, "When the Civil War ceased I was here then and sixteen years old. I'm a hundred years old. Some folks tries to make it out like it ain't so. But I reckon I oughter know."[76] These responses suggest that in spite of the lack of empirical knowledge, many formerly enslaved individuals nonetheless developed strategies for determining their ages and became committed to their accounts of their lifespans.

Scholars have debated the veracity and viability of the WPA narratives for decades.[77] Noting the power dynamics between interviewers and subjects, some have seen the narratives as representations of white coercion; others have questioned their reliability based upon the difficulties associated with long-term memory and age.[78] For example, in an essay in the 2014 *Oxford Handbook to the African American Slave Narrative*, Sharon Ann Musher cautions researchers about relying on narratives that have been excessively revised and redacted, particularly those in Mississippi and Texas, "where state editors altered the narratives to downplay masters' abuse...and to suggest a paternalistic relationship."[79] But Musher also urges researchers to avoid interviews with formerly enslaved people who were "too young to remember enslavement or too old at the time of the interview to recall it."[80] She goes so far as to suggest that researchers set "cut off dates for the interviews they analyze," suggesting the range of "eighty two and ninety eight years old" as viable.[81]

Musher's willingness to dispense with the interviews of very elderly people is striking, considering that all of the interviewees are quite old. Indeed, she notes that "two-thirds of the ex-slaves interviewed were over 80 years old and 6% were older than 100, with some reporting their age to be as old as 130. Without birth certificates, it is difficult to verify age, and as many as 17% of those interviewed reported that they were unsure of their exact age."[82] While she acknowledges the difficulty of "verifying" age, she nonetheless advocates for a scholarly practice based upon numerical age.

Given the history of age deprivation and even age expropriation that characterized the experience of slavery, we should hesitate before returning these subjects to a methodology that again devalues elderly perspectives. But even more significantly, we should be wary of subjecting these testimonies to a realm of governmentally sanctioned accuracy, reaffirming the birth certificate and census as the arbiters of truth about African American lives.[83] Demographic data on African American longevity has long been used to legitimize racist ideology. For example, in the 1840s, scientists claimed that the comparatively long lives of African American slaves revealed their biological difference from whites and indicated their fitness for Southern climes.[84] By the 1890s, demography "proved" that the race was dying out, a sign of their inferiority and devolution.[85] Thus, the census became yet another avenue for white authorities to catalog and organize black lives in ways that often obscured or devalued lived reality. Reflecting on the problems of the African American subject and the census reporter, Eric Gardner notes, "Accurate or not, her or his information might then be 'corrected' by a racist government worker's dismissal of Black intelligence."[86] Thus, rather than dispensing with those narratives that seem unbelievable due to claims of extreme age, we might focus on *precisely* those narratives for what they tell us about how slavery affected aging and age discourse. Indeed, in light of how politically fraught the question of age was for enslaved persons, the testimonies might be read not as signs of senility or unreliability but as cogent, meaningful responses to a system that co-opted the very terms of age.

White interviewers frequently register a mix of awe and disbelief upon encountering very elderly subjects who appear to have robust physical health. For example, one interviewer describes a woman named Daphney Wright, noting that "she says she is 106 years old. She comes to the door without a cane... Save for her wearing glasses and walking slowly, there are no evidences of illness or infirmities." The interviewer seems to be attempting to match her reading of her body—"no evidences"—with the seeming implausibility of her reported age. Of Mrs. Henrietta Jackson, the interviewer notes she is "very active," observing that "at the time I called, [on an] August afternoon of over 90 degrees temperature, Mrs. Jackson was busy sweeping the floor... gett[ing] around without the aid of a cane or support of any kind." The interviewer continues to note: "Just how old Mrs. Jackson is, she herself doesn't know, but she thinks she is about 105 years old. She looks much younger." Another interviewer describes the former slave Richard Mack as "a happy philosopher, 104 years old, in perfect mental and physical condition, is still working as janitor."[87] Mack also tells the interviewer about his aunt, who "lived to be 141; she saw George Washington— she told me so." Similarly, the interviewer of Sarah Gudger refers to the "almost incredible claim of Aunt Sarah Gudger, ex-slave living in Asheville, that she was born on Sept. 15, 1816," making her 121 years old at the time of the interview.[88]

While the interviewers perform incredulity at these claims to longevity, they have no recourse or means of calling the information into question.[89] Indeed, a certain irreproachability protects these claims, as the interviewers have no choice but to take their alleged ages at face value, as the formerly enslaved people wield discursive authority. The unimpeachability of these reports of age echoes William Wells Brown's observation that "few persons can arrive at anything like the age of a Negro, by mere observation, unless they are well-acquainted with the race."[90] The very illegibility that Brown ascribes to the black body becomes the basis for the manipulation of age, and that indecipherability serves as a foundation for seizing the discourse of aging itself.[91]

In their extraordinary claims, these formerly enslaved people evince the simultaneous desire to claim a relationship to numerical age but also to subvert age as an objective measure.[92] In her discussion of William Dorsey's nineteenth-century *Colored Centenarians* scrapbook, Ellen Gruber Garvey observes that Dorsey, an African American artist, used the scrapbook to make "elderly black people the *most* representative of the nation's history."[93] Garvey writes, "their claim to great age makes a place for them in print— a claim to distinction and newsworthiness."[94] Just as Dorsey devoted an entire scrapbook to cases of extreme black longevity, the testimonies of formerly enslaved people suggest that numerical age remained a charged metric for a population stripped of the right to catalog their own lives and to develop along a normative life course.[95] Furthermore, we might read in these testimonies a demand for the respect considered appropriate for the elderly, an impulse to use age in order to override the disrespect they might garner based on race.

Moreover, these extraordinarily long lives are biological refusals to accommodate the economy of slavery and ideological responses to a system that denied enslaved persons access to age norms. Indeed, if racism is "the state-sanctioned or extralegal production and exploitation of group-differentiated vulnerability to premature death," as Ruth Wilson Gilmore writes, then we might read long lives themselves as acts of resistance to the objectives of entrenched racism.[96] These individuals, interviewed in the mid-1930s, have successfully navigated the racist science, medical practices, and mob violence of the nadir, not to mention the war itself and the poverty that likely characterized their postbellum existence. Thus, their lives function as disruptive and perplexing to a system that deems them not just worthless but obstructive.

We can read these claims to extraordinary age at once as refusals to abide by mainstream assumptions about age *and* as reclamations of age as a component of identity. These individuals occupy "oceanic lifespans," a phrase Habiba Ibrahim has recently used to describe "black subjects who could exceed the normal lifespan of a (white) human."[97] As she puts it, such subjects inhabit "lived temporalities that derive from liberal humanist dispossession."[98] In other words, once a discourse used to evaluate them as chattel, age functions for these formerly enslaved people as a tool to signify their authority over their life narratives and to challenge prevailing ideas about humanity.

Such claims to longevity echo those made earlier in the century in the case of Joice Heth, an enslaved woman, who was purchased by P. T. Barnum in 1835, and purported to be 161 years old and a former nursemaid to George Washington [see Figure 2.5]. Heth was exhibited by Barnum for seven months, during which controversy ensued over the veracity of her age and even her status as a human. When she died in 1836, a public autopsy was performed to determine her age, and the penny papers ran numerous articles on this dissection of an African American woman's body, rendering her the object of the empirical gazes of both journalism and science. While the anatomist who performed the dissection declared her to be in her late seventies, the cultural obsession with Heth's advanced age underscores the extent to which elderliness itself was a significant, even transgressive, space for African Americans to inhabit.

Situated in the context of an economy that turned African American age into currency, Heth's imagined elderliness is a kind of hyberbolic

Figure 2.5. "The Greatest Natural & National Curiosity in the World: Joice Heth." Printed Handbill, *c.*1835. Courtesy of the Somers Historical Society.

demonstration of that logic. In other words, it was Heth's age that served as the site of value for Barnum. Uri McMillan has recently described Heth as a performance artist, referring to the "ontological work she performed... [as] an important (though generally overlooked) cultural actor."[99]

That is, while the case of Joice Heth is most easily read as another example of how African American age was manipulated for white profit, we might also consider Heth's own role in reimagining the meanings of age and challenging the boundaries of imaginable life narratives. Without eliding the fact of her oppression, we can nonetheless recognize that Heth's age claims exploit the white desire to scrutinize black bodies, capitalizing on the illegibility of her body and subverting age as an empirical and reliable metric.

McMillan's formulation of Heth as an actor offers a useful frame for reading the many claims formerly enslaved people made to improbable longevity. Such narratives of unfathomable longevity return age to the individual and resonate with a postmodern desire to "recast the life span in fantastical ways."[100] To cite one final example: Until his death in 1979, Charlie Smith, a formerly enslaved man, claimed to be the oldest person in the United States. He is the subject of *The Transplant: The Biography of 135-Year-Old Charlie Smith, a Former Slave* by Sherman Clifton Byrd as well as of the PBS film *Charlie Smith and the Fritter Tree* written by novelist Charles Johnson. While subsequent research has called his age and life narrative into question, Smith's claims of extraordinary longevity are perhaps more significant than their veracity. After working on the film, Johnson noted, "We saw that Smith was a fantastic yarn-spinner, a fabulist for his own life."[101] What Smith's story reveals is that age—long withheld from enslaved individuals—became a strategic site for identity formation, a narrative resource, and a vehicle for self-promotion.

Smith's story and the Federal Writers Project testimonies venerate and demand respect for their longevity even as they challenge normative ideas about age. Though these interviews invoke numerical age, they also rupture dominant understandings about what qualifies as a long life and call into question how we measure lifetimes. As Jacques Ranciere writes, "The forms of subjectivization by which individuals and groups distance themselves from the constraints of 'normal' are at once ruptures in the sensory fabric of domination *and* ways of living within its framework."[102] The extra-ordinariness of these reported ages might be read as signs that they are gauging life according to alternative criteria, as if living through slavery itself qualifies survivors to another lifetime.

Alternately, we could read these ages as reclamations of the years of life, and hours and hours, stolen by slavery.[103] Historian Robin Kelley refers to "colored people's time" as a twentieth-century strategy "to recover unpaid wages and/or compensate for low wages and mistreatment," noting that "workers figured out a way to rig the clock in order to steal time."[104] In a similar vein, these peculiarly long lifespans hint at a yearning to repossess those years unjustly appropriated by slaveholders. As historian Mark

Smith notes, "With natural time polluted, linear time ascendant, and the sound of clock time regulating work, it is little wonder that some slaves believed freedom would mean a repudiation of master's time, broadly construed." Indeed, we might read in these extraordinary accounts of age a repudiation of "master's time" and a desire to destabilize numerical age as a coherent measure of human life.[105]

*   *   *

Toni Morrison's *Beloved* is set in motion when the eponymous character, the reanimated ghost of a slain child, reappears in the present as an ostensibly grown woman. Critic Kathyrn Bond-Stockton aptly calls her "a nineteen-year-old baby-woman," noting that "Beloved, when she is dead, is a virtual child, kept alive in a watery limbo [until she returns] as a teenage infant."[106] As Bond-Stockton's description suggests, Beloved is an age-queer character; her numerical age, bodily development, and maturity are out of sync, destabilized by the regime of slavery, which enforced and produced peculiar forms of aging. Morrison conjures a nightmarish vision of how age theft and age perversion manifest as a legacy of slavery. The novel's ominous ending, its final vision of the pregnant Beloved, adumbrates a future inevitably haunted by stunted lives.

We live in that future now, a time that historian Daina Ramey Berry calls "the historic spectacle of black death." It is a moment in which African American lives are visibly and regularly brutalized and stolen by imprisonment and policing. Certainly the many stories of murdered young African American men and women that precipitated the Black Lives Matter movement remind us of this truth—that the age theft and distortion so integral to the system of slavery reverberate today in the disproportionate number of black lives denied the right to age and to accrue the cultural privileges of maturity. The *American Psychological Association* published a study in 2014 that acknowledged that "black boys can be seen as responsible for their actions at an age when white boys still benefit from the assumption that children are essentially innocent."[107] In other words, racism continues to thwart the life course, making people of color less likely to achieve longevity and reserving the privileges of childhood for white children.

Black adulthood in the early twenty-first century is still defined by the threat of death, an anxiety that one's life is not wholly in his/her possession, not guaranteed the right to mature and age without the specter of imminent theft or violence. In a recent essay, Garnette Cadogan observes, "As adults we walk without thinking, really. But as a black adult I am often returned to that moment in childhood when I'm just learning to walk. I am once again on high alert, vigilant."[108] What Cadogan is describing here is not simply the exclusion from the white privilege of leisure, from the affective experience of the *flâneur*, but rather how the experience of childhood vigilance and anxiety structures his adult experience, eroding his access to autonomy and racializing the normative experience of adulthood.

Given the persistence of the age effects instantiated by slavery, we can see how elderliness—and extreme maturity—serve as a means of evading the market logic of slavery and as a mode of claiming possession of one's life and self. Where Melville represents boyhood itself as a tactic of resistance, a refutation of capitalist imperatives, such a stance was hardly appealing for those trapped in a regime premised on non-development and racial immaturity. The following chapter explores how white women, for whom nonage was a similarly permanent rather than temporary status, negotiated their exclusion from adulthood. While white women did attain the legal age of majority in some states, gaining the rights to sign contracts and obtain emancipation from their parents, they lost many of these rights upon marriage, and they never aged into political maturity during the nineteenth century. Indeed, they were denied the rights of full adult citizens even after they reached the "age of majority."

3

Little Women, Overgrown Children, and the Problem of Female Maturity

"Woman at her best never outgrows adolescence."

G. Stanley Hall[1]

Harriet Beecher Stowe's benevolent but impotent Mr. St. Clare describes the people he enslaves as living in a "dependent, semi-childish state," but in the nineteenth century, women of all races were expected to be politically and economically dependent.[2] Without analogizing the experiences of enslaved individuals and free white women, it is crucial to acknowledge how the discourse of maturity buttressed both racial and gender hierarchies. Just as people of color were deemed perpetually child-like, so too were white women considered intellectually infantile, not sophisticated enough to vote, sign contracts, or hold office. For white women, numerical age was negated as a measure of maturity and functioned instead as a barometer for social and economic value. That is, where slavery valorized young people for their reproductive and productive potential, so too did middle-class gender ideology make youthfulness a signal aspect of white female worth, as wives were increasingly expected to function as curators of domestic life and ornamental signs of socioeconomic status.

One of the era's most celebrated female authors, Louisa May Alcott was deeply attuned to concretization of age norms and life stages over the nineteenth century and to adulthood as a cultural status reserved for men, and like Herman Melville, Frederick Douglass, and Harriet Jacobs, she wielded literature as a tool for reimagining the meanings attached to age. Alcott is often labeled as a writer of children's literature, and rightly so, as she wrote several books specifically for children.[3] However, conceiving of Alcott only in terms of her figurations of childhood limits our ability to see her contribution to the theorization of age more broadly. Alcott's interests in pedagogy, women's rights, and childhood are anchored in an enduring engagement with the meanings of age and the gendered expectations for life trajectories.

This chapter considers the exclusionary status of adulthood through close attention to Alcott's fiction, which highlights the normative—and limited—meanings associated with female aging. In her work, Alcott acknowledges numerical age as a viable measure of maturity but denaturalizes the seeming inevitability of gendered norms and the developmental teleology that underwrites them. Where *Little Women* intimates but ultimately forecloses an unconventional teleology of aging, Alcott's subsequent novel *Work* envisions alternative versions of female maturity and departs from linear models of aging as decline. This chapter argues that an analytics of age is at the core of Alcott's feminist project, which interrogates the meanings mapped onto women at various stages of the life cycle. This reconceptualization of female aging reverberates in the work of Charlotte Perkins Gilman, who was committed to the expansion of women's opportunities in the public sphere and to their full development as individuals.

Alcott acknowledged age as both a biological fact and a cultural construction that took shape differently across gender, race, and class lines. Her investment in the significance of age and its particular implications for girls and women permeates her oeuvre, but it lurks on the margins of the robust scholarship on even her most celebrated work, *Little Women.* Critics consistently address the novel's feisty tomboy heroine, Jo March, who wears boy's clothes and speaks in slang, and lament the disappointment of the novel's conservative ending.[4] For example, Ivy Schweitzer has recently written of "the feminine conditioning and constriction that the last part of the novel imposes upon Jo."[5] And Elizabeth Young observes that "Alcott's women conclude their inner civil wars with a marked victory of civility over conflict."[6] What is missing from these accounts is the acknowledgment of how age norms operate in tandem with gender norms to direct these female protagonists to their expected positions within domestic life.[7]

Little Women repeatedly exposes age and gender ideologies as mutually constitutive. When the novel begins, Alcott specifies that Jo is fifteen, and she is just becoming aware of the expectations associated with womanhood. When her older sister Meg tells her, "You are old enough to leave off boyish tricks," Jo replies, "I hate to think I've got to grow up, and be Miss March, and wear long gowns, and look as prim as a China Aster!"[8] According to this formulation, there is no way to grow up without succumbing to a rigid gender role. Significantly, it is not the biological aspect of aging that Jo fears; rather, she recoils from the expectation that she must adhere to the age and gender norms associated with adult womanhood. To grow up is to conform to a specific script, which necessitates becoming a different person with a different name ("Miss March") and a different style ("long gowns"). Jo begs, "Don't try to make me grow up before my time…Let me be a little girl as long as I can."[9] Despite the diminutive term, being a "little girl" permits her to inhabit a world of theatrical performance and relative gender equality; by contrast, womanhood signifies an unnatural regime that demands acquiescence to an appropriately gendered life schedule. *Little Women* is thus a coming-of-age novel that thematizes coming of age as unnatural, fraught, and rife with anxiety.

What is most troubling for Jo is that normative womanhood does not entail a relationship to the public sphere or to professional life. On the contrary, she associates womanhood with uselessness and domestic servitude; it means the disintegration of her family of origin and the imaginative escapades of her childhood. While the Civil War offered boys a masculine proving ground and a venue for coming-of-age, Jo laments her exclusion from this rite of passage: "I'm dying to go and fight with Papa. And I can only stay home and knit, like a poky old woman!"[10] She draws an analogy between her status as a young woman and that of a "poky old woman," suggesting that being a young woman is not significantly different from being an old woman.[11]

While boys gain rights and privileges with age, Jo recognizes that women do not acquire access to public life or to a more expansive set of possibilities. On the contrary, Alcott observes that women's lives narrow as they age: "In America, as everyone knows, girls early sign a declaration of independence, and enjoy their freedom with republican zest; but the young matrons usually abdicate with their first heir to the throne, and go into seclusion almost as close as a French nunnery."[12] This somewhat sardonic aside highlights the unusual amount of freedom American girls enjoy but also points to how they surrender that freedom when they become mothers; thus, conventional aging ushers women into a private—and unfree—existence.

Jo's plea to remain a girl is a plea for freedom from the disciplinary constraints that come with growing up. But Jo is not the only character attuned to age norms; the novel is obsessed with the idea of age propriety. In an early chapter, when the sisters act out *Pilgrim's Progress*, Marmee assures them they are "never too old for this."[13] Later, Amy is "too young to go to the theatre,"[14] while Meg is "getting too old for [acting]."[15] Later, Meg "too young too to do anything about [John Brooke] yet," and at the same time, she is anxious about becoming "a fidgeting, broken down old woman before my time."[16] The novel's attention to the rhetoric of age thus captures the core disciplinary idiom in the lives of girls and women, who must constantly calibrate their behavior and appearance to their chronological age.

The novel's concluding chapters take place on the eve of Jo's twenty-fifth birthday, suggesting Alcott's understanding of birthdays as occasions for reflecting on one's status in relation to age standards and developmental expectations. That is, the novel reveals that birthday celebrations have a regulatory function as they ask individuals to assess their lives with regard to the heteronormative life schedule. Jo's twenty-fifth birthday forces her to contemplate her failure to comply with these benchmarks, reminding her of "how little she seemed to have accomplished."[17] She laments, "At twenty-five, girls begin to talk about being old maids, but secretly resolve they never will be. At thirty they say nothing about it, but quietly accept the fact."[18] These reflections point to how the meanings of age derive from one's relationship to gender ideology; the failure to comply with heteronormativity can render a woman prematurely "old," as the pejorative term "old maid" penalizes women for non-compliance with the dual codes of age and gender. It is Jo's birthday realization—her obligatory contemplation of her age—that seems to lead to the novel's rapid resolution, as Professor Bhaer re-emerges in this same chapter, reassuring readers that Jo will not in fact become a dreaded "old maid."

Ultimately, *Little Women* affirms the conventional notion—and generic expectation—that women are grown up when they marry. As Jo swallows the bitter pill that comes with this version of maturity, she tells Laurie, "The happy old times can't come back, and we mustn't expect it. We are man and woman now, with sober work to do, for playtime is over, and we must give up frolicking."[19] This lament for "playtime" resigns them to the gender-differentiated work that defines adulthood. Indeed, with the March sisters' adherence to normative gender teleology comes the acknowledgment that their artistic and literary ambitions were merely "playtime," nothing but "castles in the air," unrealizable and unrealistic.[20]

One way to account for the almost tacked-on quality of the ending, its total and utter concession to heteronormative maturity, is the pressure Alcott faced from publishers.[21] She wrote to her uncle May: "publishers are very perverse & wont let authors have their way so my little women must grow up and be married off in a very stupid style."[22] Significantly, Alcott calls her publishers "perverse" because of their investment in traditional marriage, revealing her own conviction that there is something "perverse" about the very trajectory that defines normativity. Indeed, after the publication of the first installment of *Little Women*, Alcott wrote in her diary that readers were pressuring her to conclude the novel with Jo's marriage to Laurie: "Girls write to ask who the little women marry, as if that was the only end and aim of a woman's life. I *won't* marry Jo to Laurie to please any one."[23] Here, one senses Alcott's own perverse delight in the prospect of withholding the pleasure of the conventional ending from her readers.

WORK AND THE QUEST FOR MATURITY

In the years after *Little Women's* massive success, Alcott may have felt a bit freer to experiment with less conventional narratives. Her 1873 novel *Work: A Story of Experience* features a progressive female protagonist explicitly invested in her autonomy and self-cultivation.[24] Existing scholarship on *Work* tends to focus on its complex depiction of labor, and for these critics, the novel's unique contribution is its extended contemplation of the possibilities for women in the public sphere.[25] The limited scope of the scholarly conversation on this novel may result from the lack of critical vocabulary for discussing age, which I see as the novel's central subject, as well as a broader cultural ambivalence about women's aging.[26] Ultimately, *Work's* meditation on labor is inextricable from its interest in age, which inflects all other stratified subject positions.

Rather than portraying womanhood as a gradual decline after marriage and motherhood, *Work* reimagines the significance of numerical age and offers a new vision of the female life course that does not peak in girlhood or conclude with marriage. The benchmark birthdays of twenty-one, thirty, and forty structure the novel, but the protagonist inhabits these ages in ways that do not accord with entrenched age norms; instead, she transgresses the disciplinary regime of age in order to imagine new forms of aging and to envision an autonomous, publicly oriented adulthood that was culturally and politically off limits to women.

Work begins with protagonist Christie Devon poised to embark upon a coming-of-age journey. "There's going to be a new Declaration of Independence," she tells her aunt and uncle. Where *Little Women* referred to the "declaration of independence" as linked to the provisional and finite freedom of girlhood, *Work's* protagonist invokes the same document and concept to claim a self-determining adulthood. "Being of age, I'm going to take care of myself and not be a burden any longer."[27] Christie's description of herself as "being of age" is striking because women never truly came "of age" in the mid-nineteenth century, either legally or metaphorically. The age of majority—age twenty-one—held very little significance for women since they could not vote or run for political office. As historian Corinne T. Field explains, women were "perpetual minors," and this uneven distribution of rights thwarted female development.[28] While white men could achieve their majority and obtain citizenship rights at the age of twenty-one, women were not granted privileges as they aged. In the nineteenth-century United States, women fought to raise the age of consent for marriage as well as to universalize the age of majority; both of these battles hinged on making age a democratic and universal measure of maturity and autonomy.

Just as the very phrase "little women" suggests the paradoxical status of girlhood in Alcott's moment, so too was adult womanhood a kind of oxymoron. As Margaret Fuller opined, the disempowered nineteenth-century woman was practically an "overgrown child."[29] Many perceived womanhood as an extension of childhood, a period of prolonged dependence and servitude, but without the possibilities and play that balance the disempowerment of childhood.[30] In *Woman in America* (1844), Mrs. A. J. Graves observes that the contemporary woman is "trained up as though she were designed ... to be always a child. Nor, under these circumstances, can we deem it strange when we see so many around us who are women in growth, but children in character and in intellect."[31] As this passage reveals, adulthood is a function of "training" and "design." One does not inevitably attain maturity; on the contrary, it is strategically withheld from women and people of color.

Contrary to this cultural and legal reality, *Work*'s Christie Devon insists upon the meaning inherent in the age of twenty-one, even for women.[32] "Twenty-one tomorrow, and her inheritance a head, a heart, and a pair of hands," Alcott writes of her protagonist.[33] Christie's use of her chronological age as a reference point establishes the novel's interest in the gendered nature of aging norms and life narratives. She remarks, "I'm old enough to take care of myself; and if I'd been a boy, I should have been told to do it long ago ... I hate to be dependent."[34] This insistence on bionumerical age as a meaningful marker of maturity for women resonates with contemporary activist discourse. As Field explains, "Rather than highlight marriage as the point at which a girl became a woman, activists argued that age twenty-one should become a significant transition in women's lives, just as it had become in the lives of men."[35]

Christie's age-based decision to claim her autonomous adulthood revises of the normative female life course. Gazing at a fire, Christie compares two burning logs: one is "sizzling despondently among the cinders" and the "other glows from end to end with cheerful little flames." She reflects, "I know the end is the same, but it *does* make a difference *how* they turn to ashes, and *how* I spend my life."[36] She wants to live completely over the course of her life, not to burn out after her prime, whiling away the majority of her life in domestic drudgery. Christie seeks to imagine possibilities for aging beyond what Carolyn Dinshaw calls the "mechanistic and constricting linearity that leads bleakly, infinitely onward."[37] As she puts it, "There is a better sort of life than this dull one made up of everlasting work, with no object but money ... and I mean to get out of the treadmill."[38] In opposition to the "dull" and "everlasting" work associated with traditional domestic labor or with factory employment, Christie envisions a life of many little "flames," many adventures and stories rather than a linear descent into old age and infirmity.

The novel's episodic structure registers Alcott's interest in imagining alternatives to the existing model of aging available to women. In chapters named for the various occupations she explores, including "Servant," "Governess," "Companion," and "Actress," Christie attempts different kinds of work, affirming that novel's commitment to experimentation rather than development. Alcott's novel is not about the discovery of Christie's "true" self; rather, over time, Christie's devotion to perpetual change and movement is an end in itself. She seeks work in the name of experience, not in the service of professional ascent or normative success. Indeed, the novel eddies around different professional realms and groups of people, never quite settling, refuting the association of women with stasis and domesticity. In this way, the novel's form decenters advancement and growth and instead thematizes the accretion of selves. The conventional stages of life, delineated by marriage and reproduction, are replaced with various professional forays, suggesting the multiple public lives women can have. This organizing logic positions successive professional ventures—rather than the heteronormative teleology of development and decline—as a viable mode of female existence.

Beyond its interest in refiguring the trajectory of the female life narrative, *Work* exposes how social inequalities result in the uneven assignment of maturity. As Alcott reveals, women of color are deprived of the status typically associated with old age as well as the privileges of maturity, such as literacy, respect, and self-determination. While working as a servant, Christie meets Hepsey, a fugitive slave, employed in the same home, and she is appalled to see how the young daughter of their employer treats the older African American woman: "I suppose Katy thought her white skin gave her a right to be disrespectful to a woman old enough to be her mother just because she was black."[39] Katy's whiteness and class privilege stoke her sense of superiority over an older African American woman.

Far from being granted respect for her age, Hepsey is treated as a child by her employers, who reproduce the infantilizing conditions of slavery. Hepsey has been robbed of the opportunity to learn to read, and Christie teaches her the alphabet after hours. Christie watches her "laboriously shaping her A's and B's, or counting up on her worn fingers the wages they had earned by months of weary work, that she might purchase one treasure,—a feeble, old woman, worn out with seventy years of slavery far away there in Virginia."[40] Echoing similar scenes in Harriet Jacobs' *Incidents in the Life of a Slave Girl*, this description of Hepsey reduced to childlike counting and "shaping A's and B's" highlights adulthood as a privileged, even exclusionary status, dispensed according to other social positions.[41] While Alcott demands deference for this elderly character, her primary interest in this episode is to show how the dispensation of maturity—detached from chronological age—reaffirms existing racial hierarchies. Along with gender inequality, slavery and racism distort age relations and expose what Susan Sontag calls the "unequal distribution of adult roles."[42] Moreover, Hepsey's exclusion from normative adulthood is significantly different from Christie's, revealing how gendered forms of aging are also deeply racialized. While racial privilege enables Christie to move freely between a host of employment opportunities and gives her the opportunity to contemplate a rejection of the dominant modes of womanhood, Hepsey, as a fugitive slave, is deprived of even the constricted forms of aging that Christie finds suffocating.

In the first half of the novel, Alcott repeatedly presents suicide as the only alternative to the circumscribed model of female aging offered by a culture that deprives women of maturity. Following her stint as a governess, Christie finds work as a companion to an invalid, Helen, who takes her own life in order to avoid inheriting the insanity that has plagued all the members of her family. Just as Helen's suicide was a way of warding off a horrific, predetermined future, so too does Christie's contemplation of suicide suggest a dearth of options for adult women. While standing outside in the cold watching another woman get married, Christie observes "the sharpness of the contrast between that other woman's fate and her own."[43] It is no coincidence that she is standing on a bridge "with no desire to mingle in the crowd that waited on either side" when she considers taking her own life; it is a bridge beyond youth that she cannot imagine. There is literally no way to conceive of advancing or aging as a woman outside of marriage.

Though she does not take her own life, Christie's reflection on her appearance and age suggest that turning thirty itself is a kind of death. Just as Jo March feared the approach of her thirtieth birthday as the date of her personal and social expiration, so too does Christie, broke and bereft after laboring as a seamstress, look in the mirror and think, " 'Yes, I am growing old; my youth is nearly over, and at thirty I shall be a faded, dreary woman, like so many I see and pity.' "[44] Though Christie is only in her late twenties, this scene can usefully be read in terms of what Kathleen Woodward calls the "mirror stage of old age." As Woodward writes, "The mirror stage of old age is the inverse of the mirror stage of infancy. What is whole is felt to reside *within*, not *without*, the subject. The image in the mirror is understood as uncannily prefiguring the disintegration and nursling dependence of advanced age."[45] Christie contemplates her aging face, "wondering if it could be the same she used to see so full of youth and hope and energy."[46] While the mirror seems to highlight the self-evident, objective truth of age as decline, it actually reflects back the culture's perception of the aging face. Christie's anxiety about growing into a "faded, dreary woman" highlights the extent to which the fetishization of youth already dominated popular consciousness, dictating beauty standards and self-worth. The title of a contemporary text, "addressed to mothers and daughters," suggests that anti-aging discourse was already mainstream: *Woman: Her Health, Beauty, and Intellect, Preserved from Premature Decline: With Directions How to Avoid the Causes Which So Early Induce Old Age* (1857).

THIRTY IS THE NEW THIRTY

Against the emergent cultural preoccupation with youth, Alcott's novel offers the possibility for women to see and experience age differently. After Christie's near-suicide, the novel takes a marked turn, offering a more radical vision of what adulthood might look like for women. Christie's rebirth, described in a chapter entitled "Beginning Again," takes place at a commune, run by an older woman, Mrs. Sterling, and her son, David. "An old-fashioned cottage" served as "a sort of refuge for many women like herself; a halfway house where they could rest and recover themselves after the wrongs, defeats, and weariness that come to such in the battle of life."[47] This "weariness" with the "battle of life" refers to the harsh conditions that characterize the existence of women as they age. The cottage is also a "half-way house" in a more literal sense, a place where women can regain strength and perspective for the second half of life and recover from the culture's treatment of women who defy the ideology of age. Significantly, the cottage itself is described as "old-fashioned," a buzzword for age transgression in Alcott's oeuvre in which the culturally abandoned, or antiquated, regains meaning and value.

Indeed, Alcott frequently embraces the old-fashioned and the dated, or what Emily Apter calls the "démodé."[48] As Apter writes, the démodé serves "as a mechanism that makes possible the radical dispossession of time. There is a temporal violence to outdating; when it erupts, it loosens periodicity's possessive perimeters around spots of time and releases arrested images into the future."[49] Alcott uses the démodé as a strategy for enabling the old and young to mingle and for denaturalizing age categories, and her enduring affinity for the "old-fashioned" enables her to interrogate the notion of progress as necessarily permanent, inevitable, or positive.[50]

Christie's friendship with David Sterling reaffirms values beyond those enshrined by the paradigms of capitalism and heteronormativity. Described as "rather old-fashioned in manner and plain in speech," David offers an alternative to market-based models of masculinity. Instead of striving for wealth accumulation, David is driven by a Thoreauvian commitment to transcendentalism and nature. Perplexed by David's seeming indifference to conventional achievement, Christie broaches the topic with her mentor, Mr. Power: "Isn't it natural for a young man to have some personal aim or aspiration to live for?" Mr. Power replies, "*I* think David one of the most ambitious men I ever knew, because at thirty he has discovered this truth and taken it to heart."[51] This dialogue exposes as *unnatural* a linear life course, driven by accomplishment; instead, ambition is redefined in terms of soulfulness and self-cultivation. Indeed, it seems Mr. Powers makes specific mention of David's numerical age only to suggest that he is prematurely wise, upending the notion that maturity and numerical age are necessarily synonymous.

Just as David's version of a thirty-year-old man seems non-normative, so too does Christie find an unconventional way of inhabiting age and gender. Indeed, her experience at the cottage suggests the possibility for non-linear aging and for a life in which development and age are not sequential. Alcott challenges the notion that one's bionumerical age is necessarily a "truth" of identity; the novel acknowledges that "the age we feel is not necessarily the same as our calendrical age, nor is it the same as how we are perceived, or how we register ourselves being perceived by others."[52] Christie herself remarks, "It amuses me to be treated like a little girl again, when I am nearly thirty, and feel seventy at least."[53] Thus, according to Alcott, one can inhabit multiples ages at once. Indeed, the passage of time seems to entail the accumulation of differently aged identities and the negotiation of myriad temporalities, or what psycho-analyst André Green calls the "heterochrony" of psychic temporalities, suggesting that aging might be about the experience of anachronism, or the intrusion of ostensibly outdated selves into the present, rather than cohesion or evolution.[54]

According to the normative, middle-class life schedule, Christie should be married and a mother by thirty.[55] As Elaine Showalter writes, "The age of thirty was a significant threshold for nineteenth-century women, a moment of acknowledgment that the marriageable years were past."[56] But the novel contends that remaining unmarried and childless past thirty is far from a death sentence or a mark of failure. By devoting an entire chapter to Christie's thirtieth birthday party, Alcott underscores her investment in unsettling assumptions about numerical age. While the birthdays of founding fathers, such as Thomas Jefferson and George Washington, were often observed, along with the nation's "birthday," ordinary individuals were just beginning to celebrate birthdays in the second half of the nineteenth century.[57] The first American birthday cards, produced by the Louis Prang Company in Boston in the 1880s, bespeak the new significance of bionumerical age [see Figure 3.1].[58] The cards often feature children or cherubs against floral backdrops, lamenting the passage of youth.

May + + you + have · many = more · Birthdays and · ever · remain = as · Youthful · as · now ·

Figure 3.1. Birthday card from the Louis Prang & Co. Collection, *c.*1880. Courtesy of the American Antiquarian Society.

In one card, a young woman examines her aging reflection in a handheld mirror, just as Christie does in *Work* [see Figure 3.2]. The accompanying text explains that "youth must pass," urging women to live for "duty" in order to find "good gifts in store" in heaven. In other words, birthdays are an occasion to reevaluate and recommit to one's appropriate gender role.

Lilly Martin Spencer's 1869 painting "We Both Must Fade" espouses a similar message [see Figure 3.3]. The painting features a young woman gazing at her reflection with an expression of scrutiny. The woman is holding a rose, which is beginning to droop, and the painting is clearly aligning the young woman with the rose, suggesting that both must inevitably "fade" and decline in beauty and value. The mirror serves as the reminder and the indicator of this inevitable reality.

Alcott acknowledges the cultural exaltation of young womanhood only to flout the norms linked to bionumerical age and to reject the disciplinary work of the birthday celebration. David tells her, " 'I wished you many happy birthdays; and, if you go on getting younger every year like this, you will surely have them.' "[59] Whereas most women in the nineteenth century—like Jo in *Little Women*—may have associated aging with loss rather than gain, Alcott's heroine accumulates political conviction, a social life, and even physical beauty as she grows older.[60] She remarks, "I used to think many years would be burdensome, and just before I came here I felt

Figure 3.2. Birthday card from the Louis Prang & Co. Collection, *c.*1880. Courtesy of the American Antiquarian Society.

Figure 3.3. Lilly Martin Spencer, "We Both Must Fade," 1869. Courtesy of the Smithsonian American Art Museum.

as if I could not bear another one. But now I like to live, and hope I shall a long, long time."[61] Where earlier in the novel Christie could not bear to contemplate growing old, her reflections upon turning thirty suggest a transformation in her perspective on age, undermining the host of messages—from birthday cards to popular paintings—that conjoined biological age and the performance of gendered versions of maturity. If, as Mary Russo suggests, "not acting one's age is not only inappropriate but dangerous, exposing the female subject, especially, to ridicule, contempt, pity and scorn—the scandal of anachronism," then Alcott's novel dwells in this scandal, embracing the impropriety of subverting age norms.[62]

Even as a child, Louisa May Alcott was chafing against the expectations enmeshed in the age–gender matrix. At thirteen years old, she wrote in her diary, "I am old for my age, and don't care much for girl's things. People think I'm wild and queer."[63] As this entry suggests, to feel mismatched with one's age is to feel misaligned with one's assigned gender role, and Alcott felt her alienation from these normalizing forces as a kind of queerness. In *Work*, Alcott positions her protagonist as similarly estranged from these discourses, and Christie Devon comes to see biological age as prescriptive more than expressive, a disciplinary label that works in conjunction with gender and sexuality. [64]

Indeed, if queerness can describe the experience of being outside or apart from ostensibly natural age identifications and developmental schedules, then we might read Christie as aging queerly, or "growing sideways," a term Kathryn Bond-Stockton uses to describe "a mode of irregular growth involving odd lingerings, wayward paths, and fertile delays." As Bond-Stockton writes, " 'Growing up' may be a short-sighted, limited rendering of human growth, one that oddly would imply an end to growth when full stature (or reproduction) is achieved."[65] But where Bond-Stockton focuses on the queerness of childhood, Alcott is less concerned with childhood in a literal sense than with childhood as a psychic zone or set of portable behaviors and with "growing" as a phenomenon of aging over the course of a life.

Work suggests that growth can occur in a range of styles and contexts other than those associated with conventional gender-appropriate maturation. We are told that Christie "walked among them as happy as a child who finds it playmates again"; "her face grew young as she looked" at the flowers.[66] She feels like a "little girl whom [David] was trying to amuse."[67] Removed from mainstream society, Christie is also removed from the cultural meanings attached to age. The passage of time is not associated with the loss of opportunity but with the possibilities for self-invention.[68] Christie announces, "I feel as I had been born again."[69] And later, she asks, "Don't I look a different creature from the ghost that came here three of four months ago? And she turned her face for inspection like a child."[70] In other words, Christie's regeneration is physical as well as emotional; she is aging in reverse, or becoming new.[71]

While these descriptions of Christie might seem to celebrate women's childishness and youthful appearance, what is important is that this emphasis on youth coincides with her thirtieth birthday, typically the mark of middle age and the coronation of "old maid" status. Thus, Alcott's investment in Christie's youth in this section points to the capacity for women to inhabit disjunctive or multiple age positions and to unsettle age–maturity indices. In Alcott's utopic fantasy, women have the freedom to reinvent themselves and to reimagine their futures, experiencing rebirth at middle age rather than tipping into decline.

Though Christie marries David and gives birth to their daughter, marriage and childbirth are not granted much narrative attention. Marriage is not the sign of her maturation or entering a new stage of life.[72] Far from the end of her social development, her marriage to David, a feminized figure, barely registers. Alcott devotes a single paragraph to their union. Moreover, Christie ends up nursing David when he is wounded in the war, making him the dependent in their marriage, which is abruptly destroyed by the Civil War. The very fact that Christie loses her husband so soon after their marriage forces her to imagine a different life course, highlighting that marriage and motherhood are not the apotheosis of a woman's utility or the markers of completed maturation. Alcott thematizes this departure from narrative convention: "If she had been a regular novel heroine . . . she should have gone gray in a single night, had a dangerous illness, gone mad."[73] Because Christie is not a "regular heroine," Alcott must invent a new narrative template to accommodate her.[74]

The anti-climactic status of marriage in this novel fits with Rita Felski's definition of the feminist *Bildungsroman*. As she notes, "Marriage, as that mark of narrative closure which exemplifies the merging of individual and social interests, is . . . explicitly revealed not as the endpoint of female *Bildung, but as its very antithesis,* so that female 'youth'—the period of interior and exterior discovery and development—is located at quite different points within a female social biography."[75] In other words, "youth" may occur later in life for women; it is not a biologically bound concept. Thus, if age signifies differently for women than for men, then women's narratives might require distinctive conventions to account for trajectories that are not always linear or progressive. Furthermore, where the traditional *Bildungsroman* concludes with socialization and assumption of one's place in the world, *Work*'s ending gestures to the unsettling of social hierarchies and to the introduction of new possibilities rather than acquiescence to existing frameworks.

Christie's visit to her childhood home encapsulates the novel's ethos around age and gender. Upon seeing Christie, Uncle Enos remarks, "You be growing old, that's a fact; but somehow it's kind of becomin'. I never thought you'd be so much of a lady, and look so well after all you've been through."[76] He expresses surprise at Christie's attractive appearance "in spite of the gray hair at her temples and the lines about her mouth." In other words, age and experience are "becomin'," even for women. Indeed, this moment echoes the Christie's encounter with her aging face earlier in the book. The very same physical aspects of aging are reinterpreted at the novel's conclusion in radically different terms; they are signs of beauty and strength, suggesting the contingency of the meanings we attach to age. Where contemporaneous birthday cards and mainstream iconography of aging offer only a model of decline for women of a certain age, *Work* offers an alternative hermeneutic for reading the life course whereby the physical markers of aging are construed as gains rather than losses.

The novel's concluding chapter, entitled "At Forty," describes middle age as "the half-way house between youth and age."[77] It was precisely this stage of life that women's right reformers sought to redefine; they wanted women to reach "a peak of achievement in middle age." As an activist, Christie leads a "loving league of sisters, old and young, black and white, rich and poor, each ready to do her part." Thus, instead of a decrepit older woman, isolated in the domestic sphere, Christie is a public figure whose experiences and age have only made her more useful and effective, affirming that "no woman need lament lost youth or fear approaching age."[78] One need not acquiesce to the cultural demands of post-pubescent femininity or to the stringent "decline ideology" of the female life course.[79]

Against a culture that saw women as "perpetual minors," Alcott sought to democratize maturity, to represent the possibility for women to achieve intellectual and economic independence and autonomy. And her signpost-ing of Christie's specific ages—twenty-one, thirty, and forty—suggests that she believed, in part, that numerical age was a meaningful marker. In this sense, Alcott's *Work* can be read as participating in the cultural battle for female majority. However, while woman's rights activists insisted "that age—not gender—was a natural measure of human difference and therefore a truly democratic qualification for individual rights and opportunities," Alcott resists placing total faith in the reality of these biological deter-minations.[80] Indeed, the novel's vision of an interracial, intergenerational, cross-class female community suggests its interest in acknowledging but also overriding categories of social difference. Age, for Alcott, is not an innocuous status; rather, *Work* reveals that cultural constructions of age—as a measure of maturity—abet and inflect other oppressions.

We might read Christie's turn toward activism in her forties as a rejoinder to the cultural commonplace that links aging with a shift toward political conservatism.[81] This conventional wisdom relies on the association of age with increasing privilege, especially material comforts and social status. But this is a gender, race, and class-specific way of imagining the effects of age. After all, for young white men in the nineteenth century, age involved accruing the privileges of adulthood: the right to own property, to vote, to run for office. For women and all people of color, though, political immaturity was a permanent and involuntary political condition that neither age nor accomplishment could alter. Consequently, age might have divergent effects for these groups. As Lydia Maria Child, one of the foremost female radicals of the century, wrote, "They say people grow more conservative as they grow older but I grow more radical."[82] Alcott's *Work* suggests that women might leave youth, along with its requisite association with marriageability and domesticity, and enter into an adulthood organized around non-familial relationships and political commitments. Adulthood is thus refigured in terms of public engagement and interdependence rather than fierce individualism and self-sufficiency. The narrative return of Hepsey, the fugitive slave, as well as Bella, an upper-class white woman, show that Alcott was committed to the advancement and complete personhood of all women, although the novel concludes before envisioning the utopic future it conjures.

"A NEW GENERATION OF WOMEN": GILMAN AS AGE ACTIVIST

Alcott's desire to envision a female life course apart from a heterocentric model of decline remained a feminist concern for decades after her own career ended. Women writers continued to examine the gendered meanings of age and the barriers to female political maturity. As a champion of female independence and a suffragist, Charlotte Perkins Gilman was especially troubled by the equation of ideal womanhood with immaturity. Her most famous work, "The Yellow Wall-Paper," is recounted by a narrator, whose husband puts her on bed rest in a nursery and refers to her as a "blessed little goose" and a "little girl," making plain her exclusion from adulthood. Moreover, the circularity of the narrative itself and the narrator's ultimate act of creeping around the room on all four offers a nightmarish vision of devolution for grown woman deprived of the opportunity to accrue the privileges of maturity and to develop with age.

But for an even more sustained examination of women's exclusion from and desire for adulthood, we can look to Gilman's first novel, *What Diantha*

Did, which was serialized between 1909 and 1910 in *The Forerunner,* the periodical she wrote, edited, and published for seven years. Like Alcott's *Work, What Diantha Did* concerns women's relationship to labor and the public sphere, and scholars have read it as a critique of Victorian marriage, as an attempt to solve the "servant question," and as a kind of prelude to Gilman's utopian writings. But this novel also meditates on women's age and capacity for maturity. When the novel begins, Diantha Bell is engaged to Roscoe Warden, but they cannot proceed with their plans to marry as long as he is the sole support for his widowed mother, his four indistinguishable, pathologically dependent sisters, and struggling to pay off their heavily mortgaged house and other debts. Indeed, Roscoe and his sisters are imprisoned by the family (their last name is after all "Warden"), and limited by the old-fashioned ideology that circumscribes women within the home, laying the burden of support exclusively upon Roscoe.

Roscoe asks Diantha simply to wait for him to get the family finances in good order, refusing to allow her to work alongside him. But Diantha refuses his request and decides to embark upon her own quest to make money, claiming the right to shape her own life course in a more active way. When she expresses a desire to leave home, Diantha refers to her brother's life narrative, and her mother responds: "I don't see what that's got to do with it. Henderson's a boy, and boys have got to go, of course."[83] In other words, boys are obliged to develop and leave home in young adulthood, but no such logic applies to women, who are expected to wait, waste time, and remain undeveloped in an unremitting domestic stasis. She tells her father: "Now I am twenty-one, and self-supporting—and have a right to go."[84] By citing her age as the foundation for her "right" to leave home, she takes control of age discourse in a way that resonates with Alcott's heroine in *Work* and with women's rights activists, who acknowledged the age of majority as an arbitrary cultural convention even as they sought to claim its significance as the basis for political rights and personal freedom.

Diantha's use of her chronological age as a reference point establishes the novel's core interest in the gendered nature of aging norms and life narratives.[85] As she tells a neighbor, "I am of age and live in a free country; what you say of children no longer applies to me."[86] Diantha desires to escape a sociopolitical regime that denies women the opportunity to gain rights and privileges with age. Fuming, she thinks to herself, "one would think childhood had no limit—unless it's matrimony!"[87] While matrimony offers the only pathway to adulthood, it would mean merely another kind of dependence and perpetual immaturity, like the narrator in "The Yellow Wall-Paper." In fact, when she tells Roscoe, "I have plans that will be of a real benefit to all of us, something worthwhile to *do*—and not only for us, but for *everybody*—a real piece of progress," he tellingly refers to her as a "little girl" and a "brave, foolish child!" offering a glimpse into the unequal dynamic that would structure their marriage.[88]

In defiance of her family, Diantha leaves home, finds work as a domestic servant, gains the support of women in town, and establishes a thriving business that includes a maid service, cooked-food delivery service, a restaurant, and a hotel. She describes "cooperative housekeeping" as a way to "ennoble domestic service" and to avoid wasting labor, money, and food in individual family units.[89] Diantha's arithmetic skills prove essential to her eventual success, as she relies on a precise accounting of time and money to manage her business, appropriating the language of labor efficiency and industrialization to resignify domestic labor as actual work. Thus, in a novel rife with numbers, age is only one of the many metrics Diantha reconfigures in her struggle to invest value in women's time.

The primary benefit for the many women who utilize Diantha's business is that it gives them back their time, time for professional pursuits and education. The fact that Diantha is called Miss Bell throughout the novel indicates her function as a kind of wake-up call—an alarm—for other women. Indeed, after she gives a controversial lecture on the merits of cooperative housekeeping, one woman says, "I haven't felt so thoroughly awake in several years."[90] Another tells her, "You have waked me all up." For those less interested in social reform, her name and presence are an alarm and a warning about a possible future in which traditional gender roles are obsolete.

When the novel ends, thirty-year-old Diantha is a married mother of three, but these domestic achievements do not mark the end of her career. On the contrary, the novel's subversion of mainstream age ideology relies on reconceptualizing the female life course so that a woman is not rendered useless after motherhood. In *What Diantha Did* and in much of her work, Gilman offered visions of midlife—or what Margaret Gullette calls the "postmaternal" period—as a valuable, desirable stage of life.[91] Diantha's mother, for example, joins the business as an accountant, and "her eyes grew bright again, she held her head as she did in her keen girlhood, and her daughter felt fresh hope and power." Thus, Diantha's reorganization of domestic labor facilitates a revision of the female life course. Where in the beginning of the novel, Diantha looked at her mother, thinking, "It seemed to her an interminable dull tragedy; this graceful, eager, black-eyed woman, spending what to the girl was literally a lifetime, in the conscientious performance of duties she did not love."[92] By the novel's end, Diantha's mother announces: "I am feeling...as if I'd just begun to live!" In other words, freed from the confines of the home and its drudgery, she is able to experience the personal growth along with the kinds of emotions typically associated with youth. This also destroys the coming-of-age teleology, or suggests that it is portable and can be mapped on to any period of life and separated from marriage and reproduction.

Certainly the novel does not concern itself with the elevation or development of all women. Gilman's reformist agenda dealt with improving the lives of white, middle-class women, and in this sense, the novel continues to enshrine maturity as both a class privilege and a white privilege. As Charlotte Rich puts it, Gilman tends to "efface the racial and ethnic realities of household labor... and Diantha's project is a profitable scheme based on others performing tasks that are unavoidably menial."[93] Moreover, Gilman specifically believed that white women's enforced immaturity had negative consequences for the white race. As Kimberly Hamlin notes, "To Gilman, women's economic dependence on men was not just a personal problem for individual women; she believed it also stalled evolutionary progress for the 'race.'"[94] That is, she specifically saw female independence as essential to white racial futurity, gesturing to the ways that constructions of maturity shored up racial hierarchy.

Nonetheless, *What Diantha Did* does offer a progressive vision of female aging, positing that (white middle-class) women should neither remain permanently dependent like children nor should they view aging itself as linked to inevitable decline. In an essay entitled "The New Generation of Women," Gilman writes "women live somewhat longer than do men, but their life cycle in men's minds covered in the past only the child-bearing period; they had less childhood, less youth, and less maturity, and far more of the least desirable period, old age. Save as somebody's mother or grandmother, they ceased to be."[95] But Gilman rebuts this traditional way of thinking with the hopeful forecast of a new paradigm for women's aging. She observes, "The woman of fifty and onward has a wide free outlook; many have undertaken new trades and professions and carried them on successfully. This is a great beneficent change of status."

Even as a young girl, Gilman understood the liberatory potential of an adulthood freed from the confines of marriage and the work of childrearing and believed in the potency of old age. In her autobiography, she writes, "One day the girls were discussing what age they would rather be, for life. Most of them agreed on eighteen, which many of them were at the time. When they asked me, I said fifty. They didn't believe it. 'Why?' they demanded."[96] For her peers, it is literally unfathomable that anyone would *want* to be an older woman or middle aged. "'Because,' I explained, 'w'en I'm fifty, people will respect my opinions if they are ever going to, and I shall not be too old to work.'"[97]

Fulfilling this childhood vision, Gilman began publishing the *Forerunner* at the age of fifty, and she continued to write, edit, and manage every detail of production for almost a decade. At an age when people begin to contemplate withdrawing from the labor force, Gilman began an intensive new venture, actively embodying the notion that women need not decline with age. This is a point she makes in *Herland*, in which the utopian community includes many women "over forty ... yet they were not old women. Each was in the full bloom of rosy health, erect, serene, standing surefooted and light as any pugilist."[98] Gilman seems to be suggesting that removed from prevailing age and gender discourse, women might actually age differently.

Gilman's decision to take her own life in 1935, while suffering from terminal breast cancer, might also be read as a refusal to abide by the mainstream age ideology that came to dominate contemporary thinking in the early twentieth century. Rather than pursue longevity for the sake of it, Gilman's suicide affirms that the desire for a long life may be at odds with the possibility for a good life. As biographer Cynthia Davis puts it, "she had preferred living to life."[99] It is a radical act of ownership over her own life course, an idea that surfaces in a poem called "Body of Mine," written near the end of her life: "Body of mine that now grows old/ thin, dry, and old—flowers may wither and pets may pine/ fire of passion grow palely cold—but the living world is the frame of me—heart and soul are not found in thee—body of mine."[100] According to the poem, Gilman refuses to lament her aging body or to link her self-worth to her physical form; she chose not to overvalue her physical form over the part of herself that was social and lasting. She ends the poem: "The world, the sky, and the work of our hands, Wonderful work of our hands! Clothe my soul in a form divine/ Young forever to all demands /Ageless and deathless and boundless and free / Glory and joy do I find in thee, /Body of mine!" Gilman does not dismiss the embodied experience of aging but neither does she link her body's decline to the loss of her value. Rather the poem is an occasion for her to celebrate the agelessness of her work and the immortality of her writing.

Attending to age as a narrative strategy and ideological counterpart to gender illuminates another dimension of Gilman's oeuvre, as her investment in women's need for maturity inflected her writings on suffrage and socialism, the medical establishment and marriage. Against a culture that saw women as "perpetual minors," both Alcott and Gilman sought to democratize maturity, to represent the possibility for women to achieve intellectual and economic independence and autonomy. According to both writers, age need not consolidate or fix the subject along a declining spectrum or buttress a gendered teleology, with specific ages standing for particular life benchmarks. Instead, their fiction exposes age—and life stages themselves—as cultural constructions that operated powerfully in women's lives. They urge us to consider the politics of maturity, especially in relation to women for whom age wielded an especially pernicious, but often invisible, disciplinary power.

4

Over the Hill and Out of Sight

Locating Old Age in Regionalism

"I am on another story with an old woman in it; I only hope people wont tire of my old women."

Mary Wilkins Freeman to the editor of *Harper's Bazaar*[1]

"It seems to me that it is a great privilege to have an elderly person in one's neighborhood, in town or country."

Sarah Orne Jewett, *Deephaven*

There is a big secret about old people: nobody likes them.[2] By the end of the nineteenth century, old bodies were signifiers of the loss of that most American virtue, self-reliance, and they represented the erosion and—inherent impossibility—of Western beauty standards. Old women, in particular, were deemed unfit for circulation in an newly image-oriented public sphere, expected instead to recede into rocking chairs and to conceal themselves in drab clothing. Where the last chapter examined the elusiveness of female maturity, revealing that US culture fixed women in permanent dependence through heterocentric domesticity and political disenfranchisement, this chapter considers imaginative responses to the dominant expectations for old age as it became a site of anxiety and a scripted stage of life toward the end of the nineteenth century.

Louisa May Alcott meditates on the disciplinary function of age in both *Little Women* and *Work*, honing in on birthdays as supervisory occasions that monitor whether women are appropriately reaching the benchmarks linked to specific age. These works illuminate age as a discourse that operates in conjunction with gender to limit female autonomy and to maintain a male-dominated public sphere. In her novella *An Old-Fashioned Girl* (1869), Alcott gestures to the even more stringent demands for invisibility placed upon elderly women, who become worthless to mainstream culture once their reproductive and childrearing functions are complete. The narrative dwells on an encounter between the eponymous young girl, Polly, and a friend's grandmother. Of Grandma, Alcott writes, "She was even more old-fashioned than Polly; but people didn't seem to mind it so much in her, as her day was supposed to be over, and nothing was expected of her but to keep out of everybody's way."[3] However, Polly invents a game called "Playing Grandmother" that involves reanimating Grandma's "old furniture, pictures, books, and relics of a past for which no cared but herself," making the old times and objects meaningful again and inviting Grandma into the present.[4] Where mainstream culture sees Grandma as defunct and expects her to "keep out of everybody's way," this narrative—and Polly's game—re-centers her as interesting and worthy of attention. We might read the anachronistic performance of "playing grandmother" in terms of what Elizabeth Freeman has called "temporal drag," which she defines as "a kind of historicist jouissance, a friction of dead bodies upon live ones, obsolete constructions upon emergent ones."[5] The game reveals the porousness of the ostensibly biological barriers between generations and revalues old age as a source of potential pleasure. Polly's interest in Grandma represents a significant departure from a culture increasingly focused on managing—and concealing—elderly people.

Indeed, if the age expectations for young women were restrictive, then those for elderly people were downright punishing, leading many to dread growing old. Such sentiments percolated in women's periodicals and fiction in the second half of the nineteenth century. "The thought of becoming old myself brings always a saddened feeling, an inward shrinking—almost a shudder," writes Katie Clark Mullikin in an essay entitled "Growing Old Gracefully," which appeared in an 1875 issue of *The Ladies Repository*. She continues, "The American people . . . are entirely lacking in due and proper reverence for age and its accompaniments," and old people are "often considered burdens, spoken of as having outlived their usefulness and their day; spoken of often with thoughtless, if not heartless, lack of reverence."[6] Mullikin's sentiments convey the extent to which old age had become a stigmatized status by the end of the nineteenth century, and she registers shame, what she calls an "inward shrinking," at the idea of becoming old, which she attributes *not* to concerns about frailty or loneliness but rather to the social stigma against old age in mainstream American culture (how old people are "considered" and "spoken of").

While recent scholarship has shown how attitudes toward children changed over the course of the century, less attention has been paid in US literary studies to the concurrent shifts in perspectives toward old age. The rise of industrial capitalism, shifting demographics, and developments in science in the second half of the nineteenth century led to what historian W. Andrew Achenbaum calls a "watershed in which the overall estimation of old people's worth clearly changed."[7] That is, the latter part of the century witnessed a profound shift in the status of old people and in the meanings of age, particularly for the white middle class. As Achenbaum notes, "With growing frequency after the Civil War, American began to challenge nearly every favorable belief about the usefulness and merits of age." The rise of convalescent homes that specifically catered to older individuals relied on and reinforced this view of old age as dependent, infantile, and socially useless. While the majority of elderly people did not spend their final years in almshouses, one historian notes that "even the uninstitutionalized elderly began to be affected by the growing social differentiation of senescence."[8] By the end of the century, the stigma of old age was firmly in place.[9]

A particularly representative voice in this moment was neurologist George Miller Beard whose influential 1875 study, *Legal Responsibility in Old Age*, offered empirical evidence for the claim that old age entailed a decline in productivity. In his subsequent work, *American Nervousness* (1881), he links aging not only to declining productivity but also to decreased creativity, paving the way for the linkage of old age and obsolescence that would endure throughout the next century.[10] He laments, "I find no record of any very important invention conceived and developed after the age of 60. Edison, with his three hundred patents, is not the only young inventor. All inventors are young." Beard's book intimates the significance of numerical age as a tool for capitalism, and the establishment of mandatory retirement by the Pennsylvania Railroad in 1900 rendered this connection explicit.

Discussions of old age as pathological and feeble pervaded popular culture, as scientists and social workers classified "the elderly" as a distinct population, subject to social organization and medical scrutiny.[11] A *Harper's Weekly* cover in 1871 featured a poem entitled "Over the Hill to the Poorhouse," accompanied by illustrations, describes the plight of an elderly widow [see Figure 4.1]:

> Over the hill to the poor-house I'm trudgin' my weary way—
> I, a woman of seventy, and only a trifle gray—
> I, who am smart an' chipper, for all the years I've told,
> As many another woman that's only half as old.
>
> I am willin' and anxious an' ready any day
> To work for a decent livin', an' pay my honest way;
> For I can earn my victuals, an' more too, I'll be bound,
> If any body only is willin' to have me round.

This popular poem-turned-song draws attention to the conflation of old age with economic dependence; the poorhouse becomes the only refuge for a woman barred from employment because of her advanced age. Though able-bodied and "willin'...to work for a decent livin'," in her words, the narrator of the song is nonetheless deemed a drain on society. Indeed, she

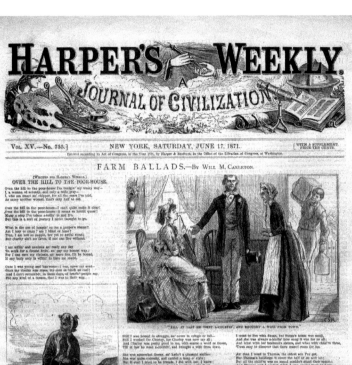

Figure 4.1. The term "over the hill" first appeared in a poem on the cover of *Harper's Weekly* in 1871. The popular poem-turned-song describes the plight of an elderly widow and draws attention to the conflation of old age with economic dependence; the poorhouse becomes the only refuge for a woman barred from employment because of her advanced age. Courtesy of the American Antiquarian Society, Worcester, MA.

is considered undesirable in spite of her chipper attitude and eagerness to work.

Popular magazines and advertisements emphasized the separateness of old age by teaching readers how to appropriately inhabit this specific stage of life [see Figure 4.2]. For example, a regular column in *Ladies Home Journal,* by Virginia Ralston, editor of the dressmaking department, regularly instructed women on how to dress for their age. Her columns included titles such as: "For Elderly Women and Semi-invalids," "The Elderly Lady at Christmas," "For the Stout and Elderly Woman," and "Dressing the Elderly Ladies."[12] She avers that elderly women "must always express dignity," as opposed to beauty, humor, smartness, or personality and explains that "along with the change in clothes comes a complete change in the style of headwear for the elderly woman; the bonnet has completely disappeared—except for those very dear old ladies with snow-white hair, who cling to tradition—but for all other women the toque and the small hat are worn exclusively." Such dictates establish how aging became enmeshed in a capitalist project of fostering insecurity in women and advocating consumption as the primary strategy for ameliorating it.

Beyond this, Ralston's columns served to entrench gendered age norms and to homogenize women along age lines, reinforcing generational barriers and disciplining women through the language of "age appropriateness."[13] Indeed, this advice literature presumes that age is a stable, biological category, even as it does the very work of producing age as a cultural construct. Ralston's column articulates what she herself calls "certain unwritten laws—laws which are known and intuitively obeyed by all women—which prohibit certain colors and styles to her who can no longer be said to be in the first flush of youth." Through these laws, Ralston's column teaches elderly women what Kathleen Woodward calls the "pedagogy of mortification," or the practice of becoming invisible. According to Woodward, older women are taught to "recede into invisibility... Surely the practice of disregard of older women is one of the reasons why in fact we have so many 'little old ladies.'"[14] By urging her older readers to consider "jet in its many varieties" and explaining that, "most elderly women require a rather plain skirt, whether the material be cloth of silk," Ralston aligns old age with discretion and diminishment. To be an old woman, she implies, one must become as diminutive and unobtrusive as possible, and such dictates mandate that only one model of old womanhood is appropriate. Thus, age, like gender, is utterly scripted by normalizing discourses.

Literary women chafed against such dictates.[15] In 1894, when *Ladies Home Journal* ran a forum called "When Is a Woman at her Best?" a variety of well-known writers, including Julia Ward Howe, Mary Wilkins (Freeman), and Rebecca Harding Davis, almost unilaterally refused to

Figure 4.2. This pamphlet, an advertisement for Shaker Extract of Roots, explains that "old age is unlovely" and juxtaposes young and older visions of individuals. The pamphlet promises that Shaker Extract of Roots will counteract the physical signs of aging, *c.*1890. Courtesy of the American Antiquarian Society, Worcester, MA.

answer the question as posed, rejecting the premise that aging necessarily entails decline.[16] For example, Davis writes, "It would be as impossible for me to find a rule applicable to the development of all women as one which would regulate all of their digestions... The only general assertion which one can safely make is that every woman is at her best in body and mind at the age when she is most fully occupied with her true work in the world." Julia Ward Howe similarly acknowledged aging as individual and idiosyncratic, noting that "the development of character does not correspond with the period of physical growth and maturity."[17] Both Davis and Howe describe chronological age as merely one attribute of identity, thereby acknowledging age as an arbitrary indicator of a woman's character or maturity. Their collective refusal to treat women's lives as quantifiable, uniform, and predictable serves as a feminist rejoinder to a culture increasingly preoccupied with aging as pathological and unattractive, especially for women.

This chapter reads New England regionalism as extension of this rejoinder and more specifically as a counterdiscourse to what Stephen Katz calls the "formation of gerontological knowledge."[18] Against this imperative to diagnose and organize elderly people into a coherent group, late nineteenth-century women writers used fiction to stage a subversive dialogue with the scientific and cultural denigration of old age and to resist the homogenizing effects of this discourse. Indeed, an 1894 article in *Harper's Bazaar* noticed this literary trend, observing that the rise of the figure of the "elderly heroine" has "added a new zest to literature."[19] The work of Mary Wilkins Freeman and Sarah Orne Jewett, in particular, challenges an emergent consensus about how to treat and conceive of an aging population. While mainstream periodicals articulated a disciplinary regime of dress and social conduct for older people, these writers rail against generational segregation, criticize benevolence movements, and refuse to sentimentalize the difficulties of old age.

Of course, I am not the first to recognize New England regionalism's preoccupation with old age. A prominent strain of scholarship reads the genre's old characters as representatives of a passing vision of New England. For example, Granville Hicks, one of Jewett's earliest critics, writes: "We may grant that her attitude is essentially elegiac, and that she writes of a dying world of old men and old women."[20] In a similar vein, Walter Berthoff refers to how "the old, the retired, the widowed, the unmarrying, the sick, the mad, the 'uncompanioned,'" exhibit the effects of a "creeping decay."[21] Another critic, Michael Holstein, writes of Dunnet Landing: "Its inhabitants are synecdoches for the region: they represent the fact of mortality."[22]

Even as feminists began to celebrate Jewett's vision of a matrifocal community, scholars continued to see the elderly characters as symbols of cultural obsolescence. More recently, scholars including Sarah Ensor and Holly Jackson have read non-reproductivity as a central motif in regionalism, linking the absence of children in the genre to contemporary concerns about "race suicide" and environmental decline.[23]

But what is striking across the long critical history on regionalism is the near universal refusal to read elderly characters as explorations of old age itself.[24] That is, scholars have overlooked or opted not to address age as a subject, perhaps the principal subject, of regionalism, choosing instead to see the thematization of old age as a metaphor for New England, the nation, or racial whiteness. Even as Heather Love's essay identifies what she terms the "spinster aesthetic" and acknowledges that Jewett "sought to represent a disregarded group of people," she never mentions old age as a crucial characteristic of Jewett's characters when it is age, as much as sexuality or gender, that marks Jewett's female characters as what Love terms "a category of person deemed unwanted."[25]

In this chapter, I want to suggest that we read the elderly characters not as metaphors for dying ways of life but *as* elderly characters.[26] First, I turn to the work of Mary Wilkins Freeman and then briefly to Sarah Orne Jewett to demonstrate what it might mean to read age as a concern for writers and readers going back to at least the early nineteenth century when chronological age became a category freighted with social and political significance. That is, I want to suggest that we as critics need new models for reading old age as a contested site, a politicized identity to be rigorously explored in its own right, rather than simply a metaphor for obsolescence or a marker of nostalgia.

MARY WILKINS FREEMAN AND BAD AGING

Mary Wilkins Freeman wrote primarily about older people. As one contemporary reviewer put it, "In the census of a Mary Wilkins village the proportion of inhabitants would approximate sixty women upwards of seventy years old, five old men, fifteen middle-aged women, eight middle-aged men, seven girls, three eligible bachelors, two children."[27] Still, scarce attention has been paid to the fact that aging, and its intersection with gender, is the central subject of her oeuvre.[28]

Freeman was the author of more than twenty-four short story collections, many of which concern women struggling against entrenched ways of thinking and impoverishment in rural New England. Widely respected by the gatekeepers of the literary establishment, Freeman frequently published in *Harper's New Monthly Magazine* and was compared by her earliest critics to Cotton Mather and Nathaniel Hawthorne.

When William Dean Howells and Elizabeth Jordan came up with the idea for a collaborative novel called *The Whole Family: A Novel by Twelve Authors*, they invited ten prominent authors to contribute, and Freeman was on the list, along with Henry James and Elizabeth Stuart Phelps. Howells intended for *The Whole Family* to center on how the engagement of a young woman affects the other members of the family, with each chapter representing a different relative's point of view.

Assigned to write the second chapter about a minor character, dubbed "old-maid aunt," Freeman refused to ascribe to this character the expected traits of docility and pathos.[29] Instead, she wields the chapter like a weapon, slicing open the narrative expectations for such a character and forcing the other contributors to piece the narrative back together after she has rendered it unrecognizable. Freeman's chapter reveals that Harry, the young man, is not actually in love with Peggy, his new fiancée, but rather with the old-maid aunt. As she explains in the voice of the old maid: "He does not care for her, at least not when I am around or when I am in his mind."[30] As the second chapter in the collaborative novel, Freeman's installment effectively de-centers the conventional young romance and positions the "old-maid aunt" as an essential figure in the narrative.

Freeman's old-maid character, Elizabeth Talbert, refuses to abide by the script for older women. Significantly, she is only in her thirties, and yet, as discussed earlier in relation to *Little Women,* the failure to comply with heteronormativity can render a woman prematurely "old," as the pejorative term "old maid" deploys age rhetoric to stigmatize women who refuse to acquiesce to gendered life-stage expectations. Observing that her family "all unanimously consider that I should dress always in black silk, and a bonnet with a neat tuft of middle-aged violets," she pronounces, "I know I am wicked to put on that pink gown and hat, but I shall do it."[31] Here, Elizabeth knowingly and provocatively disobeys the consensus in her family, and in society at large, for how older women should present themselves. Instead of donning the "middle-aged violets," she rebelliously puts on the pink hat lined with roses, delighting in her wickedness and in the attention she will garner. She refers specifically to the "eyeglasses of prejudice" through which her family sees her; they exclaim: " 'Pink at her age, and a pink hat, and a parasol lined with pink!' "[32]

We can read the pleasure that Elizabeth takes in brazenly refusing to abide by age norms as a reverberation of Freeman's own delight in derailing the plans of *The Whole Family,* upsetting narrative conventions. By making the "old-maid aunt" the love interest of the young suitor, Freeman hijacks Howells' outline for the novel and reroutes it around an older woman. As Elizabeth Jordan, a collaborator on the novel and editor of *Harper's,* wrote, "This wholly unexpected twist of the tale proved to be the explosion of a bomb-shell on our literary hearthstone."[33] While some contributors liked the unexpected turn of Freeman's chapter, others were furious, including Howells who "almost scorched the paper it was written on" and wanted to remove it from the volume.[34]

The vehemence of these responses suggests the extent to which Freeman forced the project into narrative crisis, laying bare that the novel form depends not only on narrow heteronormative conventions, as we now know, but also on disciplinary age discourses that uphold the related norms of gender and sexuality. The marriage plot is thus inseparable from age discourse. Indeed, Freeman seems to be speaking directly to Howells when the old-maid aunt herself observes that the figure of "the old maid is as much of an anomaly as a spinning-wheel, that she has ceased to exist, that she is prehistoric."[35] Suggesting that the very narrative archetype of "old-maid aunt" is old-fashioned, Freeman reveals realism's reliance on the very paradigms against which it ostensibly defined itself. As Freeman explains in a letter to Elizabeth Jordan, "Why, the whole plot of the novel must be relegated back to Miss Austin [*sic*], and *Godey's Lady's Book,* and all that sort of thing, if the old conception holds...I don't think Mr. Howells realizes this."[36] Again Freeman deems Howell's conception of the novel, reliant on worn-out gender and age paradigms, utterly old fashioned. Indeed, while realism was ostensibly premised on a shift away from such types, popular in sentimentalism and romanticism, in favor of more complex characters, she observes that it is Howells who mapped this novel out with these types as the infrastructure. Ultimately, the chapter remained in the book, and the subsequent chapters are in some sense an array of responses to Freeman's bold move. As Susanna Ashton puts it, "The ten inheritors of the Aunt Eliza problem did their best to pack her off. Nonetheless, her startling presence renders her by far the most memorable character in the novel."[37]

Critics tend to read Freeman's characterization of Elizabeth Talbert as a celebration of "the New Woman," but such an interpretation fails to take into account how Freeman's character defies age ideology as much as gender norms.[38] The "old-maid aunt" is disruptive, even perverse, specifically because she is past her supposed prime, because she wears "pink at her age," and demands attention rather than receding passively into the margins. Freeman's radical narrative act in *The Whole Family* reflects her persistent effort to unsettle narrative expectations for older women and to interrogate age as an ideological and literary problem rather than purely a biological one.

Her short fiction similarly resists the relegation of older women to the narrative sidelines and confronts the entrenchment of age norms as an effect of modernization. In "A Mistaken Charity," two elderly sisters are coerced into relocating to an "Old Ladies' Home." Charlotte and Harriet Shattuck are described as having "old rheumatic muscles," "feeble cracked old voices," and "little shriveled hands."[39] Moreover, Charlotte is blind and Harriet is deaf. However, even as they inhabit a deteriorating house and aging bodies, Harriet and Charlotte are content, and "it could not be said that they actually suffered."[40] Instead, they take much pleasure from the natural world, and Charlotte, the blind sister, delights in "chinks," her word for the "light streamin' in all of a sudden through a little hole that you hadn't known of before."[41] These chinks suggest her alternative orientation, and the story's own interest in opening up a previously overlooked, unseen reality to its readers.

The plot is set in motion when an intrusive neighbor, Mrs. Simonds, visits them one day and decides they must be relocated to an institution. Mrs. Simonds embodies a middle-class ideology that expects old women to be stationary and "comfortable." The narrator notes that "the struggle to persuade them to abandon their tottering home for a better was a terrible one."[42] The narrator further explains, "it had been hard to convince them that the 'Home' was not an almshouse under another name, and their yielding at length to anything short of actual force was only due probably to the plea, which was advanced more eloquently to Harriet, that Charlotte would be so much more comfortable."[43] Mrs. Simonds' eloquence, her plea, her "struggle to persuade" and "convince" them, and her appropriation of the term "comfortable" highlights the force of her intervention. Through her coercive use of language, Mrs. Simonds interpellates these women into the physical and ideological space of old age; she must teach them to see themselves as needy and elderly. We might read the very use of the term "Home" in this story as an indication of the extent to which the emergence of age ideology in the late nineteenth century involved the co-optation of discourse and the sentimentalization of old age in order to render it powerless and acquiescent.

For Freeman, though, old age is not about docility or pathos; instead, she underscores the ethos of resistance that can characterize elderliness. Indeed, she envisions old women as liberated from gender norms and the expectations of middle-class culture. The Shattuck sisters are staunchly outside of the frameworks of market capitalism and heteronormativity. "Neither of them had ever had a lover; they had always seemed to repel rather than attract the opposite sex," and Harriet has a "blunt, defiant manner that almost amounted to surliness."[44] Thus, in their status as spinsters, in their living arrangement, in their misalignment with conventional femininity, the sisters might be called queer, and this queerness extends even beyond their gender and sexual orientations to their broader orientation in a rapidly modernizing culture.

The sisters do not participate in a consumer economy nor do they strive to accumulate or improve their social positions.[45] As Freeman writes, "They had been, in the main, except when pressed by some temporary anxiety about their work or the payment thereof, happy and contented, with that negative kind of happiness and contentment which comes not from gratified ambition, but a lack of ambition itself."[46] This "negative kind of happiness" suggests the unconventionality of their lives, which are not structured around striving or accumulating but rather from simply having enough—a repudiation of the rapidly evolving consumer culture that linked women with fashion and materialism. Their "coarse, hearty food" and "cheap clothes" do not signify their deprivation; basic subsistence is itself a source of pride, a life not turned toward traditional middle-class comfort or external symbols of status.

Given that they are utterly dispensable and illegible to a culture that values efficiency and growth above all else, it is no surprise that the sisters' "negative kind of happiness" appears to outsiders only as impoverishment and disorder. The desire to relocate them to a "Home" is a way of standardizing their non-normative bodies, controlling their inappropriate modes of consumption and self-presentation.[47] The most explicit evidence of their misfit with the expectations for aging is in their dress. The "Home" requires them to dress more tidily, "but nothing could transform these two unpolished old women into two nice old ladies."[48] To be "nice old ladies" would entail adopting the types of etiquette and social performance outlined in *Ladies' Home Journal,* but the Shattuck sisters "did not take kindly to white lace caps and delicate neckerchiefs." And beyond that, Harriet has "a suspicion of a stubble of beard on the square chin," suggesting an utter disregard for the expectations to keep their bodies under feminine control and essentially invisible, a refusal to participate in the proper performance of elderly womanhood. As Karen Kilcup writes, "the Home attempts to obscure or erase women's—even old women's—sensuality and more, obliquely, their sexuality... prizing respectability, the Home requires the women to conceal and tidy their bodies."[49] In this sense, the Home is merely enacting the age and gender ideologies of the culture at large, and like the old-maid aunt in *The Whole Family,* these sisters reveal as unnatural the age scripts for old women and refuse to participate in the homogenizing performance of elderly womanhood.

Paradoxically, even as US culture fixated on old age as a time of sadness and decrepitude, old women were expected to diffuse good feeling, to perform a kind of affective work to counteract the bad feelings their bodies ostensibly elicited. This logic is made explicit in an 1892 column in *Ladies' Home Journal*: "If you want to keep from growing old, if you want to look young and charming, see that there come no wrinkles in your heart. Be as merry and as happy as you possibly can, finding good in everything and loveliness everywhere."[50] Such affective requirements applied even in convalescent homes [see Figure 4.3]. The Home in "A Mistaken Charity" may have been based on the Brattleboro Home for the Aged and Disabled, an institution located near Freeman's home and to whose residents she sent gifts at Christmas. The bylaws for this Home state that residents "will endeavor to diffuse cheerfulness and good feeling throughout the Home, and by consideration and forbearance promote the comfort of each other." In other words, residents living in the Home must comply with the emotional code of conduct along with the behavioral norms. To be an appropriate old woman necessitates a kind of emotional labor, a perpetual "cheerfulness and good feeling." Indeed, Kathleen Woodward observes how the affective requirements for old age serve to pacify and disengage older people from political activism. Of the cliché notion that old people should be sources of wisdom, she writes, "Wisdom carries the connotation of dignified behavior, hence the further difficulty of its association with a rhetoric of protest. It implies a kind of transcendence of the social world, a certain timelessness."[51] In other words, age-based affective expectations serve to preserve the status quo and to manufacture generational divides, keeping older people at a remove from politics and anger.

In Freeman's story, not only are Charlotte and Harriet guilty of inappropriate affect, they also eschew the very cultural work expected of older women: they are neither mothers nor widows invested in the preservation and/or reproduction of family values. Thus, they fundamentally diverge from ostensibly natural ideas about womanhood and its attendant responsibilities. When they are forced to stay at the Home, they "looked like forlorn prisoners," and just two months after their arrival, they run away. "Hobbling along, holding each other's hands," the escaping sisters are "as jubilant as children," a description that destabilizes the Home's singular definition of old people as docile and tame.[52] In another affront to the expected behavior of "nice old ladies," they hitch a ride from a stranger after underestimating the distance of the journey back to their home.

Indeed, Freeman emphasizes their rebelliousness rather than their respectability, reminding us that old age might contain a range of affects and styles, some of which might be deviant. Unlike the "nice old ladies" that reside in the Home, the Shattuck sisters refuse to abide by age norms; they might thus be described as queer subjects in their disobedience, their mismatch with ostensibly natural ideas about growing older, especially as women who are not mothers or even widows. Indeed, their version of being old allows us to see how old age might be linked to the negativity and the disregard for futurity that critics like Lee Edelman have claimed as definitional to queer identity. As scholars, such as Jane Gallop and

Figure 4.3. "The Home for the Aged & Infirm: Of District No. 1 I.O.B.B.," a lithograph by M. Thalmessinger in New York (1881). Courtesy of the American Antiquarian Society, Worcester, MA.

Cynthia Port, have suggested, elderly people inhabit a queer relationship to futurity, to reproduction, and to capitalism.[53] While there may be little to gain from simply stretching the term "queer" onto another population, it may be one of the only available epistemologies for understanding the place of elderly people in the cultural imagination, for recognizing why old age functions as what Erving Goffman calls a "spoiled identity."[54]

The story does not end in death, as one might expect, but rather with the women back at their actual home, gleefully observing the butterflies and pumpkins they have missed. The final words belong to Charlotte, who declares, "Thar is so many chinks that they air all runnin' together!"[55] ("Chinks," as we learned earlier, are those moments of light and beauty that penetrate Charlotte's blindness.) This articulation of unbounded pleasure underscores the notion that old age may encompass ineffable joys as well as perspectives unknowable to those at other points on the age continuum—it is a final vision of old age as a kind of sensory exultation; the little secret pleasures of the chinks are now dilating and encompassing their world.

The few critical treatments of Freeman that center on age tend to celebrate her elderly characters for their strength and industry or read them as abject failures. For example, Doris Turkes' relies on a binaristic logic to assess whether Freeman's aged protagonists are "successes" or "failures" according to twentieth-century life-stage theory.[56] Another critic, Susan Toth, compares the representation of old age in Jewett and Freeman's work, noting, "Miss Jewett's old ladies are usually independent, active people, who refuse to sacrifice themselves to circumstances...Mrs. Freeman's old people...reek of decay."[57] Such assessments risk judging old age according to the dictates of capitalism, implying that aging is something that can be done poorly.[58] The critical emphasis on independence and activity reinforces the repressive discourses of aging under capitalism, which vaunts home ownership and self-sufficiency as the singular markers of success and happiness. Indeed, Freeman's only biographer, Leah Blatt Glasser, observes, "A home of one's own, self-sufficiency, and control over one's fate in the later years of life were, to Freeman's mind, critical to meaningful survival."[59] What lurks in this seemingly innocuous statement is the implication that to age well is to not to age at all, not to need others, not to lose control, or even to slow down.

Such accounts not only reveal the insidious sway of capitalist ideology to set the terms for aging, but they also restore Freeman to the very paradigm she sought to deconstruct. Indeed, her work repeatedly suggests that pure autonomy—at any stage of life—may be elusive, impossible, and even undesirable. In "A Mistaken Charity," the sisters do not own their home nor are they self-sufficient. On the contrary, "meaningful survival" in the world of this story entails both dependence and disability; these women rely on one another as well as on a community of strangers, including the man who lets them live in his house rent-free and another who gives them a ride back home. And, of course, their dependence on one another forms the emotional backbone of the story. Thus, while the story criticizes a culture of benevolence that smugly assumes it knows what is best for everyone, Freeman also dismantles the notion that autonomy is the *sine qua non* of a good life or of good aging. Instead, she asks her readers to see how age ideology—its desire to naturalize and universalize seemingly innocuous values like comfort, respectability, and self-sufficiency—can do a kind of violence to the experience of aging, rendering the chinks unseeable—and thus disabling individuals at the end of their lives.

Freeman's story invites us to consider the intersections between disability and age studies.[60] Rosemarie Garland-Thomson uses the term "disability" to refer to the "socially constructed category of people whose bodily forms, functions, limitations, ambiguities, or appearances are considered to be abnormal, defective, degenerate, debilitated, deformed, ill, unfit, unhealthy, sick, obese, crippled, mad, ugly, retarded, or flawed."[61] And though old age is pervasively described in these terms, disability studies scholars have directed surprisingly little attention to age, even though age is how we often define disability. Indeed, it is largely through age that mainstream science measures whether individuals are bodily appropriate and developmentally on schedule.

While we cannot equate old age with disability, these embodied, stigmatized statuses overlap as similarly subject to discourses of regulation, rehabilitation, and pathologization, and like age, the modern concept of disability—along with race—was the product of the nineteenth century's regime of bodily classification. The field of disability studies offers a critical precedent for reading socially devalued bodies as multivalent and complex, encouraging literary critics to become attuned to how disabled bodies are put to use in narrative.[62] Sharon Snyder and David T. Mitchell refer to how disability often serves as an "opportunistic metaphoric device," a kind of "narrative prosthesis." That is, disabled characters are narratively exploited, used as signposts and markers, rather than represented as multifaceted subjects.

Old characters are often made to serve in precisely these ways. Henry James acknowledged as much in a letter to his brother, explaining that his characterization of Miss Birdeye in *The Bostonians* was merely meant to telegraph the "grotesque...humanitary and *ci-devant* transcendental tendencies...I wished to make this figure a woman, because it would be more touching, and an old, weary battered and simple-minded woman because that deepened the effect."[63] As James makes explicit, the elderly woman in his novel is not meant to be a developed, complex character; on the contrary, he uses old age, along with femininity, to make Miss Birdseye a pathetic symbol of obsolescence and exhaustion. As critics, we need to be attuned to how such characterizations of old age participate in encoding age ideology into the cultural imagination.

Perhaps the lack of attention to age in disability studies stems from the fact that old age, even able-bodied old age, is always already cast as a kind of disability by a capitalist regime premised on productivity as the only valid marker of ability. Indeed if we live in what Robert McRuer, riffing on Adrienne Rich, calls a world of "compulsory able-bodiedness," we also live in one of compulsory youth, in which the body itself becomes deviant as it ages past a certain point, no longer serving capitalism or its reproductive imperatives.[64] In this vein, Jasbir Puar's call for a scholarly shift from discussions of disability to those of debility may be a useful way to incorporate discussions of age into those that previously rendered it somewhat invisible. Puar notes that the rubric of debility "destabilizes the seamless production of abled-bodies in relation to disability . . . [A turn to debility] is about deconstructing the presumed, taken-for-granted capacities-enabled status of abled-bodies."[65] In other words, debility might allow us to conceive of a broader range of bodies that are devalued and worn out by a culture perpetually oriented toward the future and the production of new bodies and increased profit.

While Freeman's stories—like much of New England regionalism—seem to be concerned only with the mundane issues of isolated rural villages, her oeuvre actually narrates the process whereby old bodies are rendered worthless and disposable in a rapidly modernizing culture. We might thus read regionalism's elegiac strain as not merely a longing for a world before immigration, and industry, but also a culture before the modern regime of age. That is, while Peter Coviello describes Sarah Orne Jewett's world as representative of a "vanishing sociality," a world on the cusp of modernity's "normalizing force," registering the "temporal vulnerability" of a world just prior to the onset of sexual identity, New England regionalism also anticipates and reacts to the instantiation of age as a modern bureaucratic measure and disciplinary data point.[66]

Freeman's "The Village Singer," for example, begins with the revelation that Candace Whitcomb, the lead soprano in the church choir for forty years, has been replaced by a younger singer, Alma Way. Candace's abrupt displacement by a younger singer hints at the "legitimation of age discrimination and mandatory retirement, soon to be prominent features of large industrial and financial corporations as well as government bureaucracies."[67] Indeed, Freeman's story exposes how the community's benevolence masks a gendered and age-based regime premised on the logic of capitalism.

The community's decision to replace Candace reflects a new age ideology that deigns to know what is best for individuals as they get older, a perspective that is resonant with the intrusive neighbor who attempts to resettle the Shattuck sisters in "A Mistaken Charity."[68] Candace explains, "They thought the duty was getting' a little too arduous for me. H'm! I hadn't complained."[69] She points out people have begun to assume they know what it means to be old, a presumption about the experiences that are appropriate for elderly women. Thus, like "A Mistaken Charity," "A Village Singer" is about the displacement of old women, an attempt to cordon them off, segregate them, and decide how they must feel and live.

In stark contradistinction to Candace's expulsion from her role in the church are the permanence and security of the male minister and choir leader.

The choir leader, William Emmons is "elderly, stout, and smooth-faced," and similarly, the minister "was a steady-faced, fleshy old man, who had preached from that one pulpit over forty years."[70] Freeman indicates that age entitles these men to their positions of authority and respect, while growing older disqualifies women from public positions. As Marjorie Pryse observes, "Freeman describes a village which finds aging offensive in women but acceptable in men."[71] But advanced age is not merely acceptable in men; it is ennobling. That is, while aging signifies decline and erosion in women, it bolsters the status and qualifications for men.[72]

Like the Shattuck sisters, Candace staunchly refuses to acquiesce to the expectations, to gently, docilely disappear herself from the public. On the day of Alma's debut, Candace was "playing on her parlor organ, and singing, to drown out the voice of her rival."[73] From her cottage next door to the church, her voice disrupts Alma and makes it impossible for the congregation to ignore her. Her unruly voice, an analog for Freeman's own authorial expression, demands notice and attention.

Coupled with this refusal to quietly remove herself from the stage, Candace also debases the photograph album, which the congregation's gives her as a parting gift. When the minister comes to her home, he notices "Candace's feet were resting on a large red-plush photograph album."[74] Clearly intended to signify their desire to inscribe Candace herself into the past, the photograph album is a sentimental, feminine gift that she turns into a footrest, a masculine and irreverent bodily gesture.

Candace offers a prescient critique of a culture increasingly insistent on disposing of citizens no longer deemed valuable or productive. Observing the injustice of her treatment in comparison with her male peers, she asks:

> Why don't they turn him out the way they have me, an' give him a photograph album? I dunno' but it would be a good idea to send everybody, as soon as they get a little old an' gone by, an' young folks begin to push, on to some desert island, an' give 'em each a photograph album. Then they can sit down an' look at pictures the rest of their days. Mebbe government'll take it up.[75]

Her suggestions that old people might be pushed on to "some desert island" and that "mebbe government'll take it up" presage the institutionalization of elderly people and the shift from private to public care. As historian Tamara Hareven notes of the late nineteenth century, "The transfer of social-welfare functions, once concentrated in the family, to institutions in the larger society further contributed to the segregation of older people ... care transferred to specialized institutions such as asylums and reformatories."[76]

Moreover, the story suggests that generational replacement is itself a violation of Christianity, a breach of the community's implicit responsibility to its members. As Candace observes, "My voice is as good an' high today as it was twenty year ago; an' if it wa'n't, I'd like to know where the Christianity comes in."[77] In other words, she indicates that Christianity itself should oblige the church to make a place for her even if her voice had declined over time, that faith should require the community to honor her long years of service. Candace suggests that the abrupt termination of her position is fundamentally anti-social; it resonates with a corporate model of employment that devalues human feeling and responsibility in favor of profitability and usefulness.

Freeman's work discourages readers from thinking of old people as "the elderly," from reductive understandings or expectations for people based solely on chronological age. As Stephen Katz eloquently writes, "To be old merely requires that one ages. However, to be part of a population of elderly persons requires that one be absorbed into a specific discourse of differentiation."[78] It was precisely this "discourse of differentiation" that Freeman sought to resist. Her characters render old age as utterly unpredictable and unclassifiable. Indeed, the sheer range of old characters in her oeuvre stands as an affront to a popular culture that sought to circumscribe aging.

Freeman's stories fly in the face of the ageism that emerged at the close of the nineteenth century, and they also suggest a novel response to the directives and imperatives that shape old age in our contemporary moment. Freeman presages a world in which it is unacceptable to inhabit an old body, to reject the pursuit of advancement and achievement, and to jettison prevailing gender and age norms. Her characters, in their blend of frailty and zest, demand that we see old age as multifarious, neither a time of utter debility nor a period indistinct from midlife or youth.

"THE OLD FOLKS INTERESTED US MOST": JEWETT'S AGE QUEERS

If Freeman exposes as unnatural the construction of "the elderly" and resists the age regime of modernity, then Sarah Orne Jewett dismantles the age stratification that characterized the late nineteenth century and offers instead a world outside of age ideology. Indeed, Jewett's fiction, with its first-person narrators, teaches its readers how to see old people from the vantage points of youth and middle age. Both *Deephaven* (1877), her first published book, and her now canonical *The Country of the Pointed Firs* (1896), rely on narrators who visit worlds in which age norms do not apply and in which being old is not synonymous with homogenous, mainstream ideas of being elderly. These texts both denaturalize the stages of life that segregate generations and structure the course of lives.

In the United States, generational segregation became commonplace at the end of the nineteenth century and continues to serve as a dominant rubric for organizing society. As life expectancies increased and children increasingly moved away from their families of origin, more people grew old alone.[79] Such living arrangements were a sharp departure from earlier modes of social organization, and some were concerned about the effects of isolating people according to their age group.[80] For example, in his 1906 medical treatise, *Worry: The Disease of the Age*, Caleb Saleeby writes, "If old people are confined to the company of other old people, they hasten each other's downward course." He continues, "The company of youth is of the very first value for age and undoubtedly the company of age is of the utmost educative value for youth."[81]

Deephaven's premise—two twenty-four-year-old girls inhabiting the home of a recently deceased aunt and summering almost exclusively with elderly people—resists modernity's privileging of age groups and instead suggests that intimacy is not predicated on chronological age. *Deephaven* begins when two close friends, Kate Lancaster and the narrator, Helen Denis, decide to spend the summer in a small coastal town in Maine, in the home of Kate's recently deceased grand-aunt, who "died very old and was the last of her generation."[82] That Kate and Helen find the prospect of summering in her home appealing suggests their cross-generational identification and the unexpected allure of the old. As Helen, the narrator, explains, "It might be dull in Deephaven for two young ladies who were fond of gay society and dependent upon excitement, I suppose; but for two little girls who were fond of each other and could play in the boats, and dig and build houses in the sea-sand, and gather shells, and carry their dolls wherever they went, what could be pleasanter?"[83] In light of the fact that both Helen and Kate are twenty-four years old, this explanation is all the more intriguing, setting up the possibility that they have rejected normative age identification in favor of an extended childhood and the freedom that inheres in remaining in girlhood. Thus, like Jo March, they want to put off (or permanently evade) the conventional expectations for womanhood, which would entail a concern with "gay society" and hetero-sexual romance; what excites Helen and Kate are the pleasures of their friendship and rough-and-tumble adventures in the wilderness.[84]

Even before they arrive in Deephaven, it is clear that the girls are embarking on an excursion that resists the sequencing and structure of normative development and temporality. On the train ride to Deephaven, the girls strike up a friendship with an old woman named Mrs. Kew, and Helen trades places with her, remarking that she did "not mind riding backward."[85] That Helen sits backward on a train ride, itself the sign of modernity, suggests a recoil from the ostensibly forward march of progress, development, and womanhood, and instead indicates her desire to turn back toward a moment and place unstructured by the various stratifying and disciplinary schemes of modern life. Indeed, her position on the train suggests a discomfort with the supposed progress that the technologized future represents and serves as an affront to the sequential, individual-oriented life narrative celebrated by mainstream American institutions.

From the moment they arrive in Deephaven, Kate and Helen enter a kind of alternate world that liberates them from the concerns not just of urban life but also of the rigid expectations associated with gender and age. Deephaven allows Kate and Helen to inhabit age malleably, playfully, and willfully. In one particularly rich passage, Helen explains, "Sometimes in Deephaven we were between six and seven years old, but at other times we have felt irreparably grown-up, and as if we carried a crushing weight of care and duty. In reality we are both twenty-four, and it is a pleasant age, though I think next year is sure to be pleasanter, for we do not mind growing older, since we have lost nothing that we mourn about, and are gaining so much."[86] This passage establishes Deephaven as a space in which the demands for coherent identity, age-appropriate identification, and heteronormative teleology do not apply. The fact that Kate and Helen identify as "six and seven years old" and also as "irreparably grown-up" suggests the novella's complex understanding of age as both an assignment but also as performance. Furthermore, the girls' sense that "growing older" will entail "gaining so much" sets them apart from a culture that incessantly framed aging as synonymous with loss.

What is particularly significant about the girls' interest in the inhabitants of Deephaven is that it positions Helen and Kate as "other," as outsiders. That is, in Deephaven, being old is a norm rather than a denigrated or maligned social position; on the contrary, "it was impossible to imagine any children."[87] Significantly, Deephaven—like many comparable sites in regionalist literature—is described as being in some sense out of sync with the United States itself; Helen finds it reminiscent of "lazy little English seaside towns... It was not in the least American. There was no excitement about anything; there were no manufactories; nobody seemed in the least hurry."[88] The seeming un-Americanness of Deephaven and its pace matches and makes possible a culture of age non-normativity. Elizabeth Freeman describes "being normatively 'modern'" as a "matter not only of occupying an imagined place at the new end of a sequence but also of living a coordinated, carefully syncopated tempo between a quick time that seems to be enforced and a slow time that seems to be a matter of choice."[89] At a remove from industrialization and its insistence on productivity and age-based milestones, Deephaven dislodges Kate, Helen, and the residents of Deephaven from the modern regulating structures of both age as well as sexual identity.

Over the course of the novella's meandering, non-linear plot, Helen and Kate visit with various inhabitants of the town, explore the old house in which they are staying, and make forays into the ocean and woods. Their visits are almost exclusively with elderly people, often widows and widowers. As Helen notes, "The old folks interested us most."[90] And like the protagonist who "plays grandmother," in Alcott's *Old-Fashioned Girl,* Kate and Helen experience visiting with older people as a kind of transport: "We often heard quaint words and expressions which we never had known anywhere else but in old books."[91] Where the late nineteenth century witnessed the devaluation of elderly people, Jewett's protagonists are enthralled by the residents of Deephaven, piqued by the words, objects, and behaviors of older people, and as in Alcott's work, the old-fashioned and anachronistic are prized by young people interested in prior generations and older modes of being.[92]

The novella recognizes that the elderly inhabitants of *Deephaven* belong to a historical period that is fading out as modernity encroaches. Midway through the novella, Kate and Helen visit a traveling circus, which initially delights them but ultimately leaves them feeling bereft. As Helen observes, "The creatures looked tired, and as if they had been on the road for a great many years. The animals were all old, and there was a shabby great elephant whose look of general discouragement went to my heart, for it seemed as if he were miserably conscious of a misspent life."[93] The animals seem to evoke the kind of drudgery associated with factory jobs, worn out by years in an unnatural, profit-driven enterprise.

But more than the tired, old, and exploited animals, the most depressing encounter at the circus is with a woman being billed as the "Kentucky Giantess." Upon seeing her, Mrs. Kew recognizes the woman as Marilly, a woman she knew in her youth, who recounts her hard life in order to explain how she ended up traveling with the circus. As she explains, "I couldn't do nothing to earn a dollar." When they leave, she says, "I'm pleased to see somebody that remembers me as I used to be."[94] This melancholic reflection identifies Marilly as someone whose age and altered body have rendered her unrecognizable. Thus, while her unusually large size alone is the most visible sign of her deviance, we might also read the encounter with Marilly in relation to the status of elderly people as the century came to a close.

Outside of the utopic world of Deephaven, old people were increasingly compelled to rely on age-based institutions for support. Thus, the circus here may serve as a grim foreshadowing of what modern aging might entail, possibly hinting at the state of institutionalized elderly people. Moreover, the circus as "an antidomestic patriarchal institution," in Anne Romines's words, transforms deviant bodies into objects for profit, seemingly Marilly's only alternative to the familial model of support.[95] In other words, Marilly's status as a "freak" is the default position for elderly people without homes or jobs, who are forced to look beyond the home for support as they age.

In contrast to Marilly, old people in Deephaven are enfolded into the community, permitted to age and live in whatever ways they choose. The final chapters recount two visits to two different elderly women: Mrs. Bonny and Miss Chauncey. On their way to visit, Mrs. Bonny, one of the oldest women in Deephaven, the narrator observes hemlock growing along the path: "pale green of the new shoots and dark green of the old made an exquisite contrast."[96] Indeed, this slight observation encapsulates a primary ethos of the text, which recognizes and validates the profound and "exquisite" gains that lie in generational mixing and camaraderie. *Deephaven* rails against generational segregation, reveling in the pleasures and intangible benefits of cross-generational sociality and age-queer behavior.

In addition to its valuation of cross-generational sociality, *Deephaven* refuses to homogenize old age. Mrs. Bonny "wore a man's coat, cut off so that it made an odd short jacket, and a pair of men's boots" and was "so wild and unconventional... that it was like taking an afternoon walk with a good-natured Indian."[97] This get-up strays wildly from the fashion guidelines offered to elderly women in *Ladies Home Journal*. Indeed, Mrs. Bonny's behavior and appearance destabilize gender, age, and even racial categories. In opposition to Mrs. Bonny's strident independence and unconventionality, Miss Chauncey, the "last survivor of one of the most aristocratic old colonial families," depends on a servant and suffers from dementia.[98] As Kate and Helen are told, "She has been alone many years, and no one can persuade her to leave the old house, where she seems to be contented, and does not realize her troubles; though she lives mostly in the past... The town makes her an allowance every year, and she has some friends who take care that she does not suffer, though her wants are few."[99] Deephaven is thus a community that supports rather than pathologizes an elderly woman's desire to live alone in a house that is crumbling around her—an alternative to the intrusive benevolence that Freeman's characters encounter.

The visits with Mrs. Bonny and Miss Chauncey offer distinct depictions of elderly womanhood, debunking the facile assumption that "the elderly" are a homogenous group with anything other than numerical age in common. In these juxtaposed and radically different visions of old age, Jewett acknowledges that we all age but we are never the same age as other people; more precisely, our positions within a range of social hierarchies, including gender, race, and class, coupled with the idiosyncratic nature of individual identity expose as contrived the notion that we are ever the "same age" as anyone else.

In conclusion, I want to turn briefly to Jewett's most canonical work, *The Country of the Pointed Firs* (1896), which also imagines a world unmoored from age norms. The novel describes an unnamed forty-year-old narrator's visit to Dunnet Landing, a town in coastal Maine, characterized by its "unchanged shores" and populated primarily by men and women in their seventies.[100] The middle-aged narrator, the youngest character in the novel, spends the summer on the island to work on her writing and takes up residence with Almira Todd, a widow in her late sixties, described as a "landlady, herb-gatherer, and rustic philosopher."[101] Mrs. Todd, "quite absorbed in her bustling industries," is just one of several characters that challenge mainstream ideas about aging as a monolithic and knowable phenomenon.

Indeed, as if to underscore the point growing older need not signify only decline, Jewett offers a characterization of Mrs. Todd's mother, Mrs. Blackett, who is perhaps even more energetic and impressive in her capacities than her daughter. Mrs. Blackett lives alone on an island where she does all manner of housework on her own. As Mrs. Todd boasts, "Life ain't spoilt her a mite. She's eighty-six an' I'm sixty-seven, and I've seen the time I've felt a good sight the oldest."[102] She goes on to remark of her mother: "Lookin' pretty well for an old lady, ain't she." These descriptions, coupled with the references to Mrs. Todd and Mrs. Blackett's specific ages, point to Jewett's interest in portraying old women as figures of power.

Such representations run counter to the reductive interpellations of elderly people that pervaded popular periodicals at the end of the nineteenth century. For example, an article in *Scribner's* observes how "women more often than men... in the advanced years become pursy and corpulent, pale and flabby, or perhaps quite fat; their skin hangs not in wrinkles, but in rolls; and their voice, instead of rising, become gruff and husky."[103] In contrast to corpulent women conjured in this ageist screed, the women in Jewett's worlds are hardy, stoic, and wizened; the narrator looks admiringly at Mrs. Todd's "great determined shape."[104] Thus, without reifying able-bodiedness as a norm or even an ideal, it is nonetheless significant that many of Jewett's very old characters are capable of self-sufficiency and physical vigor, undermining the cultural commonsense that saw aging as a disease.

Repeatedly, the narrator ascribes youthful qualities to Mrs. Blackett, calling her "a delightful little person herself, with bright eyes and an affectionate air of expectation like a child on a holiday."[105] She offers "exquisite" hospitality to the narrator, who notices the tidiness of her home, and her daughter Mrs. Todd is surprised to find that her mother has turned over her carpets without much assistance. At the end of their visit, the narrator reflects, "As for the mother, she took on a sudden look of youth; you felt as if she promised a great future, and was beginning, not ending, her summers and their happy toils."[106] This portrayal of Mrs. Blackett undermines prevailing cultural ideas about the elderly as oriented only toward decline and decrepitude. For Jewett, aging is instead defined by non-linear development and renewal rather than deterioration.[107]

To be clear, Jewett does not depict all old people as strong and capable nor does she idealize autonomy or the notion of "successful" aging. On the contrary, most of her characters are non-productive and uninterested in the future-oriented practices mandated by capitalism; they do not accumulate, aspire, or invest. The perpetually grieving Elijah Tilley, the broken-hearted Joanna Todd, the nostalgic Captain Littlepage: these characters, as Sarah Ensor puts it, are "exclusively aged, exclusively uncoupled, and exclusively nonaspirational."[108] Furthermore, they occupy a world outside of traditional kinship structures, lacking connections to future generations and instead engaging solely in horizontal caregiving.[109]

In this sense, Jewett's characters—like those in Freeman's stories— inhabit what Jack Halberstam defines as queer temporality, their lives "unscripted by the conventions of family, inheritance, and child rearing."[110] Oddly, Halberstam defines this alternative mode of temporality in terms of an "epistemology of youth." While he sees endless possibility for queer resistance and experimentation in youth cultures, he neglects to consider how old age too might offer theoretical opportunities or ways of inhabiting time that do not merely ensure generational continuity or correlate to respectability. Indeed, he seems unable to imagine a queer temporality of old age. This fetishization of youth runs the risk of reproducing in a different register Halberstam's own critique of the narrow "gay male archive" in the work of scholars, including Lee Edelman.[111] If the understanding of queerness is sutured to the privileged categories of youth *and* masculinity, then old womanhood needlessly becomes the default category for normativity.

But what Jewett's Dunnet Landing residents teach us is to see old age as a queer time, as a space of culturally defined failure in relation to capitalism's version of success, and as a backward-oriented status. Both Jewett and Freeman remind us that being old might involve a different relation to time itself. In their work, elderliness is a mode of inhabiting time and space that deviates from the future-oriented practices of heteronormativity, the saving and planning and scheduling that define reproductive adulthood. As Jewett's narrator observes, "Even funerals in this country of the pointed firs were not without their social advantages and satisfactions."[112] This association of funerals with satisfaction, and even with society, suggests the queer orientation of Dunnet Landing, a place defined by its relation to the past rather than the future, a place where death is not a locus of dread but a fact of life.

The novel's final chapter, entitled "A Backward View," affirms the orientation of the elderly characters, validating the eccentric Captain Littlepage's perspective and refusing to see the future as the only source of meaning. The narrator reflects, "Neither of my companions was troubled by her burden of years. I hoped in my heart that I might be like them as I lived on into age, and then smiled to think that I too was no longer very young."[113] We might read this shift in perspective, the narrator's embrace of old age, as one that Jewett hopes to instill in her readers as well. Not only does the narrator come to see the inhabitants of Dunnet Landing as exemplars of aging well, but she also accepts, with a smile, her own advanced age.

If we acknowledge *The Country of the Pointed Firs* as a novel about old age, then its oft-discussed plotlessness takes on a new significance. That is, some scholars have read the novel's formal flatness as reflective of a gynocentric world in which the heteronormative teleology of romance and marriage is eschewed in favor of friendship and community.[114] But might we not also see this alternative narrative template as representative of a possible temporality of old age? That is, perhaps *The Country of the Pointed Firs* exemplifies a narrative form shaped by retirement, repose, and withdrawal rather than by marriage, reproduction, and productivity.[115]

In a sense, the construction of old age as a cultural category has affinities with the genre of regionalism itself, as a devalued social zone, separated from and rendered provincial by the march of technological progress and the development of industrial capitalism.[116] It is surely no coincidence that this literary genre emerged at the moment when old age was constituted as a separate stage of life. Jewett's elderly characters are out of sync with the global economy, remnants of a social order increasingly seen as past its prime, and in these regions, Jewett locates something rich, valuable, and at times transgressive, where a profit-driven mainstream culture see only waste, excess, and obsolescence.

As we attend to age and its intersections with disability and other hierarchies, we should, as Heather Love reminds us, "check the impulse to turn [dark] representations to good use in order to see them at all."[117] That is, we need not celebrate old age only when it aligns with the paradigms of success and beauty privileged by capitalism or refuse to acknowledge it at all. Rather, we must acknowledge the blind spot that has limited critical thinking about representations of old age—which are typically read in relation to historical change when they are not ignored altogether. We must see old age as part of a whole embodied life that is unexplored, untheorized, and is inherently oppositional to the demands of power, capitalism, and gender.

5

Beyond Mastery

Undoing Adulthood in the Work of Henry James

"These persons, it appeared, were not of the age they ought to be."
Henry James, *What Maisie Knew*

"But who's 'quite independent,' and in what sense is the term used?"
Henry James, *The Portrait of a Lady*

While Sarah Orne Jewett and Mary Wilkins Freeman sought to make narrative space for old age and to imagine alternative paradigms for growing old, Henry James seems on the surface to be invested in normative constructions of adulthood. James, for example, was appalled by Mary Wilkins Freeman's contribution to the collaborative novel, *The Whole Family*. Like William Dean Howells, he found Freeman's chapter on the "old-maid aunt" offensive and did not find humor in her irreverent disruption of conventional narrative expectations. James responded to his sense of the novel's plot derailment by making his chapter, "The Married Son," twice as long as any other contributor, hoping that an abundance of words would minimize the impact of Freeman's chapter.[1] This response to Freeman signals an allegiance to conservative ideas about the novel form as well as to age ideology; James' very conception of the novel seems to rely upon and enshrine age normativity.[2]

Indeed, James was deeply invested in the notion that the novel had a particular role to play in the construction of age norms. Where nineteenth-century US literature was largely written for and read by readers across the age spectrum, James was at the forefront of a turn toward the age categorization of literary markets, which entailed the elevation of the "adult novel" into a class of its own. As Teresa Michals observes, James was "trying to call a new adult cultural realm into being," noting that he sought "to imagine and to promote the category of the adult, a category that is not fully in place in his world."[3] Realizing this fantasy, James has earned a reputation for being one of the only mature or adult American novelists, renowned for his dense prose and his engagement with thorny moral issues.[4] As Christopher Beha recently put it, "We rightly recognize in James a maturity absent from so much of American culture not just today but a hundred years ago."[5] Even James' moniker—"the Master"—is suggestive of his status as a kind of über-adult, a solitary genius and supremely autonomous writer.[6]

While James certainly fetishizes the sophistication and complexity we now associate with literature for adults, this chapter argues that James' fiction actually destabilizes adulthood, complicating rather than consolidating this category. Indeed, he shows that the notion of adulthood as an epoch of independence and self-determination may be a fiction not unlike that of childhood innocence. As the previous chapters have demonstrated, American writers have long sought alternative ways to conceptualize age and have questioned the limited terms by which maturity is defined. While James would seem to be an outlier, a conservative proponent of conventionally defined adulthood, his fiction exposes the various inflections that compromise the autonomy of the adult subject and reminds us of the extent to which American ideas of adulthood remain exclusionary and ideological.

James' career spanned a period in which age categories crystallized. Just as the notion of elderly people as a distinct population was gaining traction, so too were children increasingly becoming a separate category of people. The end of the nineteenth century saw the emergence of the child study movement, campaigns to raise the age of consent, and the formation of pediatrics and geriatrics as discrete medical specialties. All of these efforts suggest the cultural turn toward parsing the life course into discrete stages, each demanding its own legal protections and scientific frameworks. As Marah Gubar writes, "Age mattered during this period, not as a settled and easily legible fact about one's identity, but as a site of ideological struggle like gender, race, and class."[7] James entered this ideological struggle in fiction, interrogating the meanings of adulthood and its relationship to various kinds of independence, financial, legal, and physical.

"YOU ARE OLD ENOUGH TO BE MORE REASONABLE": ELUSIVE ADULTHOOD

In *Daisy Miller,* one of his earliest works, James describes a crisis in the meanings and practices of age. The narrative begins by characterizing the Miller family as fundamentally out of step with age norms. We first encounter the Millers, who hail from Schenectady, New York, at a resort in Switzerland. Nine-year-old Randolph is described in the opening pages as "diminutive for his years" and has an "aged expression of countenance."[8]

In other words, he is smaller than he should be even as he looks older than his age in his face. Furthermore, he possesses a voice that is "immature and yet somehow not young."[9] This characterization sets up Randolph—and his family more generally—as out of step with appropriate aging; they are at once precocious and stunted, seasoned but also naïve.

Beyond his diminutive physical size and hoary expression, Randolph is losing teeth. As he explains, "It's this old Europe. It's the climate that makes them come out. In America they didn't come out."[10] In other words, the European climate has bodily consequences for this little boy; it speeds up his maturation, causing his baby teeth to fall out faster than in America. Even Mrs. Miller experiences the differences between Europe and America at the bodily level. She reports: "I suffer from the liver...I think it's this climate; it's less bracing than Schenectady, especially in the winter season."[11] Thus, James maps the differences between America and Europe, Old and New Worlds, onto the bodies of his characters, and the immaturity and precocity of America manifests at the level of faces, heights, and teeth. Indeed, it is through the Millers' irregular aging that James characterizes America itself as a place that distorts normative aging and thwarts appropriate developmental benchmarks.

An American expatriate, Frederick Winterbourne is captivated by the Miller family and their unusual deportment. He observes Randolph's extreme childishness and "wondered if he himself had been like this in his infancy, for he had been brought to Europe at about this age."[12] Winterbourne thus notices Randolph's odd age performance and wonders whether it can be attributed to his Americanness. But more than Randolph, Winterbourne's primary object of interest is Daisy, who acts with a striking disregard for European age and gender expectations. He notices that she has "certain laxity of deportment" and repeatedly refers to her as a "pretty American flirt."[13]

Daisy conducts herself with a casualness that dismays the older American women who monitor the social scene. For example, Mrs. Walker, another American expatriate, attempts to discipline Daisy for publicly socializing with Italian men. " 'You should walk with your mother, dear,' " she exhorts, but Daisy responds by telling her: " 'My mother never walked ten steps in her life. And then, you know,' she added with a laugh, 'I am more than five years old.' "[14] For Daisy, walking in public and maintaining independence from her mother are simply the privileges of any person beyond childhood. In her mind, she has achieved a stage of life that grants her the freedom to make her own choices and to socialize in whatever ways she deems desirable.

But as Mrs. Walker sees it, Daisy has entered a stage of life that demands her to act with discretion and to monitor her public behavior. Mrs. Walker insists, "'You are old enough to be more reasonable. You are old enough, dear Miss Miller, to be talked about.'"[15] For Mrs. Walker, Daisy's relationship to her age is precisely the problem; she is at an age when she *should* be more particular about how she acts in public and more thoughtful about her reputation; she is acting like a child rather than a grown woman. Their disagreement thus hinges on competing ways of understanding Daisy's age, and it underscores the extent to which age norms are far from natural; on the contrary, they are contingent on gender, national context, and socioeconomic class. Daisy's disregard for cultural norms—most notably for age expectations—eventually leads to her premature death. Indeed, her early death is her final and starkest refutation of age norms. Ultimately, we can read *Daisy Miller* as a story about the instability of age conventions and the desire for an independent adulthood that remains dangerously beyond reach for a young woman.[16]

Daisy's desire for radical independence flies in the face of European social mores, but it marks her as specifically American. American adulthood has always been defined by independence, a view with a long tradition in American political culture rooted in the Revolution and our founding documents. Since the Revolutionary era, the discourse of age has been used to naturalize the nation and its progressive linear history. Indeed, incitements for the Revolution were premised on identifying the United States as an infant nation that needed to separate from an overbearing mother country.[17] In his pamphlet *American Crisis,* Thomas Paine asked, "To know whether it be the interest of the continent to be independent, we need only ask this easy, simple question: Is it the interest of a man to be a boy all his life? The answer to one will be the answer to both."[18] For Paine, the revolution against Britain relied on analogizing the ideal development of the nation and the ideal development of the individual. Moreover, by describing the emergent nation as a "boy" ready to become "independent," Paine affirms independence as integral to American ideas about maturity and adulthood. The *Declaration of Independence* similarly deploys a naturalized teleology to describe the nation's coming of age; the references to the "course of events" and the "laws of nature" suggest that to mature is synonymous with gaining independence and becoming separate and autonomous.

But this emphasis on independence as the *sine qua non* of maturity was not merely metaphor; it became a key term in allocating citizenship rights and defining political maturity. Significantly, independence was not simply considered the inevitable product of chronological age. On the contrary, the construction of the liberal subject hinged on class. In a 1776 letter, John Adams articulates how class operates, alongside age, to determine who should qualify as a politically viable citizen. He writes:

Children have not Judgment or Will of their own. True. But will not these Reasons apply to others? Is it not equally true, that Men in general in every Society, who are wholly destitute of Property, are also too little acquainted with public Affairs to form a Right Judgment, and too dependent upon other Men to have a Will of their own?[19]

Adams sees reason and judgment as premised upon financial independence, essentially equating men "destitute of property" with children. This formulation holds that poor men lack sufficient exposure to the public sphere to actually have a "will of their own." Thus, from the founding moment, poverty was equated with immaturity, and dependence disqualified individuals, of any age, from participation in the civic realm. According to this logic, adulthood remained a status defined by class, along with race and gender.

As the century progressed, the nascent republic ostensibly moved toward a more democratic understanding of adulthood, expanding citizenship rights to all men regardless of their socioeconomic position and more officially breaking from the mores of monarchical England where inherited status and family rank were the operative criteria for political participation. States increasingly gave up property ownership as a key qualification for democratic citizenship, and age became the sole criteria for determining who had enough maturity—and independence—to vote.[20] As Corinne T. Field writes, politicians "turned to age as a measure of civic capacity because it so perfectly suited the Jacksonian impetus to cut through class bias and enfranchise the 'common man.'"[21]

But in spite of this move to make age the equalizing rubric for all men's political status and to deemphasize class as the criteria for adult citizenship, adulthood in the American imaginary remains yoked to independence and self-sufficiency. And dependence is still seen as a symptom of irresponsibility and weakness, excluding anyone who cannot care for themselves, financially and bodily, from prevailing cultural conceptions of maturity. In their genealogy of dependency, Nancy Fraser and Linda Gordon trace the feminization of dependence over the course of the nineteenth and twentieth centuries. They chart a "shift from a patriarchal preindustrial usage...to a modern, industrial, male-supremacist usage that constructed a specifically feminine sense of dependency."[22] Dependence has become increasingly deviant, even pathological, in a culture that fetishizes self-reliance and stigmatizes welfare and support programs and disciplines subjects into self-sufficiency. As this book has shown, adulthood is thus constructed as a privileged category in relation to race, gender, and ability and as a status awarded to those who successfully align with prevailing economic logic. Even in our own moment, the privilege of adulthood tacitly requires financial independence and bodily autonomy.

It is thus no surprise then that the paradigmatic American *Bildungsroman* is also a rags-to-riches story, making coming of age synonymous with class assent. Horatio Alger's *Ragged Dick* began as a serial in the magazine *The Student and Schoolmate* in 1867 and was published in book form in 1868. Alongside Benjamin Franklin's autobiography, *Ragged Dick* is deemed the quintessential celebration of grit, hard work, and individualism. It became a massive bestseller, disseminating its ideological vision of coming of age to thousands of American readers.

The first installment in the Ragged Dick series, *Ragged Dick; or, Street Life in New York with the Boot Blacks*, centers on a poor adolescent boy, an orphan, who works as a bootblack in New York City, eventually rising to the middle class through a combination of luck, pluck, and hard work. When the novel begins, Dick is fourteen years old and living on the streets. Through a serendipitous encounter, Dick ends up chaperoning a wealthy boy named Frank around the city. Where Dick is unkempt and unmotivated, Frank is refined, educated, and steeped in the teleological, capitalist vision of growing up. He tells Dick, "You won't be a bootblack all your life."[23] Dick agrees, responding, "I'm goin' to knock off when I get be ninety."[24] This dialogue encapsulates competing, class-based ways of understanding the life course. For Frank, working as a bootblack is a juvenile job that one must move beyond; he articulates and anticipates a vision of class mobility whereby one moves up a ladder into a respectable profession. Dick cannot conceive of such mobility nor does he see work as tied to development at all. Their conversation reveals that the very notion of having a "future" is a class construction and a privilege. Just as Frederick Douglass lamented that he would forever be a boy, despite the passage of time, Alger indicates that a professional, and personal, trajectory is a class privilege that is not natural or broadly available.

Dick's encounter with Frank is transformative, sparking his desire to grow up and and move up. He comes to realize he has been "brought up queer" and seeks to redirect, or straighten, his course. His sense of being "queer" is linked to his awareness of having a deviant relationship to development; he comes to see that the pathway to adulthood and respectability is linear and involves upward mobility.[25] Indeed, his desultory, non-linear development—prior to his decision to rise upward—falls under Kathryn Bond Stockton's rubric of "growing sideways," a term she uses to describe the non-normative growth and movement associated with the queerness of childhood.[26]

While *Ragged Dick* reveals that adulthood is not the product of chronological age, the novel reveals how numerical age can nonetheless usher individuals into an aspirational relationship with the ideal of adulthood. Fourteen-year-old Dick reflects on the benchmark age of twenty-one, which he identifies as the age when he should be suitably "respectable," another term for middle class.[27] As the narrator explains, "In seven years he would be a man, and, since his meeting with Frank, he felt that he would like to be a respectable man." Here he equates adulthood with the age of twenty-one even as he recognizes that numerical age is not on its own a guarantor of adulthood—one must also grow out of poverty and internalize the ethos of capitalism. As Frank's uncle, Mr. Whitney, tells Dick, "Your future position depends mainly upon yourself... It will be high or low as you choose to make it."[28] In other words, one must take responsibility for one's own destiny rather than depending on others or blaming systemic injustice for entrenched class stratification.

The *Ragged Dick* stories reveal how the coming-of-age narrative is fused with the rags-to-riches narrative in American culture so that financial independence—rather than numerical age—is still the *sine qua non* of adult status, even though legal and political requirements no longer hinge on class status. By the end of the novel, Dick dons a new suit and has been re-christened Richard Hunter, his last name evoking the kind of ruthlessness required for participation in the modern economy. Implicit but integral to this success story are Dick's statuses as white and male, prerequisites for entrance into the ranks of American adulthood.

In recent years, scholars have complicated the "Horatio Alger myth," which rests on the notion of *Ragged Dick* as a straightforward capitalist fairytale. Some have noted that Dick never truly gains "riches," while others have pointed out that the stories express anxiety about industrialization and its values rather than pure celebration. Additionally, some have noted that Dick doesn't pull himself up by his bootstraps but rather relies on a homosocial network of wealthy patrons and fellow street children.[29] While Dick's rise in status is certainly facilitated by cross-class connections and friendship, such a reading nonetheless affirms childhood as a period of dependence from which one graduates to a self-reliant adulthood. When the first novel in the series concludes, Dick is done asking for help and relying on his friends; he is a "young gentleman on the way to fame and fortune."[30] *Ragged Dick* ultimately cements the logic that the entrance into adulthood is synonymous with assent into the middle class, that independence and adulthood are interchangeable.

This conflation of coming of age with becoming independent results in a singular normative view of adulthood, one that only recognizes forms of maturity that comply with capitalism. While childhood may be a stage "inevitably passed through," as Karen Sanchez-Eppler puts it, dependence is not.[31] And yet the naturalized teleology instantiated by age categories ends up making dependence at any stage *other* than childhood seem pathological. As Martha Fineman writes, "The construction of the adult liberal subject captures only one possible developmental stage—the least vulnerable—from among the many possible stages an actual individual might pass through if s/he lives a 'normal' lifespan."[32] That is, the ideal of adulthood as an inherently independent phase of life obfuscates the array of needs and dependencies that characterize all lives.

* * *

Interestingly, Henry James himself hit a point where he had to confront the limits of his own independence as an author because of a disability. In 1897, he came to depend for the first time upon an amanuensis to type his sentences into a Remington typewriter.[33] He was fifty-four years old and suffered from a persistent, piercing pain in his wrist that made him unable to type for any extended period of time, forcing him to dictate the remainder of his works to an assistant. Though a lifelong bachelor, James himself came to understand the inexorability of dependence and the benefits of entanglement and intimacy.

Perhaps surprisingly, he found this dependence valuable. Indeed, it opened up new possibilities and advanced his style into the aesthetics that many have described as mature and masterful.[34] In her memoir of her eight years as his secretary, Theodora Bosanquet notes that James found dictation freeing rather than restrictive. As she writes, "He found dictation not only an easier but a more inspiring method of composing than writing with his own hand, and he considered that the gain in expression more than compensated for any loss of concision."[35] Bosanquet herself served as a sounding board, an audience, and a collaborator for James, reminding us that dependence and disability are not only constricting or limiting but may also be enriching. James' relationship with his assistants, particularly Bosanquet, asks us to consider the generative effects of interdependence.[36] The very fact that James' development as a novelist, his famously complex "late style," was made possible by dependence challenges the notion of the "master" as a solitary genius and complicates the notion of adulthood as a period of complete independence and self-sufficiency.[37]

The book that James was writing when he first came to depend upon an amanuensis was *What Maisie Knew*.[38] I am less interested here in how dictation may have altered James' style than in considering how his reliance on an amanuensis itself might register at the narrative level.[39] That is, how might James' fiction in fact reflect on the impossibility or problem of such autonomy as a value or ideal? And how does James envision the relationship between dependence and adulthood?

Though on the surface, *What Maisie Knew* is centrally concerned with childhood disempowerment and exploitation, I want to suggest that we may also read it as a meditation on the fact of lifelong interdependence in relation to the cultural construction of self-reliant adulthood. In the remainder of this chapter, I move beyond the title character in order to reveal how dependence and insecurity shape the lives of the novel's adult characters and to suggest that childhood is only the starting point for James' examination of the unequal dispensation of autonomy across many positions.[40]

What Maisie Knew begins with the dissolution of a marriage, which throws six-year-old Maisie into a grueling visitation schedule, shuttled between two grotesquely self-involved parents, who view her alternately as a burden or a tool. As the omniscient narrator explains, "They had wanted her not for any good they could do her, but for the harm they could, with her unconscious aid, do each other."[41] The child is thus recruited into— rather than shielded from—her parents' vicious "adult" world. Over the course of the novel, Maisie's parents remarry, and then these stepparents begin an affair, and Maisie receives care and comfort primarily from an elderly governess, and sporadically, from her stepparents.

From its first pages, the novel upends the binary between adults and children and denaturalizes the concept of "the child" as a stable, coherent subject. Upon the court's ruling of joint custody, a distant relative announces, " 'Poor little monkey!' ... The words were an epitaph on the tomb of Maisie's childhood."[42] This casual reference to Maisie as a "monkey" hints at how the death of Maisie's childhood coincides, to a certain extent, with the death of her personhood. Indeed, the term "monkey" hints at the liminal space she occupies, neither granted autonomy nor guaranteed support. Over the course of the novel Maisie is also called "goose" and "duck." What seem to be playful terms of endearment actually reveal the extent to which Maisie is excluded from personhood because of her status on the age spectrum.

Indeed, James shows how childhood is less a natural, knowable stage of a life than a constructed ideological space. The adults in the novel develop a "theory of her stupidity," which relieves them from having to protect her and from having to act like adults.[43] By ascribing stupidity to Maisie, her parents participate in a form of age inequality, shoring up a hierarchy that associates childhood with ignorance. As he writes, "She began to be called a little idiot ... She appeared not to take things in."[44] This "stupidity" is actually the titular knowledge on which the novel meditates, and James is centrally invested in the idea that children might be more knowing and aware than others assume.

The novel's free indirect narration reveals that Maisie is far more adept and insightful than the adults in the novel expect or allow. As James writes, "Maisie had practiced the art of pacific stupidity."[45] That is, she uses silence strategically and deploys ignorance as a way to avoid conflict when she actually has a cognitive edge on those who are older than her.[46] When asked about her encounter with her mother's new lover, she tells Sir Claude, "I'm afraid I didn't attend to him very much." He responds, "You were the perfection of a dunce."[47] In other words, Maisie has learned to perform childhood, to act in accordance with the pre-existing scripts of childhood ignorance and innocence.[48]

Frequently, the novel draws attention to how Maisie exceeds conventional ideas of childhood. Sir Claude refers to her as "old man" and "old fellow," telling her, "I'll never, never forsake you, old fellow."[49] He tells her, "One would think you were about sixty and that I—I don't know what any one would think *I* am."[50] The fact that he links Maisie to the age of sixty suggests the insufficiency of age as a measure of rationality, competence, or autonomy. Pamela Thurschwell makes a similar point about the denaturalization of age in *The Awkward Age*: "Age becomes an artificial act in which the differences between adults and children are finessed and broken down, paradoxically unraveling as a stable method for categorizing people."[51]

Repeatedly, Maisie displays the kind of knowingness and emotional resilience typically associated with those much older than her. As she tells Sir Claude, "'Mama doesn't care for me.' ... Child as she was, her little long history was in the words; and it was as impossible to contradict her as if she had been venerable."[52] That Maisie seems "venerable" links her with old age, suggesting the extent to which childhood is merely a construct in the world of this novel, an unstable status invested with a range of contingent meanings.

Scholarship on the novel tends to focus on Maisie's thwarted childhood, her exploitation by adults, and her partially knowing perspective on their affairs. Holly Blackford, for example, sees the narrative point of view in the novel as a tactic of defamiliarization, writing that "the 'innocent' child's perspective [is] being used to expose adult hypocrisy."[53] Kevin Ohi reads Maisie as a representative of the queerness of children, and in a similar vein, Susan Honeyman refers to Maisie as a figure for what she calls the "inaccessibility of childhood."[54] Most forcefully, Beverly Lyon Clark argues that James "abuses childhood," using Maisie in particular to "clarify his own vision."[55] While these critical perspectives illuminate the novel's interest in child subjectivity and the representational problems it poses, they also reinforce the age essentialism that I will argue James' work undermines. That is, such accounts tend to reinscribe life stages as stable, biological statuses even when they acknowledge childhood as culturally constructed.

To cite just one final example, Irene Tucker points out how *What Maisie Knew* exposes the "patent falsity" of the "liberal, promissory contract, which presumes a wholly autonomous and efficacious subject." As Tucker argues, a child, who is not self-sufficient or competent, cannot fulfill this function. For Tucker, the novel is about Maisie's "condition of profound dependency."[56] While Tucker is right to see the novel's interest in the problem of the liberal subject, she nonetheless fails to see how a slew of other characters in the novel operate from positions of partial autonomy.

Such claims reinforce the reductive commonplace understanding of childhood as the stage of life uniquely vulnerable to social precarity, prey to conditions of exploitation and circumscribed agency. But childhood is not the only dependent status of life in this novel. Indeed, if we look beyond Maisie herself, we can see how the novel ends up unifying her with a range of adults who are also reliant on others for support, who lack pure autonomy and self-determination, and who trouble the teleological vision of the life course. The very absence of any other children in the novel draws attention to the fact that Maisie's peers are other adults who depend upon her parents for financial support. Such characters give lie to the notion that one eventually and inevitably outgrows dependence with age, destabilizing the very notion of the liberal subject as autonomous and self-reliant.

What Maisie Knew not only unsettles the binary between children and adults, but it destabilizes adulthood itself, exposing the diverse set of ages and modes of existence that fall under this single rubric. Maisie thinks:

> The only mystification in this was the imposing time of life that her elders spoke of as youth. For Sir Claude then Mrs. Beale was "young," just as for Mrs. Wix Sir Claude was: that was one of the merits for which Mrs. Wix most commended him. What therefore was Maisie herself, and, in another relation to the matter, what therefore was mamma?... If she wasn't young then she was old; and this threw an odd light on her having a husband of a different generation. Mr. Farange was still older—that Maisie perfectly knew; and it brought her in due course to the perception of how much more, since Mrs. Beale was younger than Sir Claude, papa must be older than Mrs. Beale. Such discoveries were disconcerting and even a trifle confounding: these persons, it appeared, were not of the age they ought to be.[57]

Maisie ascertains that chronological age holds no absolute meaning here; rather, its significance is relational and sliding. "Youth" itself is a relative status that only has meaning in relation to other statuses. Moreover, Maisie realizes that her "elders," including mamma, Mr. Farange (Papa), Sir Claude, Mrs. Beale, and Mrs. Wix, all ostensibly inhabit the category of adulthood, and yet, their versions of adulthood are radically disparate, revealing that adulthood is not a homogenous category. For this reason, when Maisie tries to make sense of their ages in relation to their various roles in her life and their statuses in the social world, she finds it "confounding." Moreover, she is stymied when she tries to read age as a hierarchy or as a barometer for maturity. Looking at her mother's "thick colour and marked lines," Maisie cannot make sense of these visible signs of age in relation to her mother's childish and impulsive behavior.[58] She comes to see that getting older does not produce a coherent, recognizable subject nor does adulthood signal autonomy and independence.

The novel's deconstruction of adulthood as a monolithic category enables us to see dependence from an intersectional perspective, linked not only to age but also to gender, class, and ability. Indeed, this is one of the key contributions of critical age studies, which urges us to uncouple presumptions about age from ideas about autonomy, ability, and dependence. Chronological age reveals very little about one's capacities or interests, and it is reductive to presume that age can serve as a barometer for dependence. As George Agich writes, "All human beings are dependent no matter what their stage of development," and consequently, autonomy and independence are always precarious and unsustainable achievements.[59]

James reveals how independence is always made possible by invisible forms of dependence. Over the course of the novel, Maisie's parents entertain moves to the United States and South Africa with new partners, and their mobility casts Maisie's lack of agency into relief. But even more significantly, these impulsive forays abroad are only possible because of the circumscribed lives of Maisie's various caregivers, who like Maisie are beholden to the Faranges and whose lives are also constrained by age, gender, and class.

The succession of nannies and governesses that care for Maisie suggests that the work of caring for others is easily commodified and always undervalued. Maisie's nurse, Moddle, is replaced with a governess, Miss Overmore, "a lady and yet awfully poor."[60] After Miss Overmore takes up with Maisie's father, her mother hires the elderly Mrs. Wix, who refers to "the scant security she enjoyed." Maisie explains, "Mama got her for such low pay, really for nothing."[61] That Mama "got" Mrs. Wix "for nothing" suggests her value in a society that radically devalues older women as well as caregiving. Maisie "knew governesses were poor; Miss Overmore was unmentionably and Mrs. Wix ever so publicly so."[62] These nannies and nurses are upper-class strategies for addressing childhood dependency, and yet they also create a more complex web of independence and dependence among the adults themselves. The novel thus exposes how the "official" maturities are themselves dependent, contingent, propped up by the devalued labor of others.

In a world that equates financial independence with maturity, it is not surprising that being old and dependent is repeatedly described in pejorative terms, considered aberrant and unattractive. With her long gray braid and dowdy dresses, Mrs. Wix is the subject of much derision. Miss Overmore observes, " 'She's really beyond a joke!' "[63] Threatened by Mrs. Wix's staunch middle-class morality and her intimacy with Maisie, Miss Overmore obstructs their correspondence, dubbing Wix "illiterate," "unprofessional," and "ridiculous." She refers to her as "ignorant as a fish."[64] Other characters lob similar jabs, indicating a disdain both for her poverty and her age.

Critics have tended to reproduce these biases against Mrs. Wix. For example, John McCloskey refers to Mrs. Wix as "physically grotesque" and notes that she is "incompetent and nearly illiterate." Similarly, Edmund Wilson calls her a "ridiculous old governess."[65] These critical assessments conflate poverty with childishness, link formal education with maturity, and devalue the care work that Mrs. Wix performs. Indeed, these critical responses echo longstanding disdain for dependency work, emotional labor, and older women.

The novel, however, urges us to revise hastily formed prejudices about dependence and vulnerability and to see care work in more nuanced ways.[66] Maisie's reactions to Mrs. Wix are pedagogical, modeling the shift from a kneejerk disdain to an embrace.[67] Maisie first sees Mrs. Wix as a "frightening old woman"; she "struck [Maisie] at first as terrible."[68] This initial impression bespeaks the culturally conditioned way of reading old bodies; they are fear inducing because they put the provisional nature of autonomy on display, reminding everyone of the fundamental transience of bodily integrity and self-determination.

But far from "frightening," Mrs. Wix emerges as the sole source of true comfort for Maisie. "In her ugliness and her poverty, she was peculiarly and soothingly safe," and she gives Maisie the "tucked-in and kissed-for-good-night feeling" that no one else can.[69] "Something in her voice at the end of an hour touched the little girl in a spot that had never even yet been reached."[70] This description implies that Mrs. Wix is the first person to truly care for Maisie, and their rapport forces us to abandon the ageist assumptions that blinker the way we read elderly people and pathologize dependence.

Significantly, Mrs. Wix's vision is also thematized; her signal descriptive detail is her glasses. "She wore glasses which, in humble reference to a divergent obliquity of vision, she called her straighteners."[71] Though they are often read as a symbol of her moral clarity or lack thereof, these glasses do not improve faulty vision; they correct her crossed eyes in order to put *others* at ease. "The straighteners, she explained to Maisie, were put on for the sake of others, whom, as she believed, they help to recognize the bearing, otherwise doubtful, of her regard."[72] In this sense, the "straighteners" are best understood as a figural reminder of Mrs. Wix's investment in shaping her body and self to ease the experience of others. They refer to a perceived weakness that bothers others but does not bother her.

Furthermore, the very term "straighteners" links her with queerness, suggesting her point of view is non-normative. Like Ragged Dick, who is linked to queerness before he becomes self-sufficient and independent, Mrs. Wix is queer because of her dependence and her need for others. Her straighteners link her to James himself, foregrounding her lack of pure autonomy, her imperfection, and lack of complete mastery. While Mrs. Wix is the first "mother" Maisie recognizes, she is not infallible or morally perfect; she exploits her deceased daughter, Clara Matilda, nurses a tragic and unrealized crush on Sir Claude, and often responds to situations with emotional excess. Indeed, where Maisie is precociously knowing, Mrs. Wix is often childish and undisciplined in her emotions like the other adult characters.

Critic Teresa Michals observes that James' saw adulthood as a "complex and appealing psychological realm of age-specific pleasures, one that borrows the glamour of an aristocratic entitlement to pleasure."[73] Michals' definition of adulthood here is inextricable from class privilege. In fact, Michals aligns Maisie and Mrs. Wix as outside of adulthood, later noting, "Mrs. Wix and Maisie endow Maisie's absent parents and step-parents with a very thick imaginative aura indeed." The unremarked-upon pairing of Maisie and Mrs. Wix as similarly stationed ends up reifying a vision of adulthood as autonomous and exclusively upper class. After all, Mrs. Wix is incontrovertibly an adult, if one defines that status as premised on chronological age, and yet, Michals disqualifies her from the category based upon a tacit understanding of adulthood as premised on financial independence and upper-class leisure.

Far from consolidating adulthood as a domain of pleasure, *What Maisie Knew* dismantles the very notion of adulthood as a coherent age category. While the novel does align Mrs. Wix and Maisie, it is not because of their age but rather because of their dependence. "A governess who had only one frock was not likely to have either two fathers or two mothers: accordingly if even with these resources Maisie was to be in the streets, where in the name of all that was dreadful was poor Mrs. Wix to be?"[74] Mrs. Wix's anxiety about her employment and livelihood calls into question the normative conception of a life course that progresses from childhood dependence to adult independence.

While Maisie's parents are often described as playing games, Mrs. Wix and Maisie look on passively, suggesting that the pleasure of games is only available to those who can afford to play at precarity. As Mrs. Wix tells Maisie, "Well, my dear, it's her ladyship's game, and we must just hold on like grim death."[75] Mrs. Wix and Maisie are both beholden to the moves of "her ladyship"; they both lack the power to direct their own lives, excluded from pleasure and linked instead to suffering and death.

Beyond her close association with Mrs. Wix, Maisie is often compared to servants and experiences anxiety about her living situation just like these employees. Maisie's father explicitly compares Maisie's status with servants when he pressures her to travel to the United States with him: "Your mother will never again have any more to do with you than if you were a kitchen maid."[76] Ironically of course, Maisie's mother already treats her with the same detachment as she treats her employees, making this threat somewhat moot.

The novel thus underscores how the insecurity of childhood—even a privileged childhood—finds affinities with other forms of social disempowerment from which adulthood offers no escape. There is always the looming threat that the Faranges will "get rid of" the servants and/or Maisie. Mrs. Wix wonders aloud, "They'll take you, and what in the world will become of me?"[77] This concern echoes Maisie's own worry that she'll soon face "the hour when...with two fathers, two mothers, and two homes, six protections in all, she shouldn't know 'wherever' to go." In other words, those "homes" and "protections" are null, merely nominal; the failure of the biological family to provide unconditional love and caregiving reveals that Maisie shares with her parents' employees an uncertainty about her future, about where she will live, who will provide for her, how her dependent existence will be supported.

Similarly, Miss Overmore, a young single woman in the beginning of the novel, describes how utterly contingent her employment is on obeying the protocols of the Faranges: "'She says that if I e'er do such a thing as enter his service I must never expect to show my face in this house again...If I wait patiently till you come back here we shall certainly be together once more.'"[78] In other words, Miss Overmore must be obeisant to Mrs. Farange in order to gain access to Maisie. The very notion that she "must wait patiently" resonates with the discourse a parent uses with a child, as does the ultimatum that her security depends upon loyalty and emotional labor. She tells Maisie, "I can't say No, because I'm afraid of your mamma, don't you see?"[79] Here, Miss Overmore articulates her sense of being not an employee but a dependent of Mrs. Farange, emphasizing her disempowerment.

To be clear, by highlighting these similarities, I am not suggesting class and age are homologous hierarchies. Maisie's status as an upper-class child means that her disempowerment is somewhat temporary, while most of the servants occupy more entrenched positions of subservience. Their relationship is assymetrical, imbalanced, and perhaps temporary, and yet Maisie's youth—like Mrs. Wix's old age—makes her insecure and dependent; they share a fundamental need for one another. *What Maisie Knew* thus acknowledges that dependence occurs at many points in life, especially as both extremes of the age spectrum make individuals vulnerable to exploitation and reliant on others for support.

Maisie prompts us to conceive of dependence and vulnerability as aspects of life across the age spectrum. As Anna Mae Duane observes, the child has "been an instrument for demonstrating a particular form of impairment," and the representation of the child "allows us to think through how *all* subjects are dependent and vulnerable."[80] That is, renderings of childhood might spur us to think more intersectionally about the multiple forms of dependence, legal, economic, social, or physical. Maisie's school-room, for example, serves as a space for all subordinates and dependents—it is not an age-specific domain. Maisie becomes conscious of this when her mother's second husband, Sir Claude, first enters it. "The way Sir Claude looked about the schoolroom made her feel with humility as if it were not very different from the shabby attic in which she had visited Susan Ash."[81] Maisie senses that her designated space as a child is analogous to the "shabby" room of a housekeeper, suggesting that they share similarly subordinate statuses and spaces. And other adult characters frequently spend time in the schoolroom, further shoring up the overlaps between children and dependent adults. "There were hours of late evening, when she had gone to bed, that Maisie knew [Sir Claude] sat there talking with Mrs. Wix of how to meet his difficulties." Mrs. Wix and Maisie are again linked when Ida comes to the schoolroom to introduce her new lover. Mrs. Wix and Maisie are jointly described as "interrupted students," and "the conscious little schoolroom felt still more like a cage at a menagerie."[82] The fact that the schoolroom is likened to a "cage" suggests the oppressed position not just of Maisie but of all the subordinate adults who lack self-determination and power.

Significantly, these comparisons to Susan Ash and to a kitchen maid are also gendered, revealing how womanhood itself is always already subservi-ent and dependent. Indeed, James draws attention to how adult women are only ever partially autonomous, their independence limited by the patriarchal family structure. Even Maisie's mother, a figure of authority and seeming self-determination, relies on a series of suitors and husbands. As Lynn Wardley notes, "Ida remains dependent on the man she marries, or is trying to marry, or, when she is between husbands, on the legacy from her 'paralysed uncle.'"[83] Ida's reliance on men implies that Maisie herself, as a woman, will not necessarily outgrow dependence.

Conventional adulthood is achieved in this novel not through chrono-logical age or the capacity for rationality but rather through aligning oneself with the acquisitive values of capitalism and heterosexuality—and it is only partially ever available to women. When Miss Overmore marries Maisie's father and becomes Mrs. Beale, she assumes the first name of her new husband as her last name, and James suggests that the change in class and marital status endows her with maturity: "There was almost as vivid a bloom in her maturity as in mamma's." Mrs. Beale's new maturity reveals adulthood as a hetero-economic construct, not a biological status. Though this marriage grants her a semblance of stability, Mrs. Beale's attachments to Maisie's parents are her only avenues for security, and in this sense, she is reliant on Maisie's parents, just like Maisie herself and subject to the directives of those in positions of authority over her. Indeed, like Maisie, she moves horizontally from one household to the other. Lacking a first name like Mrs. Wix, Mrs. Beale must depend on others for her name, identity, and material resources; her life is thus structured in relation to the decisions, even whims, of men.

Perhaps most strikingly, even Sir Claude, a white male and fallen aristo-crat, operates from a position of dependence. Described as a "poor plastic and dependent male," Sir Claude is "ever so much younger" than Maisie's mother, who he marries and who he admits to being afraid of.[84] The fact that he is younger than his wife situates him queerly in the social economy of the novel. Mrs. Wix tells Maisie that "it was proper to [Sir Claude's] 'station' to be careless and free. That had been proper to every one's station that she had yet encountered save Mrs. Wix's own."[85] But Sir Claude is not "careless" or "free"; he is feminized by his dependence on women and by the caregiving responsibilities he assumes. When he meets Maisie, Sir Claude announces, "I am a grandmother...I like babies—I always did."[86] Referring to himself as a "grandmother," Sir Claude suggests his age and gender queer status, revealing that caregiving is an inappropriate pastime for a man. He bonds so quickly with Maisie, and assumes so much caretaking respon-sibility that Mrs. Wix remarks, "He makes up for the want of a nurse."[87]

Constrained by the needs of someone much younger than himself and subject to the various women with whom he is entangled, Sir Claude does not normatively inhabit the role of a gentleman; rather, he is a dependent adult male, which is culturally unacknowledged and inscrutable. His departure from normative manhood is highlighted by the fact that he is afraid of both Mrs. Beale and Maisie's mother. "It brought back to Maisie his confession of fear of her mother; it made her stepmother then the sec-ond lady about whom he failed of the particular virtue that was supposed most to mark a gentleman."[88] When Maisie asks Sir Claude why he isn't afraid of her, he replies, "I *should* be in fear if you were older—there! See— you already make me talk nonsense."[89] In other words, Maisie's status as a child equalizes their relationship, offsetting his misfit with upper-class masculinity and putting them on similar footing. Age is thus one of many vectors that determine power and authority in this novel.

"THE BOTHER AND BURDEN": CAREGIVING AND MATURITY

This chapter has demonstrated how the ostensibly adult characters in James' novel occupy positions of instability and dependence. More specifically, the novel reveals a network of interdependence that gives lie to the notion of adulthood as a period of inherent autonomy and self-determination. At one point, frustrated with Maisie's parents, Mrs. Wix, Maisie, and Sir Claude entertain the fantasy of a collective that shares in care work. They imagine "any sort of little lodging," says Mrs. Wix. Sir Claude adds, "But it would have to be something that would hold us all." They share a desire for an alternative domesticity that would allow them to inhabit age and class in new ways and to share in caregiving. This scene conveys the interdependence and intimacy that characterizes the relationships between these individuals, who occupy three distinct positions on the age spectrum as well as in the class hierarchy. "For the rest of the conversation [Maisie] was enclosed in Mrs. Wix's arms, and as they sat there interlocked, Sir Claude, before them with his tea-cup, looked down at them in deepening thought."[90] The words "enclosed" and "interlocked," in particular, call attention to their web of dependency and caregiving. Ultimately, their fantasy is nullified by the romance between Mrs. Beale and Sir Claude, which necessarily excludes Mrs. Wix and Maisie. The affair between Sir Claude and Mrs. Beale breaks up the queer kinship with Maisie and Mrs. Wix, reminding us that heterosexuality is an obstacle to, rather than a guarantor of, an adulthood defined by ethical obligations.

What Maisie Knew reveals the notion of independent adulthood as a class privilege, at odds with care work and premised on an unyielding individualism. Near the end of the novel, Miss Overmore tells Maisie, "[Ida] isn't your mamma any longer...Sir Claude has paid her money to cease to be...She lets him off supporting her if he'll let her off supporting you...take the whole bother and burden of you and never let her hear of you again."[91] This revelation shows how the "bother and burden" of being responsible for another person can simply be evaded with money. Indeed, the only way to be free of the problem of dependence is to buy one's way out, making conventional adulthood available only to those who can outsource care work and make their own needs invisible.

At the conclusion of the novel, Sir Claude proposes that Maisie live with him and Mrs. Beale, but Mrs. Wix insists on the immorality of such an arrangement. In response, Sir Claude refers to her as a "hideous creature" and a "horrible old woman!".[92] And Mrs. Beale calls her a "raving old demon who has filled your dreadful little mind with her wickedness."[93] These cruelties expose the thin veneer of their kindness and civility and the ageism and sexism that lurk just beneath it.

In contrast to the vindictive behavior and self-motivated accusations of these adults, Maisie registers concern about the needs of Mrs. Wix. She wonders, "If I part with her where will she go?...What will she do?"[94] Maisie recognizes that Mrs. Wix's livelihood and identity stem from their interdependence, and her accountability to another person distinguishes Maisie from her parents, who utterly disavow their obligations. This recognition of the needs of others is linked to the "moral sense" that Mrs. Wix insists upon throughout the novel and which others describe as her "frumpy old-fashioned conscience," a phrase which clearly deploys both age and femininity to stigmatize morality and duty to others. Lynne Segal writes, "We only gain any sense of ourselves through our ties to others; yet, it is just those ties of dependence that we tend to repudiate upon entering adulthood."[95] Maisie's decision to stay with Mrs. Wix, to acknowledge their mutual dependence, is deviant in a world that defines adulthood in terms of separation and unfettered individualism.

While one might be tempted to read this novel as a *Bildungsroman* and to see Maisie as having achieved awareness about the machinations of the adult world, it is more appropriate to see this novel as skeptical of the coming-of-age narrative and its positioning of adulthood as the desirable achievement of youth. James' novel is thus not teleological in the traditional sense of charting a protagonist's development from dependence to self-reliance; instead it warns against the conventional hallmarks of adulthood. If adulthood is a hetero-economic construct, by which I mean a status tied to heterosexual marriage and a patriarchal division of labor and distribution of resources, then Maisie remains staunchly outside of this paradigm, as she realizes that becoming an adult might be about realizing the hollowness of cultural constructions of that very category. In this sense, this conclusion aligns with some feminist models of development, which eschew marriage and reproduction as the signposts of successful female character formation; the biological family is finally rejected in favor of an intergenerational, cross-class partnership.[96]

Ultimately, what Maisie knows is what all children know: the experience of vulnerability and dependence. But the novel demonstrates that those states, which have long been considered the special domains of childhood, are not exclusive to children at all. The novel tells us we can learn from children—more than simply how to tap back into wonder or innocence—but rather to see dependence as a definitive aspect of human life. Moreover, instead of reinscribing commonplace ideas about maturity, *What Maisie Knew* asks us to consider age intersectionally, to see how class and gender, in particular, work alongside age to determine who has power and autonomy in the modern world and who can access the recognizable markers of maturity. By attending to adulthood as a construction, we can see new possibilities for narrative, new models for kinship and affiliation, and a range of new values, such as interdependence, vulnerability, and intimacy. And we might be able to recognize a mode of maturity—linked to caregiving and commitment—that competes with and operates alongside the more socially recognizable and revered versions of maturity.

Coda

The New Old Age

This book has charted nineteenth-century American literature's engagement with the increasing importance of chronological age as it became a key index for political participation, a tool for regulating the population, and an instrument for maintaining gender and racial hierarchies. It began by considering Herman Melville's fantasy of boyhood as a physical and ideological space apart from conventionally defined adulthood. For Melville, boyhood offered the possibility of a life lived outside of the lockstep teleological march of hetero-capitalist time. And yet, as Frederick Douglass reminds us, such anti-developmental fantasies held little appeal for those excluded from political and social forms of adulthood. Slavery made immaturity a permanent and obligatory status. Divorced from the accrual of political rights and social status, chronological age was instead a catalog of loss for enslaved people, a register of stolen time. The reclamation of age, often in spectacular hyperbole, by the Federal Writers Project interviewees half a century later performs a transgressive repossession of age and its meanings.

For white women, the cultural significance of chronological age was defined by a patriarchal investment in female youth and reproductive potential. In the work of Louisa May Alcott, Charlotte Perkins Gilman, and later regionalist fiction, we can see how women writers reimagined the meanings of middle and old age, resignifying birthdays, for example, and offering subversive new visions of post-maternal possibility and elderly embodiment. For Mary Wilkins Freeman, there is no attempt to locate a buoyantly "youthful" old age; on the contrary, she asks her to reader to adopt an unflinching gaze at elderly characters, to look squarely at need, debility, and frailty as aspects of the human condition that need not be sequestered in institutions or coated in sentimentality.

The final chapter examined a similar recognition of dependence in Henry James' work, an acknowledgment that the myth of a sovereign, rational adulthood fails to capture the vulnerability that characterizes all lives. By charting how these writers engage with the increasing political and social significance of bio-numerical age, I have sought to open up new ways of reading representations of age and the myriad discourses of developmental life stages. The writers examined in this book not only anticipate the ageism of our moment but also highlight how age expectations and biases structure and limit the lives of individuals at all points on the age continuum. In closing, I want to offer one final reading in order to pursue some of the ethical questions raised in the final two chapters, questions about the representation of elderly characters and about caregiving, individualism, and autonomy.

Charles Chesnutt's "The Wife of his Youth" (1898) tells the story of Mr. Ryder, a respected leader in the black bourgeois social world of the North during the Reconstruction era. As Chesnutt explains, Ryder "might aptly be called the dean of the Blue Veins," a black social club unofficially comprised exclusively of those light-skinned enough for their veins to be visible.[1] On the brink of his engagement to a much younger, lighter-skinned woman ("very good-looking and not over twenty-five"), Ryder is approached by an elderly, dark-skinned black woman named Liza Jane, who is searching for the man she married while enslaved twenty-five years earlier.[2] It is ultimately revealed that Ryder—previously known as Sam Taylor—is her missing husband, but he does not acknowledge their intimate shared history until the story's conclusion.

Critics have read this story in relation to contemporary discussions of atavism, the politics of marriage, and the genre of realism.[3] But little attention has been paid to Chesnutt's representation of age, despite the fact that Liza Jane's advanced age is the most salient aspect of her characterization, including her shrunken stature and her face, "crossed and re-crossed with a hundred wrinkles."[4] Her hair is "short gray wool," and she wears a gown of "ancient cut" and "an old-fashioned brass brooch."[5] Her appearance is thus singular in its superannuation, even repulsive by the entwined standards of ageism and racism that the story reveals: She "was very black—so black that her toothless gums, revealed when she opened her mouth to speak, were not red, but blue."[6]

Liza Jane is an anachronism, an uncanny and unwelcome figure, disrupting linear notions of history as progress; her dissonant reappearance in Ryder's life suggests the impossibility of moving beyond slavery, despite his changed name and circumstances.[7] As Chesnutt notes, "She looked like a bit of the old plantation life, summoned up from the past by the wave of a magician's wand."[8] This description echoes many of those in the works of Chesnutt's contemporaries, from Joel Chandler Harris to Thomas Nelson Page, white writers who peddled in plantation stereotypes.[9] The story might thus offer a statement on the failure of Reconstruction to achieve national development or to make black futures possible.[10] In this interpretation, her old age positions her as an unfortunate holdover from a past that should have died but will not.

But there is another way to read Liza Jane's advanced age, as well as Ryder's inability, at first, to recognize her, and his ultimate embrace of this long-severed attachment. Episodes of accelerated aging and subsequent misrecognition are not uncommon in nineteenth-century African American literature. In her postbellum novel, *Iola Leroy*, Frances Harper describes how the eponymous protagonist and her brother reconnect after she has been enslaved for six years. "There was something in the fairer one that reminded him forcibly of his sister, but she was much older and graver than he imagined his sister to be... 'I can hardly realize that you are our own Iola, whom I recognized as sister a half dozen years ago.'"[11] Six years of slavery have hastened Iola's aging so dramatically that she is unrecognizable to her own brother. To cite another example, Martin Delany's *Blake* describes a similar moment of failed recognition between a husband and wife. Although he comes to Cuba expressly to find his wife Maggie, Blake does not know her when he sees her: "She had a careworn expression of irreconcilable trouble,—unhappiness and sorrow, sunken eyes... her appearance was that of a woman ten years the senior of his wife."[12] These examples of accelerated aging reveal how African American literature envisioned aging as a way to index, somatically, the deprivations of enslavement, its non-normative temporality that warps developmental narratives and threatens interpersonal ties.

This is the case in Chesnutt's story in which Liza Jane's aged appearance contrasts significantly with Ryder's as a man in his seeming prime. While he has achieved social and professional success, Liza Jane has spent her years of nominal freedom searching for her lost husband and for economic sustenance. Ryder notes, she is "one upon whom advancing years and a laborious life had set their mark."[13] In other words, he sees how aging manifests unevenly and how the impact of time differs depending on one's status. In this sense, the story is attuned to the ways that women could not as seamlessly evade gender and class hierarchies; indeed, Chesnutt acknowledges how such hierarchies determine access to developmental narratives. Liza Jane is in fact ineligible for the freedom that Ryder attains; her return and her condition thus suggest both the impossibility of historical progress *as well as* the material realities that made normative aging possible for some and not for others.

While slavery devalued elderly people, who were deemed a drain on resources and insufficiently productive, Reconstruction cast many freed people into conditions of not only poverty but illness. As historian Jim Downs writes, "Tens of thousands of freed slaves became sick and died due to the unexpected problems caused by the exigencies of war and the massive dislocation triggered by emancipation."[14] Within this vulnerable population, old people, women, and those with disabilities were even more likely to succumb to disease or death.

Read with this context in mind, the story seems less about the inescapability of slavery than about the specific status of elderly black people, especially women, who were deemed economically worthless in the postwar period and suffered in the absence of resources for care and support. The federal government's "strict understanding of who qualified as a laborer left thousands of women, children, elderly, and disabled slaves unable to pursue a meaningful life of 'freedom.'"[15] This is precisely the status of Chesnutt's Liza Jane, whose reappearance is an unsettling reminder of the toll of slavery and its aftermath on the lives of elderly people and women and the particular consequences of the failure of Reconstruction for this demographic.

Moreover, this story's treatment of age markers in relation to social hierarchies and historical trauma suggests ways not only to read them critically but also to engage them ethically. When he first hears Liza Jane's story about her search for her missing husband, Ryder responds, "'Perhaps he's outgrown you, and climbed up in the world where he wouldn't care to have you find him.'"[16] This suggestion points to capitalist discourse of "growth" mapped onto class ascent, the same sense of bourgeois maturity that James thematizes in *What Maisie Knew*. Ryder's shift into light-skinned society would relegate Liza Jane's abject blackness to the past, suggesting that one must "outgrow" a historically and even physiologically defined racial identity to realize a narrative of successful American development.

But the story turns suddenly away from this potential resolution, championing instead a version of manhood that encompasses racial solidarity and cross-class affiliation.[17] The story's teleology of self-making is rerouted away from conventional heteronormative closure at the final moment, jettisoning fantasies of maturity that dispense with dependence. Ryder's initial failure to acknowledge Liza Jane and his subsequent suggestion that he may have "outgrown" her are rejected in favor of an elective embrace of entanglement; despite its inconvenience and disruption, this attachment is privileged over a future defined by the values of white American capitalism, as he permits his former wife to enter into an uncertain relation with the present.[18] In this sense, the story echoes Melville's injunction to stay true to the "dreams of thy youth," to reject the regulatory mandates of maturity to embrace the freedom and idealism typically thought to expire with adulthood.

Although "The Wife of his Youth" was well received, Chesnutt was stymied by readers' lack of empathy for Liza Jane. He wrote to *Atlantic* editor Thomas Hines Page, "It is surprising that a number of people do not seem to imagine that the old woman was entitled to any consideration whatever and yet I don't know that it is so astonishing either, in the light of history."[19] The story's insistence that an "old woman" is "entitled to" "consideration" urges its resistant readers toward an accountability to vulnerable populations, a responsibility that can seem onerous, even grotesque, in an age in which ideals of individualism, autonomy, and acquisition prevail.

The assent of neoliberalism has increasingly meant that individuals must rely upon themselves for support—rather than the government or public institutions—in times of illness, death, disability, unemployment, not to mention the demands of child care and other quotidian kinds of caregiving. Dependence has come to be regarded increasingly as deviant, even pathological, in a culture that fetishizes self-reliance and stigmatizes support programs. Chesnutt's Liza Jane, for example, represents someone who would have been disqualified from the resources of the Freedmen's Bureau due to her age, and she thus must turn to the private family to provide for her.

As we experience, again, the "graying" of the American population, there is much talk of aging well, a term which itself suggests the stealthy reach of capitalist ideology. As this book has shown, the most seemingly innocuous ideas about age are ideological, imbricated in a range of structures, but made to seem natural or like common sense. The desire to evade aging, to appear and act perpetually young, might best be understood as a kind of "cruel optimism," which Lauren Berlant' defines as the desire for something that is "actually an obstacle to your flourishing."[20] The rise of the term "successful aging" sets up busyness and independence as the signposts of doing old age correctly, and this narrow, idealized vision inevitably deems other modes of aging inadequate.

Against such an ethos, we might remember that total autonomy and relentless ambition, the signposts of successful American adulthood that serve capitalist demands, are not universal goods nor should such values colonize the entire life course. Thomas Cole rightly observes that well-intentioned critics of ageism need to be careful not to fetishize self-sufficiency, a tendency he describes as "politically dangerous."[21] A widespread cultural anxiety about old age—and a stigmatization of dependence—ends up serving the privatizing ideology of neoliberalism. The expectation that one must regulate one's unruly body, stay young and productive as long as possible, and then buy into a retirement or assisting living facility has become a mainstream developmental narrative for those privileged enough to afford the new old age. As Donald Hall, a former poet laureate of the Unites States, grimly observes, "These days most old people die in for-profit-making expiration dormitories."[22]

But it is not only "old people" who are stigmatized or interpellated by age rhetoric nor is it only the elderly whose dependence places them outside the social norms of worthiness. All life stages are defined by particular age discourses deployed in conjunction with those of class, race, gender, and sexuality to mete out access to a range of political privileges and social resources. Adulthood serves as the prize of compliance with a system that prioritizes the self over others and competition over cooperation. And yet, as this book has demonstrated, adulthood is in many ways an illusory status, a perpetually receding horizon, promising stability, recognition, and closure. For those that resist its appeal or recognize its impossibility, a multitude of other life narratives become conceivable.

Without neglecting the myriad ways mainstream US culture privileges youth, we must also attend to how maturity is unevenly dispensed and to how the discourse of age remains a potent and permissible way to subjugate women, immigrants, disabled people, and others. Thus, the meanings of chronological age must be understood intersectionally; there is no universal experience of any age. More than spark a facile awareness of ageism in American culture, I hope this book inspires a heightened attunement to the complex ways that the discourses of age shape social hierarchies and lived experience.

Endnotes

INTRODUCTION NOTES

1. Henry Wadsworth Longfellow, "Morituri Salutamus: Poem for the Fiftieth Anniversary of the Class of 1825 in Bowdoin College" in *The Complete Poetical Works of Henry Wadsworth Longfellow* (Boston, MA: Houghton Mifflin, 1893): 314.
2. Ralph Waldo Emerson, "Old Age." *The Atlantic Monthly* (January 1862): 134.
3. Walt Whitman, *Leaves of Grass*. 1881 edition. As David S. Reynolds notes, "In 1881, readers knew well enough that Walt Whitman was neither thirty-seven nor in perfect health." *Walt Whitman's America: A Cultural Biography* (New York: Random House, 2011): 535.
4. In a 2010 review essay, Leerom Medovoi notes that "systematic investigations of age as an organizing cultural category are still rare and underappreciated when they appear." "Age Trouble: A Timely Subject in American Literary and Cultural Studies." *American Literary History* 22.3 (2010): 657–72.
5. Though scholars of Victorian literature have recently begun attending to representations of age, Americanists remain conspicuously silent on the subject, perhaps reflecting a particularly American cultural phobia about aging in a nation long identified with youth. Pioneering work on the social meanings of age by Kathleen Woodward and Helen Small have laid the foundation for a handful of new studies of age in the British context by scholars, including Kay Heath, Claudia Nelson, and Devoney Looser.
6. Foundational studies on childhood in US culture include Caroline Levander, *The Cradle of Liberty: Cradle of Liberty: Race, the Child, and National Belonging from Thomas Jefferson to W. E. B. Du Bois* (Durham, NC: Duke University Press, 2006), Karen Sanchez-Eppler, *Dependent States: The Child's Part in Nineteenth-Century American Culture* (Chicago, IL: University of Chicago Press, 2005), Robin Bernstein, *Racial Innocence: Performing American Childhood from Slavery to Civil Rights* (New York: New York University Press, 2011), and Anna Mae Duane, *Suffering Childhood in Early America: Violence, Race, and the Making of the Child Victim* (Athens, GA: University of Georgia Press, 2010).
7. Margaret Morganroth Gullette, *Aged by Culture* (Chicago, IL: University of Chicago Press, 2004): 18.
8. Following Philippe Aries' influential thesis that childhood, as we know it, was a relatively recent European "invention," scholars often address childhood as a cultural, rather than biological, category. Lesley Ginsburg, for example, refers to the "unstable and airless binary of child/adult" and Caroline Levander observes that "the child emerges as not just another distinct category of identity along with class, race, gender, and sexuality but, instead, becomes a vehicle through which these elements of individual identity are stabilized and made legible as distinct aspects of the self." In a similar vein, Anna Mae Duane

cogently examines the child as a multivalent metaphor in *Suffering Childhood in Early America*. See Leslie Ginsberg, "Minority/Majority: Childhood Studies and Antebellum American Literature," in *The Children's Table: Childhood Studies and the Humanities*, ed. Anna Mae Duane (Athens, GA: University of Georgia Press, 2013): 105. Levander, *The Cradle of Liberty*, 16. See Karen Sanchez-Eppler, *Dependent States: The Child's Part in Nineteenth-Century American Culture* (Chicago, IL: University of Chicago Press, 2005).

9. While seemingly fairly straightforward, even numerical age is not an entirely stable metric, as an individual's biological age and numerical age might conflict.

10. Treas, "Age in Standards and Standards for Age: Institutionalizing Chronological Age as Biographical Necessity" in *Standards and their Stories: How Quantifying, Classifying, and Formalizing Practices Shapes Everyday Life*, ed. Martha Lampland and Susan Leigh Star (Ithaca, NY: Cornell University Press, 2009): 87.

11. Holly Brewer's *By Birth or Consent: Children, Law, and the Anglo-American Revolution in Authority* (Chapel Hill, NC: University of North Carolina Press, 2005) examines the construction of childhood in relation to the shift from status to consent as the basis of political authority. See also *Age in America: The Colonial Era to the Present*, ed. Corinne T. Field and Nicholas L. Syrett (New York: New York University Press, 2015).

12. Chudacoff, 20. Of the new attention to age in the mid-nineteenth-century, historian Joseph Kett writes, "It would be difficult to underestimate the significance of this heightened attention to chronological age as a basis of classifying people." *Rites of Passage: Adolescence in America, 1790 to the Present* (New York: Basic Books, 1977).

13. On the democratization of voting, see Jon Grinspan, *The Virgin Vote: How Young Americans Made Democracy Social, Politics Personal, and Voting Popular in the Nineteenth Century* (Chapel Hill, NC: University of North Carolina Press, 2016). On the establishment of Philadelphia's first home for the elderly, see Carole Haber, "The Old Folks at Home: The Development of Institutionalized Care for the Aged in Nineteenth-Century Philadelphia." *Pennsylvania Magazine of History and Biography* 101 (1977): 240–57.

14. While most historians agree that what we now call "ageism" was firmly in place by the turn of the twentieth century, there is some disagreement about when and why this view of elderly people as burdensome and unappealing first arose. See Carole Haber and Brian Gratton for an overview of the scholarship on old age in America. *Old Age and the Search for Security: An American Social History* (Bloomington, IN: Indiana University Press, 1994).

15. Quoted in W. Andrew Achenbaum, *Crossing Frontiers: Gerontology Emerges as a Science* (New York: Cambridge University Press, 1995): 30. Thomas Cole notes, "In England and America, the word 'senile' itself was transformed in the nineteenth century from a general term signifying old age to a medical term for the inevitably debilitated condition of the aged" (196).

16. Edward Bliss Foote, *Medical Common Sense* (New York: Published by the Author, 1868): 46.

17. Achenbaum importantly notes, "There was never a 'golden epoch' in the history of old age. The elderly once upon a time were *not* automatically granted positions of authority or invariable adoration in western civilization." On the emergence of pensions, Judith Treas writes, "The Civil War pensions enabled aging veterans to withdraw from the labor force and to live independently of kin, thus marking the beginning of the modern institution of retirement." Treas, 74. See also Carole Haber, *Beyond Sixty-Five: The Dilemma of Old Age in America's Past* (New York: Cambridge, 1985).

18. The publication of G. Stanley Hall's 1904 groundbreaking tome, *Adolescence: Its Psychology and its Relations to Physiology, Anthropology, Sociology, Sex, Crime, Religion and Education* established the modern concept of adolescence.

19. The early twentieth century saw the institutionalization of geriatrics and gerontology as discrete medical fields. In 1903, Elie Metchnikoff established "gerontology" ("the study of aging") in the *Etudes on the Nature of Man*, and Ignatz Nascher coined the term "geriatrics" in the *New York Medical Journal* in 1909, which broke with prevailing pathological models of old age and instead established it as a viable and distinct stage of life. He subsequently published *Geriatrics: The Diseases of Old Age and their Treatment, including Physiological Old Age, Home and Institutional Care, and Medico-Legal Relation* in 1914.

20. Howard P. Chudacoff, *How Old Are You?: Age Consciousness in American Culture* (Princeton, NJ: Princeton University Press, 1992):13. He notes that while "life expectancy at birth was only about forty to forty-five years," but one's chance of living to sixty increased if one survived childhood. Older people were relatively rare in New England with only 4 percent of the American population older than sixty in 1850.

21. John Harvey Kellogg, *Plain Facts for Old and Young* (Burlington, Iowa: Segner and Condit, 1881): 127.

22. Kellogg, 134.

23. Nathaniel Hawthorne, "Dr. Heidegger's Experiment" in *Twice-Told Tales* (Boston, MA: American Stationers, Co, 1837): 319.

24. Hawthorne, "Dr. Heidegger's Experiment," 326.

25. Nathaniel Hawthorne, *The Scarlet Letter* (New York: Random House, 2000): 15. This characterization of old age as worthless contrasts with Hawthorne's well-known conservatism; his children's collection *Grandfather's Chair* (1841), for example, suggests the vital role of older generations in passing on family and national heritage.

26. Hawthorne, *The Scarlet Letter*, 15.

27. Hawthorne, "Dr. Heidegger's Experiment," 325.

28. Hawthorne, "Dr. Heidegger's Experiment," 330.

29. Hawthorne, "Dr. Heidegger's Experiment," 332.

30. Hawthorne, "Dr. Heidegger's Experiment," 331.

31. In his landmark work, *The Rise of the Novel*, Ian Watt distinguishes the novel from other forms of fiction by observing that the novel is premised on a linear temporal sequence, or on the passage of time and its effects on a character.

32. Franco Moretti, *The Way of the World: The Bildungsroman in European Culture* (New York: Verso, 2000): 5.

33. Leslie Fiedler, *Love and Death in the American Novel* (Chicago: Dalkey Archive Press, 2003): 24.

34. Jed Esty, *Unseasonable Youth: Modernism, Colonialism, and the Fiction of Development* (New York: Oxford University Press, 2013): 40.

35. Patricia Ann Meyer Spacks, *The Adolescent Idea: Myths of Youth and the Adult Imagination* (New York: Basic Books, 1983): 12–13.

36. Rebecca Harding Davis, "Anne." *Harper's New Monthly Magazine* 78 (April 1889): 744–50.

37. Davis, "Anne," 746.

38. Davis, "Anne," 747.

39. Davis, "Anne," 744.

40. Davis, "Anne," 746.

41. Davis, "Anne," 747.

42. Helen Small observes, "The age we feel is not necessarily the same as our calendrical age, nor is it the same as how we are perceived, or how we register ourselves being perceived by others." Helen Small, *The Long Life* (New York: Oxford University Press, 2007): 3.

43. Leni Marshall, *Age Becomes Us: Bodies and Gender in Time* (Albany: SUNY Press, 2015): 1.

44. Amelia DeFalco, "'And then—': Narrative Identity and Uncanny Aging in *The Stone Angel*." *Canadian Literature* 198 (2008): 75–89.

45. See especially Sigmund Freud's "Three Essays on the Theory of Sexuality," which defines the teleology that results in normative adult sexuality. Also see Judith Roof's *Come as You Are: Sexuality and Narrative*, which offers a queer reading of this Freudian paradigm in relation to narrative.

46. See especially Sara Ahmed, "Orientations: Toward a Queer Phenomenology." *GLQ: A Journal of Lesbian and Gay Studies* 12.4 (2006): 554.

47. J. Jack Halberstam, *In a Queer Time and Place: Transgender Bodies, Subcultural Lives* (New York: New York University Press, 2005): 2.

48. Judith Halberstam, *In a Queer Time and Place: Transgender Bodies, Subcultural Lives* (Durham, NC: Duke University Press, 2005): 2.

49. Jane Gallop, "The View from Queer Theory." *Age Culture Humanities: An Interdisciplinary Journal* 2 (2015). Relatedly, Eve Sedgwick referred to her estrangement from generational narratives and described the "temporal disorientation" that results when people do not progress according to normative models. *Novel Gazing: Queer Readings in Fiction* (Durham, NC: Duke University Press, 1997): 26.

50. Dana Luciano, *Arranging Grief: Sacred Time and the Body in Nineteenth-Century America* (New York: New York University Press, 2007): 9.

51. Kathryn Bond-Stockton, *The Queer Child, or Growing Sideways in the Twentieth Century* (Durham, NC: Duke University Press, 2009).

52. Letter to Annie Fields in *Letters of Sarah Orne Jewett*, ed. Annie Fields (New York: Houghton Mifflin, 1911): 125.

53. Louisa May Alcott, *Louisa May Alcott: Her Life, Letters, and Journals*, ed. Ednah Cheney (Carlisle, MA: Applewood Books, 2010) 48.

54. Maturity and gender operate in tandem; legible gender serves as a privilege, prize, and sign of appropriate aging. In this sense, gender is the index of normative maturation, which is why unseemly age identifications often coincide with the queering of gender or sexual norms. A foundational precedent, Susan Fraiman's *Unbecoming Women: British Women Writers and the Novel of Development* shows how women have traditionally been excluded from the novel of development. Instead, as she points out, women have largely been made to serve as the benchmarks by which male protagonists measure their growth. Like Fraiman, I regard gender as a fundamental, perhaps the fundamental, marker and sign of development, but where Fraiman laments women's exclusion from the narrative of growing up, this book denaturalizes development and questions the gender norms associated with maturity.

55. Even after the power of coverture was diluted by the Married Women's Property Act, "it continued to rationalize the exclusion of women from full participation in political life." See Melissa Homestead, *American Women Authors and Literary Property, 1822–1869* (Philadelphia, PA: University of Pennsylvania Press, 2005): 252.

56. For an excellent study on how legal and cultural understandings of age were also always gendered, see Nicholas Syrett, *American Child Bride: A History of Minors and Marriage in the United States* (Chapel Hill, NC: University of North Carolina Press, 2016).

57. Susan Sontag, "The Double Standard of Aging." *Saturday Review* (September 23, 1972): 29–38.

58. For a discussion of how British women writers and gendered terms of development, see Susan Fraiman, *Unbecoming Women: British Women Writers and the Novel of Development* (New York: Columbia University Press, 1993).

59. Rosemarie Garland Thomson uses the term "disability" to refer to the "socially constructed category of people whose bodily forms, functions, limitations, ambiguities, or appearances are considered to be abnormal, defective, degenerate, debilitated, deformed, ill, unfit, unhealthy, sick, obese, crippled, mad, ugly, retarded, or flawed." Thomson, *Extraordinary Bodies: Figuring Physical Disability in American Culture and Literature* (New York: Columbia University Press, 1996).

60. One excellent exception is Sally Chivers, *The Silvering Screen: Old Age and Disability in Cinema* (Toronto: University of Toronto Press): 2011.

61. Robert McRuer, "Compulsory Able-bodiedness and Queer/Disabled Existence" in *The Disability Studies Reader*, ed. Lennard Davis (New York: Routledge, 2013): 88–99.

62. Howard P. Chudacoff, *How Old Are You? Age Consciousness in American Culture* (Princeton, NJ: Princeton University Press, 1989).

63. Jeffrey Arnett, *Emerging Adulthood: The Winding Road from the Late Teens through the Twenties* (New York: Oxford University Press, 2004).

64. The term was popularized by Kelly Williams Brown's bestselling *Adulting: How to Become a Grown-up in 468 Easy(ish) Steps* (New York: Hachette, 2013).

65. Steven Mintz's recent *The Prime of Life: A History of Modern Adulthood* (Cambridge, MA: Harvard University Press, 2015) is organized sequentially with chapters on marriage, divorce, and parenting, without making explicit how they are relevant to a history of adulthood. While Mintz acknowledges that "adulthood today lacks a well-defined roadmap," the book seems invested in preserving or reinstating such a map by unequivocally conflating adulthood with heteronormative, middle-class milestones.

66. Anna Mae Duane, Introduction. *The Children's Table: Childhood Studies and the Humanities.* (Athens: University of Georgia Press, 2013): 5. A similar point is made by Lennard Davis and David Morris who use the term "biocultures" to refer to culture and history's "inextricable, if highly variable, relation to biology." See Davis and Morris, "Biocultures Manifesto." *New Literary History* 38.3 (2007): 411–18.

67. See Susan Merrill Squier's *Liminal Lives: Imagining the Human at the Frontiers of Biomedicine* (Durham, NC: Duke University Press, 2004) on the transformative interchanges between biomedicine and narrative.

68. Jennifer Silva, *Coming Up Short: Working-Class Adulthood in an Age of Uncertainty* (Cambridge, MA: Harvard University Press, 2013): 6.

69. Julie Passanante Elman, *Chronic Youth: Disability, Sexuality, and US Media Cultures of Rehabilitation* (New York: New York University Press, 2014): 3.

70. Toni Calasanti, Kathleen F. Slevin, and Neal King. "Ageism and Feminism: From 'Et Cetera' to Center." *NWSA Journal* 18.1 (2006): 13–30.

71. Ruth Wilson Gilmore, *Golden Gulag: Prisons, Surplus, Crisis, and Opposition in Globalizing California* (Berkeley, CA: University of California Press, 2007): 197.

72. Socioeconomic class has similarly been linked to longevity. According to the 2016 Brookings Institute study, there is a growing gap in life expectancy between the rich and the poor. See Barry Bosworth, Gary Burtless, and Kan Zhang, "Later Retirement, Inequality in Old Age, and the Growing Gap in Longevity between Rich and Poor." See also Louise Greenspan and Julianna Deardorff, *The New Puberty: How to Navigate Early Development in Today's Girls* (New York: Rodale, 2014). The earlier onset of menstruation shows how a biological rite of passage is shaped by cultural conditions, revealing that a nexus of genetic, cultural, and biological factors produce developmental milestones and stages of life.

73. Pat Thane, *Old Age in English History* (New York: Oxford University Press, 2002): 5.

74. Pierre Bourdieu, *Distinctions: A Social Critique of the Judgment of Taste*, trans. Richard Nice (Cambridge, MA: Harvard University Press, 1984): 479.

CHAPTER 1 NOTES

1. See Robert Milder, "Melville and the Avenging Dream," *The Cambridge Companion to Herman Melville*, ed. Robert Levine (New York: Cambridge University Press, 1998): 275; Charles Haberstroh, *Melville and Male Identity* (Madison, NJ: Fairleigh Dickinson University Press, 1980): 133; and Eleanor

Metcalf, *Herman Melville: Cycle and Epicycle* (Cambridge, MA: Harvard University Press, 1953): 48–55. In addition, William Dillingham claims Melville was reminding himself "to discover the light and strength within, the primitive, Unfallen Man"; see Dillingham, *Melville's Later Novels* (Athens, GA: University of Georgia Press, 1986): 377. Martin Leonard Pops reads the quotation as indicative of Melville's preference for the heart over the head. See *The Melville Archetype* (Kent, OH: Kent State University Press, 1970): 255.

2. By the end of the century, many considered the United States to be fully mature. Urging the United States to assume its place as a world leader, one periodical columnist wrote, "This nation has been a child long enough . . . The child is now fully grown, a new career of manly responsibility is before it." "A Nation's Manhood." *The Independent* (May 12, 1898): 13.

3. Carol Smith-Rosenberg, *Disorderly Conduct: Visions of Gender in Victorian America* (New York: Knopf, 1985): 99. See also Joseph Kett, *Rites of Passage: Adolescence in America, 1790–Present* (New York: Basic Books, 1977).

4. Glenn Wallach writes, "In the 1840s and 1950s, youth for the first time became a part of a national catchphrase—Young America" (3).

5. Henry David Thoreau, *Walden: An Annotated Edition*, ed. Jeffrey S. Cramer (New Haven, CT: Yale University Press, 2004): 9.

6. Samuel Osgood, "Editor's Table: Youth and Age." *Harpers* (Jan 1860): 263.

7. See Edward Widmer's excellent treatment of this literary coterie. It is also worth noting that the terms "Young America" and "Young American" were used frequently to describe a range of beliefs, practices, and types in this period. For an in-depth examination of Young America as a political movement, see Yonatan Eyal's *The Young America Movement and the Transformation of the Democratic Party* (New York: Cambridge University Press, 2003). See also Glenn Wallach, *Obedient Sons: The Discourse of Youth and Generations in American Culture, 1630–1860* (Amherst, MA: University of Massachusetts Press, 1997).

8. Ralph Waldo Emerson, *Nature and Selected Essays* (New York: Penguin, 2003): 35.

9. George Henry Evans's *Young America* magazine "had scores of b'hoys imploring busy New Yorkers to fulfill the nation's destiny in the West." See John Beckman, *American Fun: Four Centuries of Joyous Revolt* (New York: Pantheon, 2014): 121.

10. *Pierre: or, The Ambiguities* (New York: Penguin, 1996): 255.

11. For further discussion of Melville's relationship to the literary marketplace, see David Dowling, *Literary Partnership and the Marketplace: Writers and Mentors in Nineteenth-Century America* (Baton Rouge, LA: Louisiana State University Press, 2012). See also Michael Kearns, *Writing for the Street, Writing in the Garret: Melville, Dickinson, and Private Publication* (Columbus, OH: Ohio State University Press, 2010). For a discussion of his relationship to the authorial paradigm of the Young America movement, see Priscilla Wald, *Constituting America: Cultural Anxiety and Narrative Form* (Durham, NC: Duke University Press, 1995).

12. See Michael Davitt Bell, "Melville's Redburn: Initiation and Authority." *New England Quarterly* 39.3 (1967): 279–97. See also David Reynolds, who refers

to *Redburn* as a "study of the initiation into evil" in *Beneath the American Renaissance: The Subversive Imagination in the Age of Emerson and Melville* (Cambridge, MA: Harvard University Press, 1989).

13. Other examples of failed *Bildungsromans* include Mark Twain's *The Adventures of Huckleberry Finn* and Stephen Crane's *The Red Badge of Courage.*

14. Leslie Fiedler, *Love and Death in the American Novel* (Chicago, IL: Dalkey Archive Press, 2003): 24.

15. I am agreeing with Robert K. Martin, who writes, "Fiedler's greatest weakness lies in his failure to see, or to explore, the political implications of sexuality" (9). Martin, *Hero, Captain, and Stranger: Male Friendship, Social Critique, and Literary Form in the Sea Novels of Herman Melville* (Chapel Hill, NC: University of North Carolina Press, 1986).

16. Karen Sanchez-Eppler. *Dependent States: The Child's Part in Nineteenth-Century American Culture* (Chicago, IL: University of Chicago Press, 2005): xxiii.

17. Duane, *Suffering Childhood in Early America*, 3. Bernstein, *Racial Innocence: Performing American Childhood from Slavery to Civil Rights.*

18. As historian Steven Mintz writes, "Childhood is not an unchanging biological stage of life but is, rather, a social and cultural construct that has changed radically over time." Steven Mintz, *Huck's Raft: A History of American Childhood* (Cambridge, MA: Harvard University Press, 2004): viii.

19. As discussed in the Introduction, we might understand maturity and age as somewhat analogous to gender and sex; (im)maturity, like gender, is a mode of being that need not correspond to biological fact. Indeed, life stages are constructed ways of being in the world that draw on performance in the same ways as gender, and just as non-normative gender behaviors are policed and pathologized, so too are immature, childish behaviors subject to social stigma when performed past the appropriate age. While imperfect, this analogy captures the extent to which both age and gender require that subjects adopt specific practices and behaviors that are meant to appear as natural and expressive, and in both cases, social legibility insists upon allegiance to the conventions of one's assigned group. Moreover, age and gender scripts are mutually constitutive; maturity requires compliance with gender norms, and gender performance becomes deviant when uncoupled from appropriate age performance. For a full-length study on age and performance, see Anne Davis Basting's *The Stages of Age: Performing Age in Contemporary American Culture* (Ann Arbor, MI: University of Michigan Press, 1998). Kathleen Woodward offers the intriguing point that "the very materiality of the body in age can be that at a certain point it performs us, reducing the latitude promised in part by the very concept of performance." See Kathleen Woodward, "Performing Age, Performing Gender." *NWSA Journal* 18.1 (2006): 162–89.

20. Since the economic downturn in 2008, anxieties about the status of young adults have proliferated in contemporary media, along with an associated set of terminology. See, for one example, Alan Dunn, "Failure to Launch: Adult Children Moving Back Home." *Forbes*, June 6, 2012.

21. Charles Sellers, *The Market Revolution: Jacksonian America, 1815–1846* (New York: Oxford University Press): 1994.

22. For a history of adolescence in America, see John Demos and Virginia Demos, "Adolescence in Historical Perspective." *Journal of Marriage and Family* 31.4 (Nov. 1969): 632–8.

23. Nathaniel Hawthorne, *The Scarlet Letter* (New York: Modern Library, 2000): 20.

24. E. Anthony Rotundo associates the mid-nineteenth-century with the emergence of "boy culture," a "distinct cultural world with its own rituals and its own symbols and values." He notes, "Middle-class boys of the nineteenth century had grown alienated from their fathers and from the world of adult males. This alienation cut boyhood adrift from one of its most vital connections to the adult world." Rotundo, "Boy Culture: Middle-Class Boyhood in Nineteenth-Century America" in *Meanings for Manhood: Constructions of Masculinity in Victorian America*, ed. Mark Carnes and Clyde Griffen (Chicago, IL: University of Chicago Press, 1990): 15, 33.

25. Steven Mintz, Review of *Seduced, Abandoned, and Reborn: Visions of Youth in Middle-Class America, 1780–1850* by Rodney Hessinger. *Journal of American History* 93.1 (2006): 209–10.

26. The Bowery "b'hoys" and "g'hals" make many appearances in contemporary periodicals and novels. See George G. Foster, *New York by Gas-Light with Here and There a Streak of Sunshine* (New York: Dewitt & Davenport, 1850). For scholarly discussions of this subculture, see also Sean Wilentz, *Chants Democratic: New York City and the Rise of the American Working Class, 1788–1850* (New York: Oxford University Press, 1984) and Richard Stott, *Jolly Fellows: Male Milieus in Nineteenth-Century America* (Baltimore, MD: Johns Hopkins University Press, 2009).

27. For a study of advice manuals and conduct literature in this period, see Rodney Hessinger's *Seduced, Abandoned, and Reborn: Visions of Youth in Middle-Class America, 1780–1850* (Philadelphia, PA: University of Pennsylvania Press, 2006).

28. Mark Carnes observes that the rise of secret societies and fraternal ritual in the antebellum period was a direct response to the widespread embrace of "capitalism and bourgeois sensibilities." Alongside the emergence of middle-class ideology, men were "simultaneously creating rituals whose message was largely antithetical to those relationships and values" (51). See Carnes, *Secret Ritual and Manhood in Victorian America* (New Haven, CT: Yale University Press, 1991).

29. Henry Ward Beecher, *Lectures to Young Men on Various Important Subjects* (New York: J. B. Alden, 1890): 86.

30. John Todd, *The Student's Manual* (London: Simkin, Marshall, & Co., 1840): 16.

31. Alan Wallach, "The Voyage of Life as Popular Art." *The Art Bulletin* 59.2 (June 1977): 234. According to Wallach, "In 1848, the series attracted perhaps as many as five hundred thousand people (then the equivalent of half the population of New York City) to the American Art-Union's memorial exhibition of Cole's work" (234).

32. Significantly, mainstream understandings of child and individual development are often reliant on notions of national conquest and development.

Consider, for example, that G. Stanley Hall's influential claim that human development mirrored the stages of civilization, with teenagers as "noble savages." Similarly, a twentieth-century historian like John Demos claims that adolescence, as we know it, did not exist until the end of the nineteenth century; it was, in his words, an "American discovery." Thomas Cole's *The Course of Empire* depicts five stages of civilization, thus conjoining, through aesthetic technique, normative gender development and national evolution.

33. Joy Kasson sees Cole's series as resonant with American literature's emphasis on disillusionment. See Kasson, "Thomas Cole and Romantic Disillusionment." *American Quarterly* 27.1 (Mar. 1975): 42–56. In 1847, the *United States Magazine and Democratic Review*—often considered the print vehicle of the Young America movement—published a translation of a German prose poem entitled "The Voyage of Life." *The United States Magazine and Democratic Review* 21.112 (Oct. 1847): 332–3.

34. Interestingly, as Joy Kasson notes, "Cole bitterly lamented the need to continue what he called 'pot-boiling,' painting simple Landscape views with no higher message, complaining that the public wanted 'things, not thoughts,' and protesting, 'I am not a mere leaf-painter.'" This complaint about having to placate the marketplace echoes Melville's own frustrated comments about the tastes of his middle-class readers.

35. Michael Kammen writes, "Although Cole's paintings are unquestionably the most famous rendering of the life cycle in American art, they are by no means the only version. The period from about 1825 to 1870 was especially fecund in supplying variations upon Cole's theme. The nature and extent of those variations are important for several reasons: . . . They call our attention to, and in fact highlight, a major transition in American conceptions of the life cycle following the decade 1840–1850" (45–6). Kammen, "Changing Perceptions of the Life Cycle in American Thought and Culture." *Proceedings of the Massachusetts Historical Society* 91 (1979): 35–66. Thomas Cole refers to *Voyage of Life* as a "landmark in American cultural history," noting that they were "as popular as engravings of George Washington had been in an earlier generation." Cole, *The Journey of Life: A Cultural History of Aging in America* (New York: Cambridge University Press, 1992): 111.

36. Nathaniel Currier also published the lithograph, *The Drunkard's Progress: From the First Glass to the Grave* in 1846, and Gustav S. Peters printed a German version of "The Life and Age of Man," accompanied by religious instruction in the form of an acrostic.

37. For excellent studies of US attitudes toward the annexation of Mexico, see Shelley Streeby, *American Sensations: Class, Empire, and the Production of Popular Culture* (Berkeley, CA: University of California Press, 2002) and Reginald Horsman, *Race and Manifest Destiny: The Origins of American Racial Anglo-Saxonism* (Cambridge, MA: Harvard University Press, 1981).

38. Cole, *Journey of Life*, 111.

39. Claire Perry, *Young America: Childhood in Nineteenth-Century Art and Culture* (New Haven, CT: Yale University Press, 2006): 41.

40. Jay Prosser, "Judith Butler: Queer Feminism, Transgender, and the Transubstantiation of Sex" in *The Transgender Studies Reader*, ed. Susan Stryker and Stephen Whittle (New York: Routledge, 2006): 263.

41. Jennifer Greiman theorizes circularity in Melville and Toqueville's work in relation to democracy: "For Melville, as for Toqueville, the roundness of democracy distinguishes it from other forms of social and political authority... Their circles expose a more fundamental crisis of democratic power beyond its representational need for a transcendent, absolute authority" (123). Greiman, "Circles upon Circles: Tautology, Form, and the Shape of Democracy in Tocqueville and Melville." *J19: The Journal of Nineteenth-Century Americanists* 1.1 (2013): 121–46.

42. Rodney Hessinger notes that "advice writers dramatized the transition to adulthood as a difficult passage through dangerous waters or along a treacherous path" (135).

43. Herman Melville, *Redburn: His First Voyage, Being the Sailor-Boy, Confessions and Reminiscences of the Son-of-a-Gentleman, In the Merchant Service* (New York: Modern Library, 2002): 32.

44. Melville, *Redburn*, 3–4.

45. Melville, *Redburn*, 11.

46. Melville, *Redburn*, 11.

47. Of the novel's narrative strategy, Neal Tolchin writes, Melville "exploits Redburn's conventionality to heighten the tenor of his social critique: If prissy Redburn could be driven to moral outrage, then the abuses must be damning indeed." Neal Tolchin, "The Social Construction of *Redburn*'s 'Mourning Pilgrimage.'" *Studies in the Novel* 18.2 (Summer 1986): 169.

48. Melville, *Redburn*, 41–2.

49. Melville, *Redburn*, 210.

50. *Redburn*'s ironic narrator serves as a manifestation of Melville's own sardonic attitude toward a version of manliness associated with labor and accumulation. According to David Leverenz, many of the canonical male-authored texts of the American Renaissance are double-voiced, revealing the authors' "self-consciousness of being deviant from the prevailing norms of manhood" (15).

51. Melville, *Redburn*, 101.

52. Melville, *Redburn*, 101.

53. Here my argument has affinities with David Leverenz's reading of the male writers of the American Renaissance. According to Leverenz, "Hawthorne exposes manliness as unnatural and potentially persecuting" in "The Custom House," noting that for Hawthorne, "man has become no more than his work, and his social role expresses society as mechanical order, with no awareness of feelings" (36). David Leverenz, *Manhood and the American Renaissance* (Ithaca, NY: Cornell University Press): 1990.

54. Sara Ahmed, *Queer Phenomenology: Orientations, Objects, Others* (Durham, NC: Duke University Press, 2006): 86.

55. Jeffrey Hotz, for example, reads *Redburn* as "an early study and critique of globalization and transatlantic capitalism with its roots in the slave trade."

See Hotz, "Out of Bounds, in Reverse: Melville's *Redburn* and the Painful Knowledge of the Atlantic Rim." *EAPSU Online: A Journal of Critical and Creative Work*, fall 2008.

56. Melville, *Redburn*, 167.
57. Melville, *Redburn*, 182.
58. One could also read the failure of the guidebooks in relation to the Young America movement's renunciation of the founding generation. In his introduction to the first issue of the *United States Magazine and Democratic Review*, John O'Sullivan writes, "All history has to be re-written; political science and the whole scope of all moral truth have to be considered and illustrated in the light of the democratic principle." *United States Magazine and Democratic Review* 1.1 (1837): 14.
59. Smith-Rosenberg, *Disorderly Conduct*, 88.
60. Michel Foucault, "Nietzsche, Genealogy, History" in *The Foucault Reader*, ed. Paul Rabinow (New York: Pantheon): 88. Foucault writes, "The traditional devices for constructing a comprehensive view of history and for retracing the past as a patient and continuous development must be systematically dismantled" (88).
61. Melville, *Redburn*, 250.
62. Melville, *Redburn*, 264.
63. Melville, *Redburn*, 265.
64. Melville, *Redburn*, 265.
65. Such associations were linked to a particular class trajectory, signifying a "man rising into the professional or managerial class" (Wallach 62).
66. Ian Watt, *The Rise of the Novel: Studies in Defoe, Richardson and Fielding* (Berkeley, CA: University of California Press, 2001): 22.
67. Marianne Hirsch, "The Novel of Formation as Genre: Between *Great Expectations* and *Lost Illusions*." *Genre* 7.3 (1979): 293–312.
68. Judith Roof, *Come as You Are: Sexuality and Narrative* (New York: Columbia University Press, 1996): xvii.
69. Roof, *Come as You Are*, xxiv.
70. Jed Esty's *Unseasonable Youth* is centrally concerned with the "figure of youth, increasingly untethered in the late Victorian era from the model and telos of adulthood [which] seems to symbolize the dilated, stunted adolescence of a never-quite-modernized periphery" (7). But where Esty's frame is the postcolonial, I see gender as the central idiom of development. See Jed Esty, *Unseasonable Youth: Modernism, Colonialism and the Fiction of Development* (New York: Oxford University Press, 2012).
71. Jonathan Hall writes, "At the end of *Redburn* we are given not a young man poised on the brink of a successful adulthood but an arrested development doomed to failure, to eternal circular repetition of his worst mistakes." While I agree with Hall, I view "arrested development" and "failure" as favorable alternatives to those presented as successes by the dictates of the market. See Jonathan Hall, " 'Every Man of Them Almost Was a Volume of Voyages': Writing the Self in Melville's *Redburn*." *American Transcendental Quarterly* 5.4 (1991): 259–71.

72. Roof, *Come as You Are*, xxvi.

73. Decades later, the nation was again conceived of in terms of the human life course, as the Civil War was deemed a national rite of passage, a growing pain for a nation still grappling with its independence and identity. Ralph Waldo Emerson claimed that America was "just passing through a great crisis in its history, as necessary as...puberty to the individual." Emerson's conception of the nation as undergoing "puberty," or experiencing a rocky passage, deploys the language of biological development to suture a broken United States into one body.

74. Edward Widmer coins this label for the movement's imperial turn in *Young America: The Flowering of Democracy in New York City* (New York: Oxford University Press, 1998).

75. Widmer, *Young America: The Flowering of Democracy in New York City*, 14.

76. Widmer, *Young America: The Flowering of Democracy in New York City*, 17. Widmer acknowledges that Melville exhibited some ambivalence about Young America rhetoric as early as *Mardi*, but he attributes Melville's ultimate and most complete estrangement from Young America politics in the early 1850s and to Evert Duyckinck's unenthusiastic reception of Moby-Dick (116).

77. Melville, *Redburn*, 115.

78. Melville, *Redburn*, 115.

79. Melville, *Redburn*, 115.

80. See John Bryant, introduction to *Typee: A Peep at Polynesian Life* by Herman Melville (New York: Penguin Classics, 1996.): ix–xxx.

81. Melville, *Moby-Dick: or, The White Whale* (New York: Penguin, 2001): 535.

82. *Redburn*, 74. *Redburn* prefigures the "boy books" that dominated the literary marketplace later in the century. As Bill Brown notes, boy books tend to resist developmental narratives and conjoin boyhood with a physical site "where a residual America can be preserved...where nationhood can be embodied outside history." Bill Brown, *The Material Unconscious: American Amusement, Stephen Crane, and the Economics of Play* (Cambridge, MA: Harvard University Press, 1997).

83. Hester Blum, "The Prospect of Oceanic Studies." *PMLA* 125.3 (2010): 671. For a discussion of the metaphor of the sea in antebellum literature, see Robin Miskolcze, *Women and Children First: Nineteenth-Century Sea Narratives and American Identity* (Lincoln, NE: University of Nebraska Press, 2007).

84. Melville, Redburn, 115. Relatedly, a sailor from Greenland explains that, "the nights were so many weeks long, that a Greenland baby was sometimes three months old, before it could properly be said to be a day old."

85. Melville, *Redburn*, 70. For a particularly relevant discussion of the ocean vis-à-vis age, see Habiba Ibrahim, "Any Other Age: Vampires and Oceanic Lifespans." *African American Review* 49.3 (Winter 2016): 313–27.

86. *Redburn*, 67. Of this sailor, Melville writes, "According to his own account, he had been to sea ever since he was eight years old, when he first went as a cabin-boy in an Indiaman, and ran away at Calcutta. And according to his own account, too, he had passed through every kind of dissipation and abandonment in the worst parts of the world."

87. D. H. Lawrence offered a related vision of the United States as aging in reverse: "She starts old, old, wrinkled and writhing in an old skin. And there is a gradual sloughing off of the old skin, towards a new youth. It is the myth of America." Lawrence, *Studies in Classic American Literature* (New York: Boni, 1930): 79.

88. John O'Sullivan, "The Great Nation of Futurity." *The United States Democratic Review* 6.23 (1839): 427. According to Christopher Hager, *Redburn* demonstrates the extent of Melville's disillusionment with the Young America movement—its cultural nationalism and its vigorous embrace of expansionism—well before *Moby-Dick*, which has often been associated with his disaffiliation from the movement. As Hager writes, *Redburn* "satirizes an antebellum United States that already resembles the aging and decadent empire." While I agree that *Redburn* demonstrates Melville's reservations about American expansionism, the novel seems less invested in representing the United States as overripe and prematurely old than it does in denaturalizing the logic of progress itself.

89. Wai-chee Dimock, *Empire for Liberty* (Princeton, NJ: Princeton University Press, 1989): 85, 87.

90. Melville, *Redburn*, 355.

91. Judith Halberstam, *The Queer Art of Failure* (Durham, NC: Duke University Press, 2011): 4.

92. Halberstam, *The Queer Art of Failure*, 4.

93. Melville, *Redburn*, 362.

94. Elizabeth Freeman, "Time Binds, or, Erotohistoriography." *Social Text* 23 (Fall-Winter 2005): 59. For instance, Joyce Rowe argues that "Harry's child-like qualities disable him from competing in the harshly 'masculine' society of modern commercial capitalism into which Redburn has been initiated" (58). Robert K. Martin similarly sees Harry as a homosexual figure for whom the sea is a pastoral space that can accommodate relations and possibilities fore-closed by the land-based commercial world.

95. Melville, "Letter to Lemuel Shaw" in Hershel Parker, *Herman Melville: A Biography, Volume 1, 1819–1851* (Baltimore, MD: Johns Hopkins University Press, 1996): 650.

96. The letter continues, "And while I have felt obliged to refrain from writing the kind of book I would wish to; yet, in writing these books, I have not repressed myself much—so far as *they* are concerned; but have spoken pretty much as I feel.—Being books, then, written in this way, my only desire for their 'success' (as it is called) springs from my pocket, & not from my heart. So far as I am individually concerned, & independent of my pocket, it is my earnest desire to write those sort of books which are said to 'fail.'—Pardon this egotism."

97. Melville, "The Happy Failure." (New York: Harper Collins, 2009): 112.

98. Dimock, *Empire for Liberty*, 77.

99. Herman Melville, "Bartleby" in *The Piazza Tales* (New York: Dix and Edwards, 1856): 31.

100. Melville, *Bartleby*, 34.
101. Melville, *Bartleby*, 35.
102. Melville, *Bartleby*, 36.
103. Melville, *Bartleby*, 38.
104. Melville, *Bartleby*, 39.
105. Melville, *Bartleby*, 39.
106. Melville, *Bartleby*, 47.
107. Melville, *Bartleby*, 43.
108. Melville, *Bartleby*, 43.
109. Melville, *Bartleby*, 44.
110. Melville, *Bartleby*, 32.
111. Melville, *Bartleby*, 45, 48.
112. Harvey Newcomb, *How to Be a Man: A Book for Boys, Containing Useful Hints on the Formation of Character* (Boston, MA: Gould, Kendall, and Lincoln): 4.
113. Newcomb wrote, "Indolence is a great waste of existence...never fritter away time in doing nothing" (167).
114. Rosemarie Garland Thomson observes that Bartleby "serves as a figure of disability." She observes, "That the narrator's opening revelation tells us he is 'an elderly man' nods toward a recognition of his own vulnerability to the vagaries of the body...Bartleby suggests to the narrator that a turn of circumstances can transform his vision of himself as a competent and autonomous agent of his own will into an incompetent invalid. Indeed—as the lawyer intimates— if he lives long enough, the liberal figure of autonomous self-determination will necessarily become disabled." See Rosemarie Garland-Thomson, "The Cultural Logic of Euthanasia: 'Sad Fancyings' in Herman Melville's 'Bartleby.'" *American Literature* 76.4 (2004): 777–806.
115. Toni Morrison, *Playing in the Dark: Whiteness and the Literary Imagination* (Cambridge, MA: Harvard University Press, 1992): 56. The fact that Mark Twain set this novel in the 1840s (and published it in 1885) might itself be read as a critique of a stunted, non-developed nation.
116. While in Liverpool, Redburn observes, "The negro steps with a prouder pace, and lifts his head like a man; for here, no such exaggerated feeling exists in respect to him, as in America. Three or four times, I encountered our black steward, dressed very handsomely, and walking arm in arm with a good-looking English woman. In New York, such a couple would have been mobbed in three minutes; and the steward would have been lucky to escape with whole limbs" (234).
117. Frederick Douglass, *My Bondage and my Freedom* (New York: Modern Library, 2007): 224. Orig. emphasis.
118. Douglass, *My Bondage*, 273.
119. The scholarship on how enslavers deprived enslaved people of gender norms and developmental progress is abundant. See especially Wilma King's *Stolen Childhood: Slave Youth in Nineteenth-Century America* (Bloomington, IN: Indiana University Press, 1995) and Nellie McKay, "The Girls Who

Became Women: Childhood Memories in the Autobiographies of Harriet Jacobs, Mary Church Terrell, and Anne Moody" in *Tradition and the Talents of Women*, ed. Florence Howe (Urbana, IL: University of Illinois Press, 1991). See also Karen Sanchez-Eppler's chapter in *Dependent States* on how the protagonist in *Our Nig* exploits her position as a child as a tactic of resistance.

CHAPTER 2 NOTES

1. Rosaline Rogers, Federal Writers' Project: Slave Narrative Project, Vol. 5, Indiana.
2. Douglass, *My Bondage*, 161.
3. Douglass, *My Bondage*, 229.
4. Corinne T. Field observes that Douglass drew attention to "the racial meaning embedded in popular metaphors of the life course as a voyage." Corinne T. Field, *The Struggle for Equal Adulthood: Gender, Race, Age, and the Fight for Citizenship in Antebellum America* (Chapel Hill, NC: University of North Carolina Press, 2014): 73.
5. Significantly, Douglass dons a sailor's garb to escape from slavery when he boards a train from Baltimore to Philadelphia.
6. Hortense Spillers, "Mama's Baby, Papa's Maybe: An American Grammar Book." *Diacritics* 17.2 (1987): 64–81. While scholars have not attended to age, much recent work has focused on the related issue of temporality in African American literature, especially in the literature of slavery. See especially Valerie Rohy, Lloyd Pratt, and Daylanne English. Rohy writes, "The slave is always out of time, where time designates a symbolic system governed by white culture and defined by linearity, a specificity, and publicity. He cannot keep time because his time is not his to keep." Valerie Rohy, *Anachronism and its Others: Sexuality, Race, Temporality* (Albany: SUNY Press, 2009): 25.
7. As Habiba Ibrahim has recently put it, "Modern blackness has been constituted outside of the realm of the human...Age, in this context, offers a key analytic for rethinking the limits of the human and its temporality." Ibrahim, "Any Other Age: Vampires and Oceanic Lifespans." African American Review 49.3 (Winter 2016): 313–27.
8. Douglass, *My Bondage*, 30.
9. See Daina Ramey Berry, *The Price for their Pound of Flesh: The Value of the Enslaved from Womb to Grave in the Building of a Nation* (Boston, MA: Beacon Press, 2017). Slaveholders received tax exemptions for slaves at both ends of the life cycle. See Pollard, *Complaint to the Lord*, 34.
10. Historian Marie Jenkins Schwarz writes, "Owners exhibited more concern about slaves' birth dates than did slaves. Slaveholders wanted to know the ages of any slaves they bought, and they often were required by law to maintain records of their slaves' ages, for slaves were taxable property and the rates varied by age." Marie Jenkins Schwarz, *Born in Bondage: Growing Up Enslaved in the Antebellum South* (Cambridge, MA: Harvard University Press, 2000): 15.

11. Theodore Weld, *American Slavery as It Is: Testimony of a Thousand Witnesses* (New York: American Anti-Slavery Society, 1839): 169.

12. Harriet Jacobs, *Incidents in the Life of a Slave Girl* (New York: Penguin, 2000): 8.

13. Theodore Weld notes, "In one of the preceding advertisements, out of one hundred and thirty slaves, only *three* are over forty years old! In the other, out of fifty-one slaves, only *two* are over *thirty-five;* the oldest is but thirty-nine, and the way in which he is designated in the advertisement, is an additional proof, that what to others is 'middle age,' is to the slaves in the south-west 'old age': he is advertised as '*old* Jeffrey'" (38). Daina Ramey Berry notes that "during enslavement, those who reached forty were considered elderly, unlike today, when seniors are those sixty-five or older" (130).

14. Frederick Law Olmsted, *A Journey in the Seaboard Slaves States; With Remarks on their Economy* (New York: Dix and Edwards, 1856): 93.

15. See Marion Lucas, *A History of Blacks in Kentucky: From Slavery to Segregation, 1760–1891* (Frankfort, KY: Kentucky Historical Society, 1992). As Lucas writes, "Bondsmen past their prime laboring years often proved to be of small value to slaveholders" (85). Daina Ramey Berry sees a decline in valuation for women beginning at twenty-six and for men in the early thirties.

16. "Planters often classified them as half hands (most slaves were full hands) or as the equivalent to no hand when they were unable to work, and cut the rations they received." Leslie Howard Owens, *This Species of Property: Slave Life and Culture in the Old South* (New York: Oxford University Press, 1976): 47.

17. These records are drawn from Wendell Holmes Stephenson's *Isaac Franklin, Slave Trader and Planter of the Old South; with Plantation Records* (Baton Rouge, LA: Louisiana State University Press, 1938).

18. Corinne T. Field, "What Do We Talk about When We Talk about Age in Early America?" *Common-Place* 17.2 (Winter 2017). Beyond this, these values only refer to the external values ascribed by slaveholders, not to the values of the people themselves. As Daina Ramey Berry reminds us, African Americans conceived of alternative ways of valuing their own lives so they could "restore the soul by valuing it intrinsically, instinctively, innately... immortally." Thus, the economic valuation of a human life was always only one measure of a person's worth.

19. William Wells Brown, *Clotel, or the President's Daughter* (New York: Penguin, 2003): 70. According to historian Marion Lucas, "Owners frequently covered graying hair with black shoe polish, rubbed oil on aging bodies to make them appear young and healthy, dressed bondsmen in their best clothes... Anticipating such deceptions, prospective buyers carefully examined the merchandise, whether human beings or horses, before the sale began, checking teeth, feeling muscles, and inquiring about age" (94). Marion Lucas, *A History of Blacks in Kentucky: From Slavery to Segregation, 1760–1891* (Frankfort, KY: Kentucky Historical Society, 1992).

20. Wells Brown, *Clotel, or the President's Daughter*, 21.

21. John Brown, "Slave Life in Georgia" in *I Was Born a Slave: An Anthology of Classic Slave Narratives*, ed. Yuval Taylor (Chicago, IL: Chicago Review Press, 1999): 363.

22. See George Frederickson, *The Black Image in the White Mind: The Debate on Afro-American Character and Destiny, 1817–1914* (Middletown, CT: Wesleyan University Press, 1971).
23. Ibrahim, 313.
24. Jacobs, *Incidents in the Life of a Slave Girl*, 81.
25. Jacobs, *Incidents in the Life of a Slave Girl*, 203.
26. Stowe, *Uncle Tom's Cabin, or Life among the Lowly* (New York: Penguin, 1981): 68.
27. Stowe, *Uncle Tom's Cabin*, 68.
28. Stowe, *Uncle Tom's Cabin*, 172.
29. For Stowe, it is women, particularly elderly women, and children that serve as benevolent, moral forces. At the Quaker Settlement where Eliza and her child seek safety, Stowe describes Rachel Halliday in terms that glorify female maturity: "She might be fifty-five or sixty; but hers was one of those faces that time seems to touch only to brighten and adorn." Stowe makes her valorization of old women explicit when she asks, "So much has been said and sung of beautiful young girls, why don't somebody wake up to the beauty of old women?"
30. Stowe, *Uncle Tom's Cabin*, 279.
31. Stowe, *Uncle Tom's Cabin*, 384–5.
32. Lora Romero, *Home Fronts: Domesticity and its Critics in the Antebellum United States* (Durham, NC: Duke University Press, 1997): 79.
33. Eva is not the only character to undergo rapid aging in the literature of slavery. In her postbellum novel, *Iola Leroy*, Frances Harper describes how the eponymous protagonist and her brother reconnect after she has been enslaved for six years. "There was something in the fairer one that reminded him forcibly of his sister, but she was much older and graver than he imagined his sister to be...I can hardly realize that you are our own Iola, whom I recognized as sister a half dozen years ago." Thus, six years of slavery have accelerated Iola's aging so dramatically that she is unrecognizable to her own brother. This hastened aging suggests the physical toll of slavery but also the way its dehumanizing effects manifest through age.
34. See Lesley Ginsburg's discussion of George Fitzhugh's assertion allying slaves, women, and children in their inability for self-care. Ginsburg, "Of Babies, Beasts, and Bondage: Slavery and the Question of Citizenship in the Antebellum American Children's Literature," in *The American Child: A Cultural Studies Reader*, ed. Caroline F. Levander and Carol J. Singley (New Brunswick, NJ: Rutgers University Press, 2003): 91–2.
35. Harriet Beecher Stowe, *Uncle Tom's Cabin or, Life among the Lowly* (New York: Penguin, 1981): 267.
36. Stowe, *Uncle Tom's Cabin*, 318.
37. Robin Bernstein describes how romantic understandings of childhood made innocence "the exclusive property of the vulnerable white child" (68). By contrast, "the libelous, de-childed pickaninny was interdependent with the libel of the 'childlike Negro.'" See Bernstein, *Racial Innocence: Performing American Childhood from Slavery to Civil Rights*.

38. Jo-Ann Morgan and Nathaniel Windon have both observed that Uncle Tom ages dramatically in the novel's myriad adaptations and republications, particularly as the century draws to a close. Windon writes, "By the turn of the century Uncle Tom had become much older in illustrations for the novel and in American popular culture more broadly: his hair changed from black to grey and balding, his face wrinkled, and his body stooped." Morgan likewise argues that "Tom's evolution from the hearty adult of 1850s prints into the decrepit old geezer he became speaks volumes about how mainstream culture chose to view and remember former slaves in the aftermath of emancipation, declared in 1863." Nathaniel Windon, "A Tale of Two Uncles: The Old Age of Uncle Tom and Uncle Remus." *Common-Place: A Journal of Early American Life* 17.2 (Winter 2017). Jo-Ann Morgan, *Uncle Tom's Cabin as Visual Culture* (Columbia, MO: University of Missouri Press, 2007).

39. Of the African American coming-of-age novel, Claudine Raynaud notes that "the discovery of American society's racism is the major event in the protagonist's development and in his 'education.'" Claudine Raynaud, "Coming of Age in the African American Novel" in *The Cambridge Companion to the African American Novel*, ed. Maryemma Graham (New York: Cambridge University Press, 2004): 106.

40. Douglass, *My Bondage*, 224. Orig. emphasis.

41. Douglass, *My Bondage*, 273.

42. Interestingly, Harriet Jacobs' enters the "loophole of retreat" and becomes a fugitive at the age of twenty-one, and the reward notice issued by Dr. Norcum specifies this age; thus, just as Douglass recognized the age of twenty-one as linked to freedom and adulthood, so too did Jacobs seize upon the age of twenty-one as an opportune moment to claim agency and assert her independence.

43. Jacobs, *Incidents in the Life of a Slave Girl*, 33.

44. Nazera Wright refers to the text as a "teaching apparatus" and a "strategy for encouraging white female readers to commiserate with slave girls who were beaten and raped and lend their support to the abolition movement." Wright, *Black Girlhood in the Nineteenth Century* (Urbana, IL: University of Illinois Press, 2016): 83–5.

45. Jacobs, *Incidents in the Life of a Slave Girl*, 57.

46. Jacobs, *Incidents in the Life of a Slave Girl*, 30.

47. Jacobs, *Incidents in the Life of a Slave Girl*, 39.

48. Jacobs, *Incidents in the Life of a Slave Girl*, 68.

49. Jacobs, *Incidents in the Life of a Slave Girl*, 173.

50. Jacobs, *Incidents in the Life of a Slave Girl*, 223.

51. As Claudine Raynaud notes, coming-of-age in African American literature is often a "distorted or reversed process [in which] . . . motherhood takes place before girlhood." Claudine Raynaud, "Coming of Age in the African American Novel" in *The Cambridge Companion to the African American Novel*, ed. Maryemma Graham (New York: Cambridge University Press, 2004): 109.

52. Jacobs, *Incidents in the Life of a Slave Girl*, 18.

53. Daina Ramey Berry uses the term "ghost values" to refer to the financial value of black cadavers, "which became tradable goods that were part of a

clandestine traffic in bodies used for anatomical education." As she grimly notes, "The life cycle of the enslaved is much longer than we realized."

54. See *Child Slavery before and after Emancipation: An Argument for Child-Centered Slavery Studies*, ed. Anna Mae Duane (New York: Cambridge University Press, 2017). See also King, *Stolen Childhood* and Schwartz, *Born in Bondage*.

55. Berry, *The Price for their Pound of Flesh*, 132.

56. Douglass, *My Bondage*, 54.

57. This steadfast respect for elderly people might suggest the persistence of West African culture, "with its tenacious respect patterns, strong kinship bonds, and esteem for the elderly who play a vital role in the social structure of the community" (Pollard 21). Leslie Pollard notes that "old and infirm slaves were venerated by the young and derived status from their roles as well as their age" (32).

58. Solomon Northrup similarly touches on the particular brutality of slavery for elderly individuals, "It is pitiable, sometimes, to see him chastising, for instance, the venerable Uncle Abram. He will call the old man to account, and if in his childish judgment it is necessary, sentence him to a certain number of lashes." Significantly, he refers to the white slaveholder as "childish."

59. Douglass, *My Bondage*, 97.

60. Dea Boster, *African American Slavery and Disability: Bodies, Property and Power in the Antebellum South, 1800–1860* (New York: Routledge, 2012): 65.

61. Stacey Close writes, "Rather than pondering the possibilities of manumission of female slaves or providing for them in their wills, some owners chose to sell their old female slaves in order to rid themselves of inefficient workers or in hopes of buying a younger slave lot from the proceeds of the sale" (89). She observes that old age "did not necessarily guarantee docility or acquiescence to the wishes of the white southerners." Stacey K. Close, *Elderly Slaves of the Plantation South* (New York: Routledge, 1996).

62. Significantly, the Civil War would soon introduce pensions into US culture, formally compensating veterans for their service. As Theda Skopcol explains, "Over several decades, Civil War pensions evolved from a restricted program to compensate disabled veterans and the dependents of those killed or injured in military service into an open-ended system of disability, old-age, and survivors' benefits for anyone who could claim minimal service time on the northern side of the Civil War." Theda Skopcol, *Protecting Soldiers and Mothers: The Political Origins of Social Policy in the United States* (Cambridge, MA: Belknap Press of Harvard University Press, 1992): 102.

63. Jacobs, *Incidents in the Life of a Slave Girl*, 104.

64. Douglass, *My Bondage*, 55.

65. Douglass, *My Bondage*, 54.

66. As Marie Jenkins Schwarz writes, "Although no birthday celebrations occurred in the slave cabin or quarter and lists of birth dates recorded by owners remain of dubious accuracy, archival and other sources reveal a vocabulary used by slaves and owners to depict the various stages of child development." According to Schwartz, enslaved people used terms, including

"in her lap," "creepin' days," "little tot," "a little pig-tailed," "shirt-tail," "big missy" and "half grown," to refer to age and development. Schwartz, *Born in Bondage*, 15–16.

67. These positive descriptions resonate with Daina Ramey Berry's point that elderly people had "low external values" but "their soul values excelled." As she writes, "They carried great wisdom and stability for the community and were respected by younger enslaved family and friends" (131).

68. Leslie Pollard, *Complaint to the Lord: Historical Perspectives on the African American Elderly* (Selinsgrove PA: Susquehanna UP, 1996): 32.

69. Leslie Howard Owens, *This Species of Property: Slave Life and Culture in the Old South* (New York: Oxford University Press, 1976): 47. According to Owens, "Many slaveholders viewed the presence of some of the old ones as a tax on plantation resources. A lifetime of vigorous labors had exhausted much of their physical reserves making them of little use in a culture in which physical labor defined one's existence."

70. Ben Brown, Federal Writers' Project: Slave Narrative Project, Vol. 12, Ohio.

71. Edward Taylor, Federal Writers' Project: Slave Narrative Project, Vol. 10, Missouri.

72. While some historians have thrown the "authenticity" of these interviews into question, I refer to them here less as way of conjuring an accurate picture of slavery and more as a way of revealing the complicated effects of slavery on the logic of age.

73. Some additional examples of how formerly enslaved people used the Civil War to establish their ages: In his interview Robert Wilson responded: "How old am I? Accordin' to my recollection I was twenty-three years old befo' the war started. Old master tole me how old I was. I'm a hundred and one now. Yes'm I knows I am" (Robert Wilson, Federal Writers' Project: Slave Narrative Project, Vol. 2, Arkansas). In his interview, former slave Isaac Adams explained, "I was born in Louisiana, way before the War. I think it was about ten years before, because I can remember everything so well about the start of the War and I believe I was about ten years old" (Isaac Adams, Federal Writers' Project: Slave Narrative Project, Vol. 13, Oklahoma). Rose Adway: "I was born three year 'fore surrender. That's what my people told me" (Rose Adway, Federal Writers' Project: Slave Narrative Project, Vol. 2, Arkansas).

74. George Greene, Federal Writers' Project: Slave Narrative Project, Vol. 2, Arkansas, Part 3.

75. Chaney Hews, Federal Writers' Project: Slave Narrative Project, Vol. 11, North Carolina, Part 1.

76. Ella Wilson, Federal Writers' Project: Slave Narrative Project, Vol. 2, Arkansas, Part 7.

77. Sharon Ann Musher writes, "The extreme longevity of the former slaves interviewed also suggests that the WPA ex-slaves were atypical and perhaps received better treatment than their enslaved peers. While slaves born in 1850 typically lived fewer than 50 years, scholar John Blassingame points out that almost two-thirds of the WPA interviewees were 80 or older" (102).

78. For a discussion of the WPA narratives as a scholarly source, see Saidiya V. Hartman, *Scenes of Subjection: Terror, Slavery, and Self-Making in Nineteenth-Century America* (New York: Oxford University Press, 1997). Sharon Ann Musher observes, "The former slaves frequently engaged in what Mark Twain called 'corn pone'—telling white what they wanted to hear rather than what they honestly experienced." She notes that the "racial climate of the 1930s discouraged former slaves from honestly answering their interviewers about slave days" (113–14). Also see Stephanie Shaw for an overview of the scholarly concerns with the WPA narratives.

79. Sharon Ann Musher, "The Other Slave Narratives: The Works Progress Administration Interviews" in *The Oxford Handbook of the African American Slave Narrative*, ed. John Ernest (New York: Oxford University Press, 2014): 107.

80. Musher, "The Other Slave Narratives," 111.

81. Musher, "The Other Slave Narratives," 111.

82. Musher, "The Other Slave Narratives," 110. For example, James Cape: "I's bo'n in yonder southeast Texas and I don' know what month or de year for sho', but 'twas more dan 100 years ago. My mammy and pappy was bo'n in Africa, dats what dey's tol' me. Dey was owned by Marster Bob Houston and him had de ranch down dere, whar dey have cattle and hosses."

83. Daina Ramey Berry notes, "We know that census records often undercounted African Americans" (108).

84. For example, in 1844 issue of the *New York Journal of Medicine*, Samuel Forry observes that there are a greater proportion of centenarians in the African American population but observes that the "representations of aged blacks... must be received with many grains of allowance," as "they have no family registers." He concludes, "It is thus satisfactorily shown that of all attempts hitherto made by a certain class of philosophers to establish a distinction of species between the Caucasion and African, the present one, based upon the ration of centenarians, is truly the most absurd." Samuel Forry, "On the Relative Proportion of Centenarians, of Deaf and Dumb, of Blind, and of Insane in the Races of European and African Origin," *New York Journal of Medicine and the Collateral Sciences* 2 (May 1844): 313.

85. In his enormously popular *Race Traits and Tendencies of the American Negro* (1896), Frederick Hoffman wrote, "It is not in the conditions of life, but in the race traits and tendencies that we find the causes of excessive mortality."

86. Eric Gardner, "Slave Narratives and Archival Research" in *The Oxford Handbook of the African American Slave Narrative* (New York: Oxford University Press): 47.

87. Richard Mack, Federal Writers' Project: Slave Narrative Project, Vol. 14, South Carolina, Part 3.

88. Interview with Sarah Gudger, Federal Writers' Project: Slave Narrative Project, Vol. 11, North Carolina, Part 1.

89. Of George Womble, the interviewer notes: "From all appearances Mr. Womble looks to be fifty-three years of age instead of the ripe old age of ninety-three

that he claims." Of Henry Wright, the interviewer notes: "Although Mr. Wright is 99 years of age, his appearance is that of a much younger man."

90. Wells Brown, *Clotel, or the President's Daughter*, 70.

91. Brown's claim resonates with the contemporary adage that "black don't crack." For a contemporary reference to this phrase, see Jonathan Capehart, "Michelle Obama knows 'Black don't crack, but . . .'" *Washington Post* January 15, 2014.

92. Judith Treas writes, "Unique biographical and historical situations render some individuals 'ageless.' These uncertainties about chronological age constitute breakdowns for classification systems that rely on chronological age as the basis for standards that assign rights, verify entitlements, and enforce responsibilities." She goes on to observe that "having a chronological age that is unknown or inconsistent causes a breakdown of classificatory mechanisms."

93. Ellen Grubey Garvey, *Writing with Scissors: American Scrapbooks from the Civil War to the Harlem Renaissance* (New York: Oxford UP, 2012): 141. Uri McMillan makes a similar point in his discussion of Joice Heth and subsequent elderly black female performance artists: "These elderly black women performed as embodied vessels of history, signs of generational shifts . . . they became iconic emblems of American identity itself." Uri McMillan, *Embodied Avatars: Genealogies of Black Feminist Art and Performance* (New York: NYU Press, 2015).

94. Garvey, *Writing with Scissors*, 141.

95. The Schomburg Library of Nineteenth-Century Black Women Writers includes a text entitled *Silvia Dubois, (Now 116 Yers Old), A Biografy of the Slav Who Whipt Her Mistres and Gand Her Freedom*. Written by C. W. Larison, M.D., the editor Jared Lobdell notes that Silvia "was not 116, but about 94" and also observes that "the book is not a biography, and when she whipped her mistress (if she did), she may or may not have been a slave." Nonetheless, the text's reference to extreme longevity provides another example of how age functioned as a charged and politically significant metric in the literature of slavery.

96. Gilmore, *Golden Gulag*, 28. Echoing this point in a 2014 essay in the *Atlantic Monthly*, entitled "Black Boy interrupted," Ta-Nehisi Coates refers to the "all the changes that so many black boys never see, for the death tax which their country has long levied upon them."

97. Ibrahim, "Any Other Age: Vampires and Oceanic Lifespans,".

98. Ibrahim, 314. had been lost through national progress for which audiences were nostalgic."

99. McMillan, *Embodied Avatars*, 26. McMillan situates Heth within a "tradition of other black historical figures who made theatrical careers out of performing hyperbolic roles" and observes that her work can be read as agential as well as coerced. For an excellent book-length analysis of P. T. Barnum and Joice Heth, see Benjamin Reiss, *The Showman and the Slave, Race, Death, and Memory in Barnum's America*. (Cambridge: Harvard University Press, 2001).

100. Stephen Katz, "Imagining the Life-Span: From Premodern Miracles to Postmodern Fantasies" in *Images of Aging: Cultural Representations of Later Life*, ed. Mike Featherstone and Andrew Vernick (New York: Routledge, 2003): 32.

101. Charles Richard Johnson, *Passing the Three Gates: Interviews with Charles Johnson* (Seattle, WA: University of Washington Press, 2003): 14.

102. Jacques Ranciere, "In What Time Do We Live?" in *The State of Things* (*Office for Contemporary Art Norway OCA*, London: Koenig Books, 2012).

103. In her discussion of William Henry Dorsey's *Colored Centenarians* scrapbook, Ellen Gruber Garvey makes a related point about the extraordinary African American life spans, observing that for formerly enslaved people, "their recompense takes the form of living long enough to see freedom and outliving their former masters."

104. Robin Kelley, *Race Rebels: Culture, Politics, and the Black Working Class* (New York: Simon and Schuster): 20. Mark Smith echoes this point: "CPT is a useful shorthand to describe how African Americans as a class of laborers resisted planter-defined time during and after slavery…They both accommodated and resisted their masters' attempts to inculcate a modern clock-based time sensibility during slavery." Mark Smith, *Mastered by the Clock: Time, Slavery, and Freedom in the American South* (Chapel Hill, NC: University of North Carolina Press, 1997): 130.

105. Daylanne English writes, "Understanding African American literature's tropes of timekeeping either as always-oppressive regulatory instruments or as inevitably tools of modern capitalist exploitation of labor belies their range and power." English, *Each Hour Redeem: Time and Justice in African American Literature* (Minneapolis, MN: University of Minnesota Press, 2013).

106. Kathryn Bond-Stockton, *Beautiful Bottom, Beautiful Shame: Where "Black" Meets "Queer."* (Durham, NC: Duke University Press, 2006): 184.

107. http://www.apa.org/news/press/releases/2014/03/black-boys-older.aspx.

108. Garnette Cadogan, "Walking While Black." *Literary Hub* (July 2016).

CHAPTER 3 NOTES

1. G. Stanley Hall, *Youth: Its Education, Regimen, and Hygiene* (New York: D. Appleton and Company, 1908): 293.

2. Stowe, *Uncle Tom's Cabin*, 303.

3. For recent scholarship on Alcott's children's fiction, see Cathlin M. Davis, "An Easy and Well-Ordered Way to Learn: Schooling at Home in Louisa May Alcott's *Eight Cousins* and *Jack and Jill*." *Children's Literature In Education: An International Quarterly* 42.4 (Dec. 2011): 340–53 and Lorinda B. Cohoon, "'A Highly Satisfactory Chinaman': Orientalism and American Girlhood in Louisa May Alcott's *Eight Cousins*." *Children's Literature* 36 (2008): 49–71 and Hugh McElaney, "Alcott's Freaking of Boyhood: The Perplex of Gender and Disability in *Under the Lilacs*." *Children's Literature* 34 (2006): 139–60.

4. Voicing an opposing opinion, Elizabeth Langland writes, "*Little Women* romanticizes the process by which girls become women and good wives." See Langland, "Female Stories of Experience: Alcott's Little Women in Light of Work" in *The Voyage in: Fictions of Female Development*, ed. Elizabeth Abel and Marianne Hirsch (Hanover, NH: University Press of New England, 1983): 112–27.

5. Ivy Schweitzer, "Most Pleasurable Reading We're Not Doing: Louisa May Alcott's *Little Women*." *J19: The Journal of Nineteenth-Century Americanists* 2.1 (Spring 2014): 13–24.

6. Elizabeth Young, *Disarming the Nation: Women's Writing and the American Civil War* (Chicago, IL: University of Chicago Press, 1999): 107. In a similar vein, Elizabeth Barnes describes *Little Men* and *Jo's Boys* as "pedagogical coming-of-age stories...that focus on the development of its heroines and heroes from impetuous children to responsible adults." Barnes argues that Alcott's postbellum novels "sound a sympathetic echo...for boyish exuberance even as they repeatedly resign such exuberance to its predetermined fate." Barnes, *Love's Whipping Boy: Violence and Sentimentality in the American Imagination* (Chapel Hill, NC: University of North Carolina Press, 2011): 126.

7. Scholars have long remarked upon Jo's tomboyism, but little attention has been paid to how this gender non-normativity functions in relation to age. See Michelle Abate's *Tomboys: A Literary and Cultural History* (Philadelphia, PA: Temple University Press, 2008). See also Karen Quimby, "The Story of Jo: Literary Tomboys, *Little Women*, and the Sexual-Textual Politics of Narrative Desire." *GLQ: A Journal of Lesbian and Gay Studies* 10.1 (2003) 1–22.

8. Louisa May Alcott, *Little Women* (New York: Penguin, 1989): 3.

9. Alcott, *Little Women*, 153.

10. Alcott, *Little Women*, 3.

11. Of nineteenth-century girlhood, Melanie Dawson notes that "because girls are encouraged to act out scenes of maturity, take on domestic duties, and develop self-monitoring skills, girlhood appears nearly indistinct from womanhood" (66). See Melanie Dawson, "The Miniaturizing of Girlhood: Nineteenth-Century Playtime and Gendered Theories of Development" in *The American Child: A Cultural Studies Reader*, ed. Caroline Levander and Carol Singley (New Brunswick, NJ: Rutgers University Press, 2003): 63–84.

12. Alcott, *Little Women*, 388.

13. Alcott, *Little Women*, 10.

14. Alcott, *Little Women*, 16.

15. Alcott, *Little Women*, 5–6.

16. Alcott, *Little Women*, 209.

17. Alcott, *Little Women*, 440.

18. Alcott, *Little Women*, 440.

19. Alcott, *Little Women*, 422.

20. Alcott, *Little Women*, 489.

21. Karen Quimby smartly characterizes the consensus response to *Little Women*'s ending: "Even though *Little Women* brings its tomboy heroine to the expected end of marriage, this conclusion is so unsatisfying and incoherent that most readers reject it in favor of the far more queer middle of Jo's plot, where meanings do not line up into a seamless, univocal whole." Quimby, *GLQ: A Journal of Lesbian and Gay Studies* 10.1 (2003): 1–22.

22. Alcott, qtd. in Madeleine B. Stern, *Louisa May Alcott: A Biography* (Boston, MA: Northeastern University Press, 1999): 184.

23. Louisa May Alcott, *Louisa May Alcott: Her Life, Letters, and Journals*, ed. Ednah Cheney (Carlisle, MA: Applewoods Books, 2010): 201.

24. Alcott began writing *Work* in 1861 but did not finish it until 1873. Amy Schrager Lang notes that *Work* "reverses" the progress toward maternity and marriage laid out in *Little Women*. Lang, *The Syntax of Class: Writing Inequality in Nineteenth-Century America* (Princeton, NJ: Princeton University Press): 115.

25. For example, Sarah Lahey writes, "Alcott's novel depicts a culture redeemed but also burdened by work, and its crucial insight is the assertion that leisure can be as productive as the busy bee's most industrious efforts." Sarah Lahey, "Honeybees and Discontented Workers: A Critique of Industry in the Fiction of Louisa May Alcott." *American Literary Realism* 44.2 (Winter 2012): 133–56. In a related vein, Mary Rigsby reads *Work* as invested in "an American dream based on communitarian rather than capitalistic values." Mary Rigsby, "'So Like Women!': Louisa May Alcott's *Work* and the Ideology of Relations" in *Redefining the Political Novel: American Women Writers, 1797–1901*, ed. Sharon Harris (Knoxville, TN: University of Tennessee Press, 1995): 109. And Gregory Eiselein argues that "*Work* represents women workers as desirable and desiring, and it envisions multiple romantic-erotic possibilities for women in the workplace." See Gregory Eiselein, "Sentimental Discourse and the Bisexual Erotics of Work." *Texas Studies in Literature and Language* 41.3 (Fall 1999): 203–35. See also Lynn Alexander, "Unsexed by Labor: Middle-Class Women and the Need to Work." *American Transcendental Quarterly* 22.4 (2008): 593–608 and Tara Fitzpatrick, "Love's Labor's Reward: The Sentimental Economy of Louisa May Alcott's *Work*." *NWSA Journal* 5.1 (March 1993): 28–44 and Toby Widdicombe, "A 'Declaration of Independence': Alcott's *Work* as Transcendental Manifesto." *ESQ* 38 (1992): 207–25.

26. One notable exception is Glenn Hendler's analysis of *Work* in terms of its engagement with sympathy and the generic limits and possibilities of sentimentalism. See Glenn Hendler, *Public Sentiments: Structures of Feeling in Nineteenth-Century* (Chapel Hill, NC: University of North Carolina Press, 2001).

27. Louisa May Alcott, *Work: A Story of Experience* (New York: Penguin, 1994): 5.

28. Corinne T. Field, "'Are Women...All Minors?': Woman's Rights and the Politics of Aging in the Antebellum United States." *Journal of Women's History* (Winter 2001): 113–37. As Field writes, "States defined twenty-one as the age at which an individual was free to sign contracts and the age at which a man, if he met property qualifications, could cast a vote under previous state

constitutions" (116). During much of the eighteenth and nineteenth centuries, the right to vote was reserved for white male property owners, and the voting age was twenty-one. See Alexander Keyssar, *The Right to Vote: The Contested History of Democracy in the United States* (New York: Basic Books, 2000). See also Grinspan, *The Virgin Vote: How Young Americans Made Democracy Social, Politics Personal, and Voting Popular in the Nineteenth Century*.

29. Margaret Fuller, *Woman in the Nineteenth Century* (New York: Greeley and McElrath, 1845): 161. Fuller's understanding of contemporary womanhood as a perpetual state of immaturity echoes Immanuel Kant's critique of a civilization in which enlightenment and maturity remain elusive to most individuals. In "What is Enlightenment?" Kant writes, "Only a few have succeeded, by cultivating their own minds, in freeing themselves from immaturity and pursuing a secure course." Kant, "What is Enlightenment?" in *The Portable Enlightenment Reader*, ed. Isaac Kramnick (New York: Penguin, 1995): 1–7.

30. Karen Kilcup observes, "The suggestion of immaturity was leveled against many women writers in this period, in part as a way of dismissing their apparently disproportionate investment in emotion rather than (mature and masculine) reason" (4). See Karen L. Kilcup and Thomas S. Edwards (eds), *Jewett and her Contemporaries: Reshaping the Canon* (Gainesville: University Press of Florida, 1999).

31. Mrs. A. J. Graves, *Woman in America* (New York: Harpers and Brothers, 1844): 248.

32. Just as Christie appropriates the age of majority as a relevant marker of female maturity, Alcott borrows the male coming-of-age narrative to tell a woman's story. As Elizabeth Langland writes, "*Work* presents a female tale of development strikingly like that of the male novel of development." See Langland, "Female Stories of Experience: Alcott's Little Women in Light of Work," in *The Voyage in: Fictions of Female Development*, ed. Elizabeth Abel and Marianne Hirsch (Hanover, NH: University Press of New England, 1983): 112–27.

33. Alcott, *Work*, 12.

34. Alcott, *Work*, 5.

35. Field, "'Are Women…All Minors?': Women's rights and the Politics of Aging in the Antebellum United States." *Journal of Women's History* (Winter 2001): 120.

36. Alcott, *Work*, 9.

37. Carolyn Dinshaw, *How Soon Is Now?: Medieval Texts, Amateur Readers, and the Queerness of Time* (Durham, NC: Duke University Press, 2012): 3.

38. Alcott, *Work*, 11.

39. Alcott, *Work*, 22.

40. Alcott, *Work*, 27.

41. See Robin Bernstein's related argument about how nineteenth-century African American children were denied access to "childhood innocence." As she writes, "In many cases, angelic white children were contrasted with pickaninnies so grotesque as to suggest that only white children *were* children." Bernstein, *Racial Innocence: Performing American Childhood from Slavery to Civil Rights*, 16.

42. Susan Sontag, "The Double Standard of Aging." *Saturday Review* (September 23, 1972): 29.

43. Alcott, *Work,* 122.

44. Alcott, *Work,* 119.

45. Kathleen Woodward, *Aging and its Discontents: Freud and Other Fictions* (Bloomington, IN: Indiana University Press, 1991): 67.

46. Alcott, *Work,* 119.

47. Alcott, *Work,* 191.

48. Emily Apter considers the démodé "as an aesthetic function of women's time" and notes its relation to Susan Sontag's definition of camp as well as Nietzsche's theorization of the untimely. See Apter, " 'Women's Time' in Theory." *differences* 21.1 (2010): 1–18.

49. Apter, " 'Women's Time' in Theory," 16.

50. The "old-fashioned" was a pervasive theme in Alcott's oeuvre. She published the story "An Old-Fashioned Thanksgiving" in 1881.

51. Alcott, *Work,* 195.

52. Helen Small, *The Long Life* (New York: Oxford University Press, 2007): 3.

53. Alcott, *Work,* 185.

54. As Lynne Segal writes, "There are devious means by which we always live with those passions of the past in the strange mutations of mental life in the present, whatever our age" (4). Segal, *Out of Time: The Pleasure and Perils of Ageing* (New York: Verso, 2014).

55. Women in New England married at an average age of twenty-two or twenty-three in the mid-nineteenth century. See Nancy F. Cott, *The Bonds of Womanhood: "Woman's Sphere" in New England, 1780–1835* (New Haven, CT: Yale University Press, 1977): 13–14. This sense of thirty as a woman's marriage deadline serves as the primary anxiety of Edith Wharton's *The House of Mirth*; Lily Bart, we learn on the first page, "was nine-and-twenty and still Miss Bart," implying that she is dangerously close to thirty to be unmarried.

56. Showalter, Introduction. *Alternative Alcott* (New Brunswick, NJ: Rutgers University Press, 1988): xix.

57. Birthdays were typically occasions for reflection rather than celebration, opportunities for odes and well wishes, but not parties. A fictional dialogue, published in 1836 in the *Christian Watchman* (reprinted from the *Youth's Friend*), exemplifies this attitude toward the appropriate way to observe birthdays: "Mother, is it right to keep our birth-days?" Her mother explains that birthdays are for reminding us of the "goodness of God in creating us at first, and in preserving us so long in life and comfort," not as "seasons of sinful mirth."

58. The "birthday book" also became a popular commodity during this period. Such books were used to assemble names and birthdays of friends and family alongside quotations from canonical authors. As Maura Ives notes, "By 1899, over 270 birthday books had been published, including nearly 100 single-author themed books." *Women Writers and the Artifacts of Celebrity in the Long Nineteenth Century*, ed. Maura Ives and Ann R. Hawkins (Abingdon: Routledge, 2016): 101.

59. Alcott, *Work*, 200.
60. Alcott was perhaps especially attentive to the significance of birthdays, as she shared her birthday with her father, Bronson Alcott, with whom she had an intense relationship.
61. Alcott, *Work*, 200.
62. Mary Russo, "Aging and the Scandal of Anachronism" in *Figuring Age: Women, Bodies, Generations*, ed. Kathleen Woodward (Bloomington, IN: Indiana University Press, 1999): 20.
63. Louisa May Alcott, *Louisa May Alcott: Her Life, Letters, and Journals*, ed. Ednah Cheney (Carlisle, MA: Applewoods Books, 2010): 48.
64. *Work*'s episodic, desultory plot structure deviates from the linear life course that Sara Ahmed links with heteronormativity: "For a life to count as a good life, it must return the debt of its life by taking on the direction promised as a social good, which means imagining one's futurity in terms of reaching certain points along a life course. Such points accumulate, creating the impression of a straight line. To follow such a line might be a way to become straight, by not deviating at any point." Ahmed, "Orientations: Toward a Queer Phenomenology." *GLQ: A Journal of Lesbian and Gay Studies* 12.4 (2006): 554.
65. Kathryn Bond-Stockton, *The Queer Child, or Growing Sideways in the Twentieth Century* (Durham, NC: Duke University Press, 2009): 11.
66. Alcott, *Work*, 177, 178.
67. Alcott, *Work*, 179.
68. Emily Dickinson echoed this sentiment in a letter to Louise Norcross in 1872: "Affection is like bread, unnoticed till we starve, and then we dream of it, and sing of it, and paint it, when every urchin in the street has more than he can eat. We turn not older with the years, but newer everyday. Of all these things we tried to talk, but the time refused us. Longing, it may be, is the gift no other gift supplies." Qtd. in Cynthia Griffin Wolff, *Emily Dickinson* (New York: Knopf, 1988): 552.
69. Alcott, *Work*, 194.
70. Alcott, *Work*, 194.
71. Amelia Defalco's formulation of aging as antithetical to coherent subjectivity is useful here. She writes, "Aging involves perpetual transformation that unsettles any claim to secure identity, allowing strange newness to intrude into a subject's vision of a familiar self." "'And Then—': Narrative Identity and Uncanny Aging in *The Stone Angel*." *Canadian Literature* (Autumn 2008): 76.
72. Rita Felski, *Beyond Feminist Aesthetics: Feminist Literature and Social Change* (Cambridge, MA: Harvard University Press, 1989): 138.
73. Alcott, *Work*, 239.
74. Indeed, observing the novel's formal inconsistencies, Jean Fagan Yellin deems *Work* a "failure" and lacking in vitality. Yellin, "From Success to Experience: Louisa May Alcott's *Work*." *The Massachusetts Review* 21.3 (1980): 527–39. Yellin wonders "whether the conventions of the sentimental novel prevented [*Work*] from becoming a vehicle for serious social criticism."
75. Felski, *Beyond Feminist Aesthetics*, 138.
76. Alcott, *Work*, 325.

77. Alcott, *Work*, 329.

78. Alcott, *Work*, 327.

79. Gullette, *Aged By Culture*, 122.

80. Field, "Perpetual Minors," 120.

81. This pop wisdom is perhaps best captured by Winston Churchill's declaration: "Show me a young Conservative and I'll show you someone with no heart. Show me an old Liberal and I'll show you someone with no brains."

82. Gloria Steinem makes this point forcefully in her 1983 essay collection, noting that young women "outgrow the limited power allotted to them as sex objects and child bearers...[they] haven't yet experienced the injustices of inequality in the paid labour force, the unequal burden of child rearing and work in the home, and the double standard of ageing." Gloria Steinem, *Outrageous Acts and Everyday Rebellions* (New York: Henry Holt and Co., 1983): xiii.

83. Charlotte Perkins Gilman, *What Diantha Did* (Durham: Duke University Press, 2005): 43.

84. Gilman, *Diantha,* 47.

85. See also the Feb. 1915 issue of *The Forerunner*, which includes a story called "Spoken To": "It's no use mother. I'm of age. I'm self-supporting." Lucille, who goes by Luke, tells her family: "Mother dear—...you are only forty-two—do you know it? I'm twenty-one. We hope—we confidently expect—that you will live as long as the rest of the family. Grandma, as you know, is as lively as a kitten, at sixty. Great-grandma is only seventy-eight. Great-great-grandma lived to be nearly a hundred...now what I want to ask is—at what age are you willing your little girl shall be allowed to go out alone—at night?"

86. Gilman, *Diantha,* 47.

87. Gilman, *Diantha,* 53.

88. Gilman, *Diantha,* 61.

89. Gilman, *Diantha,* 100.

90. Gilman, *Diantha,* 105.

91. Margaret Morganroth Gullette, "Inventing the 'Postmaternal' Woman, 1898–1927: Idle, Unwanted, and out of a Job." *Feminist Studies* 21.2 (Summer, 1995): 221–53.

92. Gilman, *Diantha,* 39.

93. Charlotte Rich, Introduction. *What Diantha Did* (Durham, NC: Duke University Press, 2005): 22.

94. Kimberly A. Hamlin, "Sexual Selection and the Economics of Marriage: 'Female Choice' in the Writings of Edward Bellamy and Charlotte Perkins Gilman" in *America's Darwin: Darwinian Theory and US Literary Culture*, ed. Tina Gianquitto and Lydia Fisher (Athens, GA: University of Georgia Press): 168.

95. Charlotte Perkins Gilman, "A New Generation of Women." *Current* History 18 (August 1923): 736.

96. Charlotte Perkins Gilman, *The Living of Charlotte Perkins Gilman: An Autobiography* (Madison, WI: University of Wisconsin Press, 1975): 74.

97. Gilman, The Living of Charlotte Perkins Gilman, 74.

98. Charlotte Perkins Gilman, *Herland and Other Writings*, ed. Beth Sutton-Rampseck (New York: Broadview, 2012): 50.

99. Cynthia Davis, *Charlotte Perkins Gilman: A Biography* (Stanford, CA: Stanford University Press, 2010): 397.

100. Charlotte Perkins Gilman, *The Later Poetry of Charlotte Perkins Gilman*, ed. Denise D. Knight (Newark, DE: University of Delaware Press, 1996): 119–20.

CHAPTER 4 NOTES

1. Mary E. Wilkins Freeman, *The Infant Sphinx: Collected Letters of Mary E. Wilkins Freeman*, ed. Brent L. Kendrick (Lanham, MD: Scarecrow Press, 1985): 61.

2. I am borrowing this formulation from Leo Bersani, who begins his classic essay with the provocation: "There is a big secret about sex: most people don't like it." While Bersani's essay describes how penetrative sex—particularly queer sex—instantiates the erosion of the coherent self, we might also imagine how growing old similarly involves a kind of self-shattering and a disintegration of the ego; thus aging bodies might occupy a queer space in the willful or compulsory surrender of autonomy that mainstream US culture views as deviant and unduly chaotic. Leo Bersani, "Is the Rectum a Grave?" *October* (Winter, 1987): 197.

3. Louisa May Alcott, *An Old-Fashioned Girl* (Boston, MA: Roberts Brothers, 1870): 40.

4. Contrary to Lee Edelman's claim that the child must always stand for the future, Alcott's "old-fashioned girl" is affiliated with the past. Lee Edelman, *No Future: Queer Theory and the Death Drive* (Durham, NC: Duke University Press, 2004).

5. Elizabeth Freeman, "Time Binds, or, Erotohistoriography," *Social Text* 23.3–4 (Winter 2005): 66.

6. Katie Clark Mullikin, "Growing Old Gracefully." *The Ladies Repository* 1.4 (April 1875): 335–42.

7. W. Andrew Achenbaum, *Old Age in the New Land: The American Experience Since 1790* (Baltimore: Johns Hopkins University Press, 1978): 40.

8. Haber, *Beyond Sixty-Five: The Dilemma of Old Age in America's Past*, 108.

9. Historians have disagreed about what caused old age to lose cultural prestige. While many link the erosion of elder regard to industrialization, David Hackett Fischer posits a shift in cultural beliefs much earlier than changes in capitalism. Thomas Cole claims that the Second Great Awakening changed belief systems and that evangelical ministers emphasized importance of youth; he writes, "the elderly... had become irrelevant to the culture of self-improvement." Thomas Cole, *The Voyage of Life: A Cultural History of Aging in America* (New York: Cambridge University Press, 1992): 169. Another theory is proffered by Carole Haber, who argues that the diminishing respect for old age emerged as a product of the professionalization of medicine and science. Other scholars, including Philip Greven, question the notion that old people ever had much esteem in US culture.

10. Tamara Hareven notes that "Beard's investigation represented the first attempt at a scientific inquiry into the relationship between aging and efficiency, and it set the stage for the concept of the 'superannuated man' that was to come."

11. In 1920, G. Stanley Hall, famous for his tome on adolescence, published *Senescence*, in which he sought to reclaim old age as an achievement, a status of maturity, a consolidation rather than a period of disease and decline.

12. *Ladies' Home Journal* (Dec. 1904): 65; *Ladies' Home Journal* (March 1906): 77.

13. Travis Foster has discussed the influence of *Ladies' Home Journal*, noting, "It taught readers how to fashion and recognize themselves as white American women, and it cathected that subject position with meaning and social cohesiveness." See Foster, "How to Read Regionalism and the *Ladies' Homes Journal*" in *The Oxford Handbook of Nineteenth-Century American Literature*. Ed. Russ Castronovo (New York: Oxford UP, 2014): 292.

14. Kathleen Woodward, *Figuring Age: Women, Bodies, Generations* (Bloomington, IN: Indiana University Press, 1999): x–xi.

15. As age ideology became pervasive, a corresponding literature of old age emerged, tapping into the new market of elderly readers and responding to the denigration of age. In the preface to *Past Meridian* (1854), Lydia Sigourney declares her book is for all those "who have achieved more than half life's journey," observing that "we are in the same category—a joint stock concern that admits no partners." Explicitly referring to stage of life as a "category" of identity, Sigourney strives "to prove that age, though deemed unlovely, can be happy and holy." Similarly, Lydia Maria Child's anthology *Looking toward Sunset* (1865) includes excerpts from Elizabeth Gaskell's *Cranford,* part of a speech by Cicero, poetry by Whittier and Longfellow, and many of her own meditations on old age.

16. *Ladies' Home Journal* XI.12 (Nov. 1894).

17. Gail Hamilton responds: "At her marriage, especially if that involves, as is not uncommon, her dotage." Mary Mapes Dodge: "a woman is 'at her best,' mentally and physically, when she is at 'at her best,'—and that is all there is about it." Mary Wilkins Freeman responds: "We cannot establish an unswerving rule for their times, since they depend upon the capability of individual plants for grasping and making use of the conditions of growth."

18. Stephen Katz writes, "The almshouse, pensions, and retirement, and the social survey, together with modern discourses of reform, the life-course regime, and alarmist demography, disciplined old age and brought it into the domain of power/knowledge relations." Katz, *Disciplining Old Age: The Formation of Gerontological Knowledge* (Charlottesville, VA: University of Virginia Press, 1996): 76.

19. "The Elderly Heroine." *Harper's Bazaar* (November 17, 1894): 918.

20. Granville Hicks, *The Great Tradition: An Interpretation of American Literature Since the Civil War* (New York: Macmillan, 1933): 105.

21. Walter Berthoff, "The Art of Jewett's Pointed Firs." *New England Quarterly* 32.1 (March 1959): 37–9.

22. Michael Holstein, "Art and Archetype: Jewett's Pointed Firs and the Dunnet Landing Stories." *Nineteenth-Century Literature* 42.2 (Sept. 1987): 188–202.

23. See Sarah Ensor, "Spinster Ecology: Rachel Carson, Sarah Orne Jewett, and Nonreproductive Futurity." *American Literature* 84.2 (2012): 409–35 and Holly Jackson, "'So We Die before our Own Eyes': Willful Sterility in *The Country of the Pointed Firs.*" *The New England Quarterly* LXXXII, 2 (June 2009): 264–84.

24. The few exceptions include Lisa Ashby's excellent unpublished dissertation and essays by Susan Toth and Helen Westra. Westra notes that *Country* depicts old age as a "vital stage in the continuum of life," offering a "celebration of age... not only in her positively presented elderly characters but also in the setting, events, and details she selects to underscore advancing years as a stage of life." Helen Westra, "Age and Life's 'Great Prospects' in Sarah Orne Jewett's *The Country of the Pointed Firs.*" *Colby Quarterly* 26.3 (Sept. 1990): 161–70. See also Susan Toth, "The Value of Age in the Fiction of Sarah Orne Jewett." *Studies in Short Fiction* 8 (Summer 1971): 433–41. Lisa Ashby, "Age in Sarah Orne Jewett's Short Fiction." Dissertation, University of Nebraska, Lincoln, 1998.

25. Heather Love, "Gyn/Apology: Sarah Orne Jewett's Spinster Aesthetics." 55.3–4 *ESQ: A Journal of the American Renaissance* (2009): 305–34.

26. In his discussion of British literature, Jacob Jewusiak exemplifies what this kind of work might entail, noting "a larger critical tendency to abstract old age from developmental narratives." Jacob Jewusiak, "No Plots for Old Men." *Novel* 46.2 (2012): 193–213.

27. Mary Moss, "Some Representative American Story Tellers." *The Bookman* Vol. XXIV (September, 1906).

28. One notable exception is Samaine Lockwood, whose recent book acknowledges age as a central concern and theme in regionalism. She writes, "Freeman seems well aware of how prejudices about gender, age, and poverty shaped New England women's experiences over time." Lockwood, *Archives of Desire: The Queer Historical Work of New England Regionalism* (Chapel Hill, NC: University of North Carolina Press, 2015). See also Marjorie Pryse, "The Humanity of Women in Freeman's 'A Village Singer.'" *Colby Quarterly* 19.2 (1983): 69–77.

29. Alfred Bendixen notes that while Freeman "had a great deal of respect and admiration for Howells... apparently his remarks on women in the first chapter, particularly his treatment of the old-maid aunt, irritated her... Freeman felt that Howells's conception of the aunt was based on outdated values that condemned a single woman in her thirties to an eternal and dowdy spinsterhood." Bendixen, Introduction. *The Whole Family: A Novel by Twelve Authors* (Durham, NC: Duke University Press, 2001): xxii.

30. Mary E. Wilkins Freeman, "The Old-Maid Aunt" in *The Whole Family*, 38.

31. Freeman, "The Old-Maid Aunt" in *The Whole Family*, 45.

32. Freeman, "The Old-Maid Aunt" in *The Whole Family*, 45.

33. Elizabeth Jordan, qtd. in *Publishing the Family* by June Howard (Durham, NC: Duke University Press, 2001): 15.

34. Elizabeth Jordan, qtd. in *Publishing the Family*, 15.

35. Freeman, "The Old-Maid Aunt" in *The Whole Family*, 33. Karen Kilcup considers Freeman's contribution to *The Whole Family* in terms of its critique of the masculine literary establishment: "Freeman's chapter offered to men like Howells and James (and many of their more conventional female counterparts) nothing less than a wake-up call and a battle cry." Kilcup, *Soft Canons: American Women Writers and Masculine Tradition* (Iowa City, IO: University of Iowa Press, 1999): 8–9.

36. Mary E. Wilkins Freeman, *The Infant Sphinx: Collected Letters of Mary E. Wilkins Freeman*, ed. Brent L. Kendrick (Metuchen, NJ: Scarecrow Press, 1985): 313.

37. Susanna Ashton, "Veribly a Purple Cow: *The Whole Family* and the Collaborative Search for Coherence." *Studies in the Novel* 33.1 (Spring 2001): 51–79.

38. For example, June Howard writes, "It was Mary Wilkins Freeman, speaking in the voice of that unimportant old maid, who forced *The Whole Family* to confront the figure of the woman who makes up her own mind and cannot be contained by the family" (167).

39. Mary Wilkins Freeman, "A Mistaken Charity" in *A Humble Romance and Other Stories* (New York: Harpers & Brothers, 1887): 234.

40. Freeman, "A Mistaken Charity," 237.

41. Freeman, "A Mistaken Charity," 241.

42. Freeman, "A Mistaken Charity," 243.

43. Freeman, "A Mistaken Charity," 243.

44. Freeman, "A Mistaken Charity," 236.

45. Jennifer Ansley describes the communities in Freeman's work as queer, noting that they "do not adhere to normative systems of capitalist accumulation, including wage-work, the consumption of mass-produced consumer goods, and the sale of property." Ansley, "Geographies of Intimacy in Mary Wilkins Freeman's Short Fiction." *New England Quarterly* 87.3 (2014): 434–63.

46. Freeman, "A Mistaken Charity," 237.

47. Debra Bernardi writes about Freeman's commitment to privacy in the face of an increasingly invasive charity movement. Debra Bernardi, " 'The Right to Be Let Alone': Mary Wilkins Freeman and the Right to a 'Private Share'" in *Our Sisters' Keepers: Nineteenth-Century Benevolence Literature by American Women*, ed. Jill Bergman and Debra Bernardi (Tuscaloosa, AL: University of Alabama Press, 2005): 135–56.

48. Freeman, "A Mistaken Charity," 244.

49. Karen Kilcup, *Fallen Forests: Emotion, Embodiment, and Ethics in American Women's Environmental Writing, 1781–1924* (Athens, GA: University of Georgia Press, 2013): 243. Kilcup links the civilization of the Shattuck sisters to the "civilizing" treatment of Native American girls: "Consciously or not, Freeman invokes associations between and among elderly women, children, and Native Americans, all regarded as uncivilized, natural beings."

50. Isabel A. Mallon, "Dress Hints for Elderly Women." *Ladies Home Journal* (Sept. 1892): 21.

51. Kathleen Woodward, "Against Wisdom: The Social Politics of Anger and Aging." *Journal of Aging Studies* 17 (2003): 63.

52. Freeman, "A Mistaken Charity," 246.

53. See Jane Gallop, "The View from Queer Theory." *Age Culture Humanities* 2 (2015). As Cynthia Port puts it, "No longer employed, not reproducing, perhaps technologically illiterate, and frequently without disposable income, the old are often, like queers, figured by the cultural imagination as being outside mainstream temporalities and standing in the way of, rather than contributing to, the promise of the future." Port, "No Future? Aging, Temporality, History, and Reverse Chronologies." *Occasion: Interdisciplinary Studies in the Humanities* 4 (May 2012).

54. Erving Goffman refers to "spoiled identity" in his classic sociological text, *Stigma: Notes on the Management of Spoiled Identity* (Englewood Cliffs, NJ: Prentice-Hall, 1963).

55. Freeman, "A Mistaken Charity," 249.

56. See Doris Turkes, "Must Age Equal Failure?: Sociology Looks at Mary Wilkins Freeman's Old Women." *ATQ* 13.3 (1999): 197–214.

57. Susan A. Toth, "The Value of Age in the Fiction of Sarah Orne Jewett." *Studies in Short Fiction* 8 (1971): 433–41.

58. Karen Kilcup writes, "Although the theme of New England in decline was well established in literature by Jewett's time, appearing in such culturally normative periodicals as *Harper's Magazine*, Matthiessen and Brooks were not merely reiterating a myth, they were creating one ... Jewett was irretrievably bound to a limited past rather than looking outward to a lively and masculine future." Kilcup and Edwards, *Jewett and her Contemporaries*, 4.

59. Leah Blatt Glasser, *In a Closet Hidden: The Life and Work of Mary E. Wilkins Freeman* (Amherst, MA: University of Massachusetts Press, 1996): 207.

60. Ansley observes, "At the same time, capitalism required able-bodied industrial workers; thus, the white middle-class home served as a site for the reproduction of the able-bodied subject. Disability and illness—such as that the Shattucks embody—were, in this context, viewed as forms of deviance." Ansley, "Geographies of Intimacy in Mary Wilkins Freeman's Short Fiction."

61. Rosemarie Garland-Thomson, "The Cultural Logic of Euthanasia: 'Sad Fancyings' in Herman Melville's 'Bartleby.'" *American Literature* 76.4 (Dec. 2004): 780.

62. See Rosemarie Garland-Thomson, for example, who notes that critics "look at disabled characters," but "they often interpret them metaphorically or aesthetically, reading them without political awareness as conventional elements of the sentimental, romantic, Gothic, or grotesque tradition." Garland-Thompson, *Extraordinary Bodies: Figuring Physical Disability in American Culture and Literature* (New York: Columbia University Press, 1997): 9–10. See also David T. Mitchell and Sharon L. Snyder, *Narrative Prosthesis: Disability and the Dependencies of Discourse* (Ann Arbor, MI: University of Michigan Press, 2000). My call to read age as a subject, rather than a metaphor, also echoes Hester Blum's call to examine the material

conditions of the ocean as a body of water rather than simply a symbolic space. She writes, "The sea is not a metaphor," urging critics to attend to "material conditions" and to draw on the "epistemological structures provided by the lives and writings from those for whom the sea was simultaneously workplace, home, passage, penitentiary, and promise." Hester Blum, "The Prospect of Oceanic Studies." *PMLA* 125.3 (May 2010): 670–7.

63. William James expressed concern that the character of Miss Birdseye in *The Bostonians* was an unflattering portrait of Elizabeth Peabody, James explained, "I should be very sorry—in fact deadly sick, or fatally ill—if I thought Miss Peabody *herself* supposed I intended to represent her…She was not in the smallest degree my starting point or example." *Henry James: A Life in Letters*, ed. Philip Horne (New York: Penguin, 2001): 170.

64. Robert McRuer, "Compulsory Able-bodiedness and Queer/Disabled Existence" in *The Disability Studies Reader*, ed. Lennard Davis (New York: Routledge, 2013): 88–99.

65. Jasbir Puar, *The Right to Maim: Debility, Capacity, Disability* (Durham, NC: Duke University Press, 2017): 68.

66. Peter M. Coviello, *Tomorrow's Parties: Sex and the Untimely in Nineteenth-Century America* (New York: NYU, 2013): 81.

67. Thomas Cole describes the late nineteenth-century as a period in which "chronological age [became] a tool for regulating the life course and for managing generational replacement in primary labor markets." Cole, *The Voyage of Life: A Cultural History of Aging in America* (New York: Cambridge University Press: 1992): 169. See also Haber, *Beyond Sixty-Five: The Dilemma of Old Age in America's Past*. She writes, "Mandatory retirement and the age-based pensions…not only arose out of changing ideas about the elderly's need and ability to work but legitimated the demand that the aged should no longer be employed" (124).

68. As Katz writes, "The elderly population was made knowable on the basis of supposedly behavioral, physical, and moral ills specific to the age of its members. Old age was posited as a separate, subjective existence." Stephen Katz, *Disciplining Old Age: The Formation of Gerontological Knowledge* (Charlottesville, VA: University of Virginia Press, 1996): 59.

69. Mary Wilkins Freeman, "The Village Singer" in *A New England Nun and Other Stories* (New York: Harper and Brothers, 1891): 27.

70. Freeman, "The Village Singer," 20.

71. Marjorie Pryse, "The Humanity of Women in Freeman's 'A Village Singer.'" *Colby Quarterly* 19.2 (June 1983): 70.

72. Such gendered views of aging were increasingly permeating popular science. Braxton Hicks in 1877 said that menopause led to a "tendency to revert to a neutral man-woman state" while male sexuality was immune to aging.

73. Freeman, "The Village Singer," 19.

74. Freeman, "The Village Singer," 25.

75. Freeman, "The Village Singer," 19.

76. Tamara K. Hareven, "Changing Images of Aging and the Social Construction of the Life Course" in *Images of Aging: Cultural Representations of Later Life*, ed. Mike Featherstone and Andrew Wernick.

77. Freeman, "The Village Singer," 25.

78. Stephen Katz, *Disciplining Old Age: The Formation of Gerontological Knowledge* (Charlottesville, VA: University of Virgina Press, 1996): 91.

79. See Haber, *Beyond Sixty-Five: The Dilemma of Old Age in America's Past.* These demographic changes also gave rise to the life stage of "middle age," which became linked with the period after childbearing but before senescence.

80. See Steven Ruggles, "The Decline of Intergenerational Co-residence in the United States, 1850 to 2000." *American Sociological Review* 72 (2007): 964–89. Ruggles argues that "the decline of intergenerational co-residence is linked to the rise of wage labor and mass education and the decline of household-based production."

81. As ecologist Helena Norberg-Hodge writes, "With the process of industrialization or modernization, societies around the world conform to an economic model that imposes a segregation of age groups. From childhood, people are separated into groups according to age and these divisions remain throughout their lives." See Helena Norberg-Hodge and Peter Matthiessen, *Ancient Futures: Lessons from Ladakh for a Globalizing World* (San Francisco, CA: Sierra Club Books: 2009).

82. Sarah Orne Jewett, *Deephaven* (New York: Houghton Mifflin, 1877): 11.

83. Jewett, *Deephaven*, 12.

84. Judith Wittenberg reads their identification with immaturity as part of the novella's interest in representing the authorial process: "The flexibility of their vision is appropriate for embryonic artists; complete maturity might be psychically constraining."

85. Jewett, *Deephaven*, 16.

86. Jewett, *Deephaven*, 42.

87. Jewett, *Deephaven*, 22.

88. Jewett, *Deephaven*, 98.

89. Elizabeth Freeman, *Time Binds: Queer Temporalities, Queer Histories* (Durham, NC: Duke University Press: 2010): xii.

90. Jewett, *Deephaven*, 76.

91. Jewett, *Deephaven*, 79.

92. Samaine Lockwood reads this interest in the old-fashioned, and specifically the colonial past, as a preoccupation of regionalism. She sees in this genre a "forward-looking lament about the unrealized potential of the consolidated nation-state, a dream about what the colonial moment might have meant for women's democratic citizenship, particularly their freedom to affiliate as they might choose." Lockwood, *Archives of Desire: The Queer Historical Work of New England Regionalism, 16.*

93. Jewett, *Deephaven*, 130.

94. Jewett, *Deephaven*, 141.

95. Anne Romines, *The Home Plot: Women, Writing, and Domestic Ritual* (Amherst, MA: University of Massachusetts Press, 1992): 37.

96. Jewett, *Deephaven*, 193.

97. Jewett, *Deephaven*, 203.

98. Jewett, *Deephaven*, 227.

99. Jewett, *Deephaven*, 229.

100. Sarah Orne Jewett, *The Country of the Pointed Firs* (New York: Broadview, 2010): 41.

101. Jewett, *The Country of the Pointed Firs*, 65.

102. Jewett, *The Country of the Pointed Firs*, 63.

103. Jewett, *The Country of the Pointed Firs*, 77–8.

104. Jewett, *The Country of the Pointed Firs*, 68.

105. Eugene Thomas, "The Curiosity of Longevity." *Scribner's Monthly* 11.1 (1875): 32–42.

106. Jewett, *The Country of the Pointed Firs*, 70.

107. This point is emphasized when Mrs. Todd explains to the narrator upon observing an ash tree: "Grown trees act that way sometimes, same's folks; then they'll put themselves right to it and strike their roots off into new ground and start all over again with real good courage ... Every such tree has got its own livin' spring; there's folks made to match 'em" (111). The notion of a "livin' spring" that enables perpetual growth and seasonal change encapsulates Jewett's theory of aging.

108. Sarah Ensor, "Spinster Ecology: Rachel Carson, Sarah Orne Jewett, and Nonreproductive Futurity." *American Literature* 84.2 (2012): 409–35.

109. Samaine Lockwood writes, "Rather than producing children or mothering them, the New England regionalists took up the significant work of historical generation, imagining their historicist acts as tied to alternative forms of feeling." Lockwood, *Archives of Desire: The Queer Historical Work of New England Regionalism*, 20.

110. J. Jack Halberstam, *In a Queer Time and Place: Transgender Bodies, Subcultural Lives* (New York: New York University Press, 2005): 2.

111. See Judith Halberstam, "The Politics of Negativity in Recent Queer Theory." *PMLA* 121.3 (May 2006): 823–5.

112. Jewett, *The Country of the Pointed Firs*, 124.

113. Jewett, *The Country of the Pointed Firs*, 126.

114. For an overview of the critical history on Jewett, see Marjorie Pryse, "Sex, Class, and 'Category Crisis': Reading Jewett's Transitivity." *American Literature* 70.3 (Sept. 1998): 517–49.

115. Barbara Frey Waxman has coined the term "novel of ripening," or *Reifungsroman*, to describe narratives that link age with fulfillment rather than decline. While this term does not exactly describe Jewett's novel, it is nonetheless a useful starting point for thinking about how narratives that center on old characters might necessitate alternative plots and taxonomies. Waxman, *From the Hearth to the Open Road: A Feminist Study of Aging in Contemporary Literature* (Westport, CT: Greenwood Press, 1990).

116. Unsurprisingly, age discourse has conditioned critical responses to regionalism. As Stephanie Foote smartly observes, "Traditional critiques of regional writing have tended to feminize and diminish this 'minor' genre, appreciating its aesthetic dimensions while noting its childish, although perhaps charming, inability to fully come to terms with its contemporary conditions of mature capitalism, urban unrest, and expanding immigration and imperialism." Foote, "'I Feared to Find Myself a Foreigner': Revisiting Regionalism in

Sarah Orne Jewett's *The Country of the Pointed Firs." Arizona Quarterly: A Journal of American Literature, Culture, and Theory* 52.2 (1996): 37–61.

117. Heather Love, *Feeling Backward: Loss and the Politics of Queer History* (Cambridge: Harvard University Press, 2004): 4.

CHAPTER 5 NOTES

1. As Alfred Bendixen notes, James "urged [Elizabeth] Jordan to let him 'take over the elements' of the novel, pleading that he 'hated to see them so helplessly muddled away when, oh, one could one self (according to one's fatuous thought!) have made them mean something, given them sense, direction, and form'" (xxx). Alfred Bendixen, Introduction, *The Whole Family.* Similarly, Dale Bauer notes, "Henry James's section, 'The Married Son,' is the most curious, not for what it says about Elizabeth but for its refusal to come to terms with the spinster." Dale Bauer, "The Politics of Collaboration in The Whole Family" in *Old Maids to Radical Spinsters: Unmarried Women in the Twentieth-Century Novel* (Champagne, IL: University of Illinois Press, 1990): 116.

2. Samaine Lockwood refers to James' declamation: "I hate 'old New England stories'!—which are lean and pale and poor and ugly." For Lockwood, this "epistolary outburst offers an early example of a critic constellating agedness, New England, and women's artistic inadequacy." Lockwood, *Archives of Desire: The Queer Historical Work of New England Regionalism,* 61.

3. Marah Gubar refers to a "campaign waged by turn-of-the-century writers and intellectuals (including and especially Henry James) to differentiate serious 'adult' literature from popular works aimed at mixed audiences—to effect a strict bifurcation between child and adult audiences, children's books and books for grown-ups." Gubar, *Artful Dodgers,* 125–6. See also Beverly Lyon Clark, *Kiddie Lit: The Cultural Construction of Children's Literature in America* (Baltimore, MD: Johns Hopkins University Press, 2005).

4. See the special issue of the *Henry James Review* on illness, aging, and death. Particularly relevant to critical age studies is Melanie Dawson's discussion of age rejuvenation in "Interventions into Aging: Rejuvenation in *The Portrait of a Lady* and *The Sacred Fount." Henry James Review* 37.3 (292–304). Consider also James' story, "The Diary of a Man of Fifty," in which a middle-aged narrator encounters a young man reminiscent of his own younger self and must come to terms with his own misreading of his life. His nostalgic backward glance ultimately reveals the finality of aging and the irrevocability of one's actions, thus adhering to the normative conception aging as teleological, linear, and oriented toward decline and loss.

5. Christopher Beha makes this point passionately, "Putting down 'Harry Potter' for Henry James is not one of adulthood's obligations, like flossing and mortgage payments; it's one of its rewards, like autonomy and sex. It seems to me not embarrassing or shameful but just self-defeating and a little sad to forego such pleasures in favor of reading a book that might just as easily be enjoyed by a child." "Henry James and the Great Y.A. Debate." *New Yorker* (September 18, 2014).

6. Significantly, as scholars have noted, his oeuvre is indebted—dependent upon—the work of George Eliot and others, thus giving lie to the notion of utterly self-generated mastery. See especially Sarah Daugherty, "Henry James and George Eliot: The Price of Mastery." *The Henry James Review* 10.3 (Fall 1989): 153–66.

7. Marah Gubar, "Entertaining Children of All Ages: Nineteenth-Century Popular Theater as Children's Theater." *American Quarterly* 66.1 (March 2014): 1–34.

8. Henry James, *Daisy Miller* (New York: Broadview, 1987): 45.

9. *Daisy Miller*, 46.

10. *Daisy Miller*, 46.

11. *Daisy Miller*, 72.

12. *Daisy Miller*, 46.

13. *Daisy Miller*, 52.

14. *Daisy Miller*, 80.

15. *Daisy Miller*, 80.

16. *The Portrait of a Lady* similarly meditates on the meaning of independence for a young woman. Early on in the novel, Ralph Touchett first hears his distant cousin Isabel Archer described as "independent" and wonders: "But who's 'quite independent,' and in what sense is the term used?...Is it used in a moral or in a financial sense? Does it mean they've been left well off, or that they wish to be under no obligations? Or does it simply mean that they're fond of their own way?"

17. See Jay Fliegelman's *Prodigals and Pilgrims: The American Revolution against Patriarchal Authority 1750–1800* (Cambridge: Cambridge University Press, 1982).

18. Thomas Paine, "The Crisis" in *The Political Writings of Thomas Paine* (New York: George H. Evans, 1835): 105.

19. John Adams, Letter to John Sullivan. 26 May 1776 in *Founding the Republic: A Documentary History*, ed. John J. Patrick (Westport, CT: Greenwood Press, 1995): 82.

20. For more on the democratization of voting, see Jon Grinspan's *The Virgin Vote: How Young Americans Made Democracy Social, Politics Personal, and Voting Popular in the Nineteenth Century*.

21. Corinne T. Field, *The Struggle for Equal Adulthood: Gender, Race, Age, and the Fight for Citizenship in Antebellum America*, 53. Field writes, "Counting birthdays was a truly democratic form of accumulation."

22. Nancy Fraser and Linda Gordon, "A Genealogy of Dependency: Tracing a Keyword of the US Welfare State." *Signs* 19.2 (Winter 1994): 309–36.

23. Horatio Alger, *Ragged Dick; or, Street Life in New York with the Boot Blacks* (New York: Modern Library, 2005): 33.

24. Alger, *Ragged Dick*, 34.

25. For a discussion of homoerotic undertones in Alger's work, see Michael Moon's "'The Gentle Boy from the Dangerous Classes': Pederasty, Domesticity, and Capitalism in Horatio Alger." *Representations* 19 (Summer 1987): 87–110.

26. Kathryn Bond-Stockton, *The Queer Child, or Growing Sideways in the Twentieth Century* (Durham, NC: Duke University Press, 2009).

27. Alger, *Ragged Dick*, 80.
28. Alger, *Ragged Dick*, 66.
29. For example, Michael Zuckerman writes, "Beneath his celebration of self-reliance [is] a craving to be taken care of and yearning to surrender the terrible burden of independence." See Michael Zuckerman, "The Nursery Tales of Horatio Alger." *American Quarterly* 24.2 (May 1972): 209. In this sense, even our most emblematic, ideological coming-of-age story reveals the fissures in the American idealization of independence as the core feature of adulthood.
30. Alger, *Ragged Dick*, 153.
31. Karen Sanchez-Eppler, *Dependent States.*
32. Martha Fineman, *The Autonomy Myth: A Theory of Dependency* (New York: The New Press, 2005).
33. His first assistant was William MacAlpine, who was followed by Mary Weld, and finally Theodora Bosanquet, with whom he developed a particularly close rapport.
34. Scholars have debated the extent to which the difficulty of James' late style can be attributed to this shift in the mode of composition. See David Hoover, "Modes of Composition in Henry James: Dictation, Style, and *What Maisie Knew.*" *Henry James Review* 35.3 (2014): 257–77.
35. Theodora Bosanquet, *Henry James at Work* (Ann Arbor, MI: University of Michigan Press, 2006): 34.
36. Bosanquet wrote her own memoir, suggesting that for her, too, the experience was intellectually and personally fruitful.
37. For a discussion of James' late style, see David McWhirter's *Desire and Love in Henry James: A Study of the Late Novels* (New York: Cambridge University Press, 1989).
38. Of James' biographer James Wood writes, "Leon Edel wrote that James's friends swore they could identify the very chapter in *What Maisie Knew* that marked his new method of writing."
39. Even before his own need for a secretary, James had much experience with disability. As Talia Schaffer puts it, "Henry James was part of a family deeply involved with illness and modes of caregiving... Virtually every member of the family experienced sustained periods of invalidism." (Talia Schaffer, "The Silent Treatment of *The Wings of the Dove*: Ethics of Care and Late-James Style," *Henry James Review* 37.3 (Fall 2016): 233–45.) His father, William James Senior, experienced ongoing mental trouble and physical ailments; his sister, Alice was often on bed rest, and James himself of course suffered from his "obscure hurt," debilitating wrist pain, and various other afflictions. Despite the fact that "disability looms large in James's personal history and fiction," as Mary Eyring, notes, surprisingly little scholarship exists on how these experiences resonate in his fiction, with the exception of isolated discussions of Ralph Touchett in *The Portrait of a Lady* and Millie Theale in *The Wings of the Dove*, both of whom suffer from fatal illnesses.
40. Rachel Bowlby notes that "Sir Claude and Mrs. Beale, joyously together with Maisie, get jointly excited about the idea of going out and getting themselves an education... as if they all need to know, or are all on the same educational

level, parents and child alike." Rachel Bowlby, *A Child of One's Own: Parental Stories* (New York: Oxford University Press, 2013): 199.

41. Henry James, *What Maisie Knew* (New York: Penguin, 1985): 36.

42. James, *What Maisie Knew*, 36.

43. James, *What Maisie Knew*, 43.

44. James, *What Maisie Knew*, 43.

45. James, *What Maisie Knew*, 18.

46. Rachel Murray makes the related point that "Jamesian stupidity may be nothing other than the tactical concealment of intelligence." Rachel Murray, "Delightfully Dense: The Art of Stupidity in Late James." *Henry James Review* 37.2 (2016): 192.

47. James, *What Maisie Knew*, 134.

48. For a discussion of childhood innocence as a nineteenth-century cultural construction and white privilege, see Bernstein, *Racial Innocence: Performing American Childhood from Slavery to Civil Rights*.

49. James, *What Maisie Knew*, 101.

50. James, *What Maisie Knew*, 247.

51. Pamela Thurschwell, "Bringing Nanda forward, or Acting your Age in *The Awkward Age*." *Critical Quarterly* 58.2 (2016): 72–90.

52. James, *What Maisie Knew*, 86.

53. Holly Blackford, "Child Consciousness in the American Novel: *Adventures of Huckleberry Finn* (1885), *What Maisie Knew* (1897), and the Birth of Child Psychology" in *Enterprising Youth: Social Values and Acculturation in Nineteenth-Century American Children's Literature*, ed. Monika Elbert (New York: Routledge, 2008): 253.

54. Susan Honeyman, *Elusive Childhood: Impossible Representation in Modern Fiction*. Kevin Ohi, "Narrating the Child's Queerness in *What Maisie Knew*," in *Curiouser: On the Queerness of Children*, ed. Steven Bruhm and Natasha Hurley (Minneapolis, MN: University of Minnesota Press, 2004).

55. Lyon Clark, *Kiddie Lit: The Cultural Construction of Children's Literature in America*, 43, 46.

56. Irene Tucker, "What Maisie Promised: Realism, Liberalism, and the Ends of Contract." *Yale Journal of Criticism* 11.2 (1998): 335–64.

57. James, *What Maisie Knew*, 85.

58. James, *What Maisie Knew*, 84.

59. George Agich, *Dependence and Autonomy in Old Age: An Ethical Framework for Long-term Care* (New York: Cambridge University Press, 1993): 104.

60. James, *What Maisie Knew*, 17.

61. James, *What Maisie Knew*, 50.

62. James, *What Maisie Knew*, 50.

63. James, *What Maisie Knew*, 60.

64. James, *What Maisie Knew*, 68.

65. Juliet Mitchell argues that she is "quite simply one of James's nastiest characterizations." Mitchell, "*What Maisie Knew*: Portrait of the Artist as a Young Girl." in *The Air of Reality: New Essays on Henry James*, ed. John Goode (London: Methuen, 1972): 168–89.

66. Talia Schaffer makes a related point in her reading of *Wings of the Dove* in which she argues that "James ends up developing something we might call a narrative theory of care."

67. As Juliet Mitchell notes, "Participation in a James novel is a process of initiation into vision." Mitchell, "*What Maisie Knew*: Portrait of the Artist as a Young Girl."

68. James, *What Maisie Knew*, 48.

69. James, *What Maisie Knew*, 50.

70. James, *What Maisie Knew*, 50.

71. James, *What Maisie Knew*, 49.

72. James, *What Maisie Knew*, 49.

73. Teresa Michals, "Henry James and the Invention of Adulthood." *Novel: A Forum on Fiction* 44.2 (Summer 2011): 236–7.

74. James, *What Maisie Knew*, 96.

75. James, *What Maisie Knew*, 90.

76. James, *What Maisie Knew*, 117.

77. James, *What Maisie Knew*, 108.

78. James, *What Maisie Knew*, 46.

79. James, *What Maisie Knew*, 45.

80. Duane, *Suffering Childhood in Early America*, 7. As Karen Sanchez-Eppler writes, "Independence may generally be overrated as a desideratum of civic society; interdependence or partial independence may be far more accurate terms for understanding civic life" (xxv). *Dependent States*.

81. James, *What Maisie Knew*, 82.

82. James, *What Maisie Knew*, 92.

83. Lynn Wardley, "Fear of Falling and the Rise of Girls: Lamarck's Knowledge in *What Maisie Knew*." *American Literary History* 28.2 (April 2016): 246–70.

84. James, *What Maisie Knew*, 202.

85. James, *What Maisie Knew*, 89.

86. James, *What Maisie Knew*, 74.

87. James, *What Maisie Knew*, 114. Tessa Hadley reads Sir Claude's predilection for calling Maisie "boy" and "old man" as a sign that she is a "relief from sexual complications." However, this tendency more explicitly signals the inversion of age norms.

88. James, *What Maisie Knew*, 193.

89. James, *What Maisie Knew*, 106.

90. James, *What Maisie Knew*, 99.

91. James, *What Maisie Knew*, 229.

92. James, *What Maisie Knew*, 268.

93. James, *What Maisie Knew*, 264.

94. James, *What Maisie Knew*, 252.

95. Lynne Segal, "The Coming of Age Studies." *Age Culture Humanities* 1 (2014). http://ageculturehumanities.org/WP/the-coming-of-age-studies/.

96. Lynn Wardley writes, "As her nuclear family falls apart, Maisie does not cling to the adult couple at hand, whose attachment to her would prove as unreliable as Beale and Ida's. Instead, she is made safe by—'well-attached' to—Mrs. Wix

and even to the crafty aunt, the fairy godmother at Maisie's cradle." Lynn Wardley, "Fear of Falling and the Rise of Girls: Lamarck's Knowledge in *What Maisie Knew*." *American Literary History* 28.2 (April 2016): 265.

CODA NOTES

1. Charles Chesnutt, "The Wife of his Youth" in *Conjure Tales and Stories of the Color Line*, ed. William L. Andrews (New York: Penguin, 1992): 103.
2. Chesnutt, "The Wife of his Youth," 105.
3. Monika Elbert and Wendy Ryden note that the story seems like a "quaint tale about moral choice [but becomes] becomes an allegory for atavism explored through gothic imagery, in which the dark-skinned slave wife left behind by light-skinned Mr. Ryder uncannily resurfaces from the past to make stubborn claim on him as he prepares to embrace a future in which she is forgotten and erased." Monika Elbert and Wendy Ryden, "American Gothic Realism and Naturalism" in *The Cambridge Companion to the American Gothic*, ed. Jeffrey Weinstock (New York: Cambridge University Press, 2017): 53. See also Tess Chakkalakal, "Wedded to the Color Line: Charles Chesnutt's Stories of Segregation," in *Representing Segregation: Toward an Aesthetics of Living Jim Crow, and Other Forms of Racial Division*, ed. Brian Norman and Piper Kendrix Williams (Albany, NY: State University of New York Press, 2010).
4. Chesnutt, "The Wife of his Youth," 107.
5. Chesnutt, "The Wife of his Youth," 107.
6. Chesnutt, "The Wife of his Youth," 108.
7. Holly Jackson observes that the story is about how post-Emancipation African Americans are "hamstrung by the far-reaching afterlife of slavery from achieving upward mobility as defined by white society." Jackson, *American Blood: The Ends of the Family in American Literature* (New York: Oxford University Press, 2014): 136.
8. Chesnutt, "The Wife of his Youth," 108.
9. But unlike these figures, Liza Jane is not loyal to an old master; on the contrary, she is loyal to her husband. As Elizabeth Duquette puts it, "Her lasting attachment is to her spouse, not her former master; nor does she spend her life patiently awaiting his return." Duquette, *Loyal Subjects: Bonds of Nation, Race, and Allegiance in Nineteenth-Century America* (New Brunswick, NJ: Rutgers University Press, 2010): 165.
10. For a reading of the story in the context of Reconstruction, see Elizabeth Duquette's trenchant analysis in *Loyal Subjects*.
11. Frances Watkins Harper, *Iola Leroy, Or, Shadows Uplifted* (Philadelphia, PA: Garrigues Brothers, 1892): 193.
12. Martin Delany, *Blake or the Huts of America* (Cambridge: Harvard University Press, 2017): 182.
13. Chesnutt, "The Wife of his Youth," 113.
14. Jim Downs, *Sick from Freedom: African-American Illness and Suffering during the Civil War and Reconstruction* (New York: Oxford University Press, 2012): 7.

15. Downs, *Sick from Freedom*, 145.

16. Chesnutt, "The Wife of his Youth," 110.

17. Before he decides to acknowledge "the wife of youth," Mr. Ryder "stood for a long time before the mirror of his dressing-case, gazing thoughtfully at the reflection of his own face." This moment notably presents a striking contrast with most scenes of mirror gazing. As I discussed in the third chapter, Louisa May Alcott's *Work* describes the protagonist's encounter with the mirror as inciting a kind of self-shattering, a feeling of personal fragmentation and loss, as she is unrecognizable to herself. For Ryder, however, the mirror leads to a moment of reckoning that inspires return and reconnection with a prior self.

18. Catherine Keyser makes a similar point, noting, "The old woman revises the would-be heroic narrative of masculinist bourgeois individualism." Catherine Keyser, "'The Wave of a Magician's Wand': Romance, Storytelling, and the Myth of History in 'The Wife of His Youth.'" *American Literary Realism* 44.3 (Spring 2012): 213.

19. Charles Chesnutt, *"To Be an Author": Letters of Charles W. Chesnutt, 1889–1905*, ed. Joseph McElrath Jr. and Robert C. Leitz III (Princeton, NJ: Princeton University Press, 2014): 115.

20. Lauren Berlant, *Cruel Optimism* (Durham, NC: Duke University Press, 2011): 1.

21. Thomas R. Cole, Introduction. *What Does It Mean to Grow Old?: Reflections from the Humanities*, ed. Thomas R. Cole and Sally A. Gadow (Durham, NC: Duke University Press, 1987): 7.

22. Donald Hall, *Essays after Eighty* (New York: Houghton Mifflin Harcourt, 2014): 96.

Index

Note: Page numbers in *italics* indicate illustrations.